American Pragmatism:

PEIRCE, JAMES, AND DEWEY

American Pragmatism:

PEIRCE, JAMES, AND DEWEY

By Edward C. Moore

New York 1961
COLUMBIA UNIVERSITY PRESS

For Eileen,
Mike, and Jim

Preface

This book is a discussion of American pragmatism as it is found in the writings of its three major advocates: Charles S. Peirce, William James, and John Dewey. The intent of the book is to state the pragmatism of each in some detail and to show how each of them applied pragmatism to one basic concept. In the case of Peirce his theory of reality is examined, in James the notion of truth, and in Dewey the concept of the good. Aside from the pragmatism, the remainder of the philosophy of each is indicated briefly, in order that the reader may have some acquaintance with it.

Pragmatism is the only unique contribution American philosophy has made to the tradition known as Western philosophy. All other movements in American thought either originated in or were correlated with corresponding movements in European philosophy. In spite of its significance in this respect, no effort has yet been made to write the history of the movement. One reason for this has doubtless been the necessity for attaining some historical perspective. As a position of general concern in American thought, pragmatism belongs to the first fifty years of the twentieth century. The record is not yet complete. Previously unknown items are regularly being discovered. However, with the death of John Dewey in 1952 and with the publication of the bulk of the papers of Charles S. Peirce in the 1930s, the main items may now be considered available.

A second reason no history of the movement has appeared is probably due to the fact that pragmatism has been a philosophy that engendered intense feelings of partisanship. Most American philosophers have felt strongly either for or against it. The heat of controversy is now somewhat abated, and it may be possible to begin formulating the main issues with some degree of objectivity.

It should be said that there are other philosophers besides the three studied in this book whose work would have to be taken into account in any complete history of pragmatism. The neglect of them should not be construed as implying that their contributions were negligible, but what I have sought in this book is an examination of the basic doctrines of pragmatism. Refinements and elaborations are valuable, and I hope that some readers—particularly those with personal knowledge of the issues—may be moved to make them; but my primary aim has been simplicity of statement. I hasten to add that no reader can be more conscious than I am of the degree to which I fall short of this goal. Pragmatism is not, unfortunately, a simple doctrine. The constant complaint of its advocates that its opponents do not understand what is being said is an index of the fact that the pragmatists are saying something either new or subtle or both. It is my opinion that the views of Peirce are extremely subtle, and that those of James and Dewey represent positions for which no philosophical precedent can be found. Accordingly the discussion in this book is constantly threading its way along a narrow path. On one side is the danger of over-elaboration caused by the necessity of giving detailed insight into a new or subtle doctrine; on the other side is the danger of over-simplification caused by the necessity of laying bare the bones of the argument. It is hardly likely that the discussion has been able to avoid both of these pitfalls in all cases. It is my hope that it has succeeded in most cases.

It is a pleasure to acknowledge my intellectual obligation in the section on Peirce to Arthur W. Burks, who first introduced me to Peirce, and whose philosophical abilities and personal friendship have been a source of great inspiration to me. It is scarcely necessary to add that only the author can be held accountable for the interpretations set forth in the book.

Thanks are also due to my wife without whom, in many ways, this book would never have been written.

EDWARD C. MOORE

University of Idaho
September, 1960

Acknowledgments

The author is grateful to the following publishers for permitting him to use quotations from works published or controlled by them as indicated below:

The Belknap Press of the Harvard University Press: *Collected Papers of Charles Sanders Peirce,* Volumes I–VI, edited by Charles Hartshorne and Paul Weiss, copyright 1931, 1932 (1959, 1960), 1933, 1935 by the President and Fellows of Harvard College.

Harvard University Press: *Collected Papers of Charles Sanders Peirce,* Volumes VII and VIII, edited by Arthur Walter Burks, copyright 1958 by the President and Fellows of Harvard College.

Henry Holt and Company: *Logic: The Theory of Inquiry,* by John Dewey, copyright 1938. *Human Nature and Conduct,* by John Dewey, copyright 1922. *The Influence of Darwin on Philosophy,* by John Dewey, copyright 1910. *Reconstruction in Philosophy,* by John Dewey, copyright 1920.

Philosophical Library: *Problems of Men,* by John Dewey, copyright 1946. *From Copernicus to Einstein,* by Hans Reichenbach, copyright 1942.

Hauser Printing Co. and James K. Feibleman: *An Introduc-*

tion to Peirce's Philosophy, by James K. Feibleman, copyright 1946.

The editor of *Philosophy and Phenomenological Research:* "The Scholastic Realism of C. S. Peirce," by Edward C. Moore, Volume XII, March, 1952.

The editors of *The Journal of Philosophy:* "Charles S. Peirce at the Johns Hopkins," by Christine Ladd-Franklin, from *The Journal of Philosophy, Psychology and Scientific Method,* Volume XII, 1916. "Positivism and Potentiality," by Edward C. Moore, *The Journal of Philosophy,* Volume XLVIII, July 19, 1951.

Paul R. Reynolds and Son (599 Fifth Avenue, New York, N.Y.): *Pragmatism,* by William James, copyright 1907. *The Meaning of Truth,* by William James, copyright 1909. *A Pluralistic Universe,* by William James, copyright 1909. *Memories and Studies,* by William James, copyright 1911. *Essays in Radical Empiricism,* by William James, copyright 1912.

Harvard University Press and Henry James: *The Thought and Character of William James,* 2 volumes, by Ralph Barton Perry, copyright 1935.

The Macmillan Company: *Democracy and Education,* by John Dewey, copyright 1916. *The Life and Letters of Edwin Lawrence Godkin,* edited by Rollow Ogden, copyright 1907.

Beacon Press: *Knowing and the Known,* by John Dewey and Arthur F. Bentley, copyright 1949.

G. P. Putnam's Sons: For Minton, Balch: *The Quest for Certainty,* by John Dewey, copyright 1929 (copyright renewed 1957). *Philosophy and Civilization,* by John Dewey, copyright 1931 (copyright renewed 1959).

Mrs. Sarah Y. Keyser: *Mathematical Philosophy,* by C. J. Keyser, copyright 1922.

Contents

Theory is the most practical thing in the world.

OLIVER WENDELL HOLMES, JR.

I

Introduction

As a movement in American philosophy, pragmatism had its origins in the article "How to Make Our Ideas Clear" written by Charles Peirce and published in the *Popular Science Monthly* for January, 1878. This article excited little comment at the time of its publication, and its central doctrine went unnoticed for a period of twenty years. On August 26, 1898, William James delivered a lecture titled "Philosophical Conceptions and Practical Results" before the Philosophical Union of the University of California. In this lecture he revived Peirce's doctrine and initiated the movement in American thought known as pragmatism.

From its inception the new movement was attacked on all sides. Fighting back vigorously during the first quarter of the twentieth century, it established itself, through the writings of William James and John Dewey, as an important position in American philosophy. By the 1930s a degree of tranquillity was returning to the philosophical scene when European philosophers seeking refuge in this country from the German dictatorship introduced the philosophical movement known as logical positivism. The old issues came alive again. While pragmatism and logical positivism have never merged, they have reinforced one another. As a result of their common emphasis, philosophers in our own day have been stimulated to a more persistent attempt to grapple with the type of problem first raised, in this country, by pragmatism. Accordingly the story of the development of American pragmatism has not only an historical interest but is also of value as a source of insight into contemporary philosophy.

No philosophical movement appears full-blown from the minds of its advocates. In the background of pragmatism there are three developments which were of primary influence in determining the ultimate formulation of the view. These developments were in the areas of science, religion, and philosophy.

THE INFLUENCE OF SCIENCE

The last half of the nineteenth century was a period when science reached into the thoughts of more people than in perhaps any previous period in history. Newtonian physics had reached its climactic in a mechanistic determinism that was the source of much controversy in ethics and religion; the impact of Darwin's theory of evolution and the increasing development of psychology as a science seemed to be reducing all of man's fondest hopes and most cherished aspirations to the level of a purposeless flux of matter and energy. In our own day the issue between science and religion is argued mainly by scientists and theologians. In the nineteenth century most scientists and theologians were philosophers, and the discussion was carried on as a philosophical problem. Peirce and James and Dewey were all participants in the controversy, and each in his own way had to make peace with the issues involved.

Peirce and James had intimate contacts with experimental science. Peirce received a degree in chemistry from Harvard University in 1863 and was employed for thirty years as a physicist by the United States Coast and Geodetic Survey. James was one of the first Americans to become seriously interested in the physiological psychology of Wundt and began his teaching career at Harvard as a teacher of physiology. Dewey seems to have studied experimental psychology quite intensively with G. S. Hall at Johns Hopkins in 1882 to 1884, although Dewey's interests seem to have been more with the theoretical than with the experimental aspects of psychology. This scientific background was sufficient to give each of these men a keen interest in the problems that were appearing in science. In addition to a scientific knowledge that exceeded that of most philosophers of their day, they each demonstrated a strong predilection for philosophy. Peirce studied a good deal of philosophy with his father, Benjamin Peirce, who taught mathematics at Harvard. James in mid-career switched his primary interest from psychology to philosophy, and Dewey had always been more interested in philosophy than in pure science.

One of the problems in the area between philosophy and science was the question of mechanical determinism, suggested by the success of science in explaining natural phenomena on mechanistic principles. The question was whether or not the universe was a machine; the mechanists held that the universe was a clock, designed and set in operation by its Maker at the time of creation and simply running down in accord with the Second Law of Thermodynamics. All three of the pragmatists rejected this view. Dewey says that "Nature *has* a mechanism. . . . But only a philosophy which hypostatizes isolated results . . . concludes that nature *is* a mechanism and only a mechanism" (*Quest for Certainty*, p. 248). With this Peirce and James would agree. There is law and order in the universe, but this law and order, the mechanical aspect, is not the ultimate nature of things; it is only a tool, an instrument, subservient to a larger purpose.

The second development in science that influenced each of these philosophers was Darwin's theory of evolution. Each was sufficiently aware of scientific method to avoid making the mistake made by those philosophers of the nineteenth century who interpreted the theory of evolution as evidence that, since the history of life in the universe culminated in man, therefore life was attaining ever nobler forms. In short, they did not interpret evolution as progress. Dewey refers slightingly to this view as the argument from design on an installment plan. But although they all claim to recognize that Darwin's theory gives no basis for such a belief, they all believe in progress and believe that it is demonstrated in the universe. We must postpone a discussion of their reasons for so believing.

A final aspect of scientific development that influenced the pragmatists considerably was the great interest in psychology that was evident in this country in the latter half of the nineteenth century. The most important of Peirce's early articles was a series published in *The Journal of Speculative Philosophy* in 1868, dealing with "Questions Concerning Certain Faculties Claimed for Man," which treated psychological problems of perception in considerable detail. James, of course, began his career as a physiologist and psychologist, and his first published book was his *Psychology*. We have already mentioned Dewey's studies in psychology under Hall. Dewey's first book was a text in psychology which was published in 1887; his third, of which he was co-author, was a text, *Applied Psychology*, in 1889. The number of his contributions to education demonstrates his constant preoccupation with psychological problems. The interest of these philosophers in psychology was to leave its imprint on their pragmatism.

No reference to the influence of scientific thought on pragmatism would be complete without a reference to positivism.

Positivism was not a position in science but in the philosophy of science. Since it has become in our day closely affiliated with pragmatism, it is of more than historical interest. The founder of positivism in its nineteenth century form was Auguste Comte, a French philosopher. According to Comte, there are three stages in the history of thought. The first is the theological stage in which the universe is explained in terms of the purposes of anthropomorphic deities. The second stage is the metaphysical in which natural phenomena are explained by referring them to abstract principles which, while no longer anthropomorphic or godlike, are nevertheless personified. This stage is a modification of the first stage and not a real break with it. The third stage is the scientific, or positive stage. In this stage natural phenomena are not explained by reference to any personified abstractions but observers are content with merely recording the uniformities which do occur and recognizing them as descriptions of how nature behaves without feeling impelled to read into the phenomena any evidence of purpose or design or consciousness. Thus the positivist interprets a scientific law not as a demonstration of some divine power working in the universe nor even as an exemplification of some abstract principle working out its function in material entities. He thinks of a law simply as a statement of how objects have been observed to behave. Accordingly the positivist tends to refer the meaning of all terms to what is found in experience.[1] There is no evidence that Peirce or James studied Comte's work in any detail. However, John Stuart Mill was closely allied to Comte's position, and they knew his views. Even more direct, however, was the influence of the American, Chauncey Wright, who seems to have subscribed to a positivism in many ways anticipatory of the view

---

[1] For a more extended statement of positivism the interested reader is referred to Alfred J. Ayer, *Language, Truth and Logic* (London: Gollancz, 1947).

prevailing today. Wright was a close friend of William James and of the James family. He also knew Peirce well. Peirce wrote of Wright: "He and I used to have long and very lively and *close* disputations lasting two or three hours daily for many years." [2]

Wright left no systematic statement of his views, but, from what can be pieced together from bits here and there, his position was a remarkable anticipation of many ideas that can be found in current philosophic writing. In defending his view against James's objections, Wright defined his position as "rather a discipline than a positive doctrine; an exorcism of the vague; a criticism of questions which by habit have passed beyond the real practical grounds of causes of questions" (*William James*, II, 720).

Wright, in a telling metaphor, spoke of the behavior of phenomena in the universe as "cosmic weather," meaning thereby that there was no more order in phenomena than there was in weather and that what order was found was put there by the observer, who selected certain aspects and by his process of selection instilled the order. In speaking of science Wright takes a position that would be agreeable to most contemporary positivists. He says, "Thus, while ideal or transcendental elements are admitted into scientific researches, though in themselves insusceptible of simple verification, they must still show credentials from the senses, either by affording from themselves consequences capable of sensuous verification, or by yielding such consequences in conjunction with ideas which by themselves are verifiable." [3]

Wright died at the early age of forty-five. Had he lived he might very well have exercised a dominant influence on the

[2] Letter to Christine Ladd-Franklin, *Journal of Philosophy, Psychology and Scientific Method*, XIII (1916), 719–20.

[3] Chauncey Wright, *Philosophical Discussions*, ed. Charles Eliot Norton (New York: Holt, 1877), p. 47.

development of American philosophy. Although both Peirce and James rejected positivism, Wright continually sought to force them to recognize the imperativeness of coming to grips with experience. Both of them had a tendency to philosophize in Comte's metaphysical stage, and Wright's efforts were always to bring them to the positive stage. There can be little doubt that his influence left its mark on the final formulation of pragmatism.

THE RELIGIOUS INFLUENCE

Peirce and James and Dewey were all natives of New England. During the nineteenth century New England was the hub of the American philosophic universe. The religious cast of New England thought left its mark on most of the philosophers of that day. The pragmatists were no exception.

One of the ways in which this influence was felt was in the emphasis common to both pragmatism and protestantism on the right of the individual to insist that old truths be brought to terms with the thoughts of each new thinker. No truth was valid for any man except in so far as it was grasped and accepted by him. While the pragmatists all recognize the social aspect of investigation, they each emphasize the right of the individual to come to this recognition in his own way. Pragmatism could hardly have come to fruition in a social order which denied the right of the individual to seek the truth for himself.

A more direct influence, however, was the influence of American religious idealism. Religious idealism, or moral idealism, must be distinguished from metaphysical idealism. The latter is the view that the ultimate nature of the universe is somehow or other of the nature of mind or idea, rather than matter. While Peirce, for example, was an idealist in this latter sense, it is not that view which is presently under discussion. Moral idealism is the view that whether the ultimate nature of the universe be mental or material, there is in the universe, as one of the primitive elements of it, purpose, and that this purpose is striving for a morally good goal. Moral idealism argues that the universe is not the mere blind scurrying of matter but that there is somehow somewhere a purpose which is exemplified in and being worked out through the medium of matter and motion. A philosophy which emphasizes purpose in this sense is said to be teleological. Peirce, of all the pragmatists, is most insistent on a teleological feature in the universe. James, while holding firmly to this view, is less philosophic in his insistence. By the time Dewey comes to formulate his pragmatism the element of purpose is no longer supernatural but natural. It nevertheless plays a dominant role in his thought.

The importance of moral idealism on American philosophy has been noted by most writers on the subject. For example, Townsend says: "There is one dominant note in American philosophy, i.e., idealism. The word must not be taken, however, either as an epithet of praise or as a narrowly technical label. It is intended only to characterize the central tendency in our philosophy to approximate the ancient doctrine that the invisible kingdoms furnish the foundation for the visible."[4]

Perry Miller characterizes this tendency as a dominant feature of the New England mind: "Wherever the heirs of Augustine appear, they are men for whom a sense of the continuous dependence of matter upon the spirit takes precedence over all other values, and always they verge so close to pantheism that it takes all their ingenuity to restrain themselves from identifying God with the creation."[5]

[4] H. G. Townsend, *Philosophical Ideas in the United States* (New York: American Book Co., 1934), p. 4.
[5] Perry Miller, *The New England Mind* (New York: Macmillan, 1939), p. 15.

As New Englanders and Americans, the pragmatists had to come to grips, each in his own way, with moral idealism. Whether their solutions are sublimations or degradations of moral idealism depends largely on one's own point of view, but no account of the historical background of pragmatism would be complete without an acknowledgment of the influence of religious thought on the ultimate formulation of the position.

THE PHILOSOPHICAL INFLUENCE

The primary philosophical influence on pragmatism was in the area of language problems, or what today are called problems of meaning. The fact that language problems occupy a dominant place in contemporary philosophical discussions is in itself a favorable omen, for problems of meaning have been of primary importance in every period of philosophical fertility. Today we have a new terminology for discussing the problems, but the problems in a different guise are as old as philosophy itself. Of primary interest to an understanding of these problems, and to an understanding of pragmatism, are the positions taken in Greek philosophy by Plato and Aristotle, and in the Middle Ages the controversy over the nature of universals.

Western philosophy itself is generally considered to have begun about 600 B.C. with the teachings of Thales of Miletus. Problems of meaning immediately began to appear. By 400 B.C., when Socrates, Plato, and Aristotle were stimulating the minds of the Greeks, they had assumed overwhelming importance. Socrates was continually asking for the meaning of terms, and many of the Platonic dialogues are devoted to efforts to find the meaning of some particular term. Thus the *Symposium* discusses love, the *Republic* justice, the *Charmides* friendship, and so on. A basic problem in this discussion, and one that determined the whole course of Platonic philosophy, was the problem of the meaning of general terms. A general term is one which does not apply just to one particular situation or object, but to all members of a class or group of objects. Thus, consider a term such as "triangularity." "Triangularity" does not apply just to this triangle or that triangle, but to any and every triangle. Generality of this order is a property of many of the terms that we use. The problem here was this: we do have and use general terms such has "triangularity," these terms must have a meaning to us or we could not use them meaningfully, also, a concept that is applied meaningfully to the external world must have something corresponding to it in the external world, what is there, then, in the external world that corresponds to the general concept of triangularity in my mind? Plato took the view that when I am thinking of triangularity, I am not thinking of just this triangle or that triangle, but of a property independent of all existing triangles, for, in his view, triangularity referred to properties not fully embodied in any existing triangle. He argued that since general terms do have a meaning they must refer to something, and since the meaning of a general term is not completely stated by reference to the class of, say, triangles in the real physical world, there must somewhere be an ideal non-physical realm in which there are entities corresponding to any general term such as "triangularity," and it is to an entity in this realm that I am referring whenever I use a general term. The total of such entities constitutes the famous Platonic Realm of Ideas.

What the Greek philosophers were trying to avoid was a position that would reduce general terms to the status of referring merely to figments of our imaginations. Thus the term "unicorn" refers to a figment of the human imagination, or, to use a more common term, to a fiction. There is not anything in the external world which corresponds to it. When we talk of unicorns we are talking only about ideas in the human mind.

But we do not wish to relegate general concepts such as triangularity or circularity or humanity to the status of fictions, for most of our knowledge is expressed in general terms; and if general terms are fictions, if they refer only to ideas in our own minds, then most of our knowledge does not refer to the external world at all and can tell us nothing about it. To avoid this conclusion, Plato held that an entity corresponding to each general idea was to be found in the Realm of Ideas. In this life we find physical objects none of which completely embodies any general idea but each of which partially embodies one. Thus by experiencing objects in the physical world we are able to perceive dimly the ideal form which exists only in the Realm of Ideas but which is recalled to mind when we study its imperfect counterpart as we find it here on earth.

Plato's theory of knowledge was a queer mixture of rationalism and empiricism. His pupil Aristotle rejected the rationalistic elements and sought for a more consistently empirical approach. Aristotle rejected the Platonic Realm of Ideas. He admitted that if our general terms were to have any meaning there must be in the world some object of a general nature which corresponded to them, but, consistently with his empiricism, he held that this object must be something found in its entirety in experience. In brief, he held that there was something in each object, its form, which was of a general nature and which was given to us in experience, and that it was to this that we referred when using general terms. Aristotle's position is not amenable to a simple treatment. The enduring features of his position in terms of the present discussion are that he rejected the Platonic Realm of Ideas and that he held that whatever the object of a general term was it would have to be something found in experience.

The philosophy of Plato contained many elements that were highly congenial to Christianity. A philosophical position that held that there was another realm in which everything was perfectly set forth and which looked upon the earth and earthly existence as an imperfect approach that dimly revealed a greater perfection beyond this life was easily adapted to Christian thought. A revival of Platonism in the Neoplatonic philosophy of Plotinus in the third century A.D. exercised a considerable influence on St. Augustine in the fourth century and through him became a continuing current in Christian thought. With the coming of the Middle Ages, however, and the rediscovery of the works of Aristotle, most of which had been lost to Western philosophy for over a thousand years, the problem of the referent of general terms received a new impetus. Neoplatonism met a worthy rival in the revived Aristotelianism, and the controversy began anew. The Middle Ages used its own terminology but the problem was the same. In the medieval terminology the object of a general term—which Plato had called an Idea and Aristotle a form—was now called a universal. A general term was called a universal term, and the problem now was whether there was any universal in the world which corresponded to, or was the object of, a universal term.

Out of this controversy there developed a position advocated in slightly different forms by Thomas Aquinas and Duns Scotus. In general, their position conformed to the Aristotelian tradition that the object of a general term is to be found in each particular to which it is applicable. It was, in considerable part, his interest in the medieval discussion that led Peirce to formulate pragmatism. In the next chapter we shall examine the medieval controversy in more detail in connection with its influence on Peirce.

As Peirce was led in the direction of pragmatism by a study of the medieval discussion, William James was led into a similar view by his study of the British empiricists of the seventeenth and eighteenth centuries. John Locke set the tenor of the discussion for the British empiricists. Locke tells us that

"All things that exist are only particulars"; but "ideas become general, by separating from them the circumstances of time, and place, and any other ideas, that may determine them to this or that particular existence." [6] He says that the general idea of triangularity is of a triangle that is "neither oblique nor rectangle, neither equilateral, equicrural, nor scalenon; but all and none of these at once." [7] To argue that an idea can have all of these properties and none of them at the same time is to take a position that is obviously difficult.

George Berkeley attacked Locke's view at this point and showed its untenability. In setting forth his own view, Berkeley did not "deny absolutely that there are general ideas, but only that there are any *abstract* general ideas. . . . An idea (or 'word') which considered in itself is particular becomes general by being made to represent or stand for all other particular ideas of the same sort." [8]

What Berkeley neglects to account for in this approach is that the idea of representing or standing for is itself a general idea which cannot be reduced to a particular idea. David Hume agrees with Berkeley's objections against Locke but finds Berkeley's own position unsatisfactory because there is nothing in any particular idea that represents any other idea. He sees clearly that the concept of representation is not found in the particular sense experience—the sense experience does not represent anything which is like it; it just is. The representation or resemblance is something put into the experience by the perceiving mind. This is the custom or habit of the mind for associating experiences which in themselves are completely isolated. This analysis results in a completely dissociated uni-

[6] John Locke, *An Essay on Human Understanding*, Bk. III, chap. III, sec. 6.

[7] Locke, *Human Understanding*, Bk. IV, chap. VII, sec. 9.

[8] George Berkeley, *Principles of Human Knowledge*, Introduction, sec. 12.

verse with all of the associations being introduced by the mind.

Philosophers ever since Hume have made repeated assaults upon his position with a notable lack of success. The basic difficulty with Hume's position is the problem of the origin of the custom of associating objects which are not themselves associated. If all knowledge comes from experience and experience is completely atomistic, how does the mind ever get the idea of associating objects? It was this aspect of the problem that led James into his pragmatism. He argued that Hume's general empirical position was sound but that his analysis of what was given in experience was faulty. James's view, as we shall see in greater detail when we come to study him, was that experience is not atomistic, that associations, "conjunctive relations," are given in experience just as completely as are particular objects. Thus James is also led to look to the external world for the counterpart of our general ideas.

Peirce, James, and Dewey all agree in rejecting Hume's atomistic universe. They all, however, accept the method of empiricism and seek for a solution to the impasse that Hume's efforts resulted in, by arguing that experience does not give isolated phenomena of the sort suggested by Hume's atomism. They all endeavor to "purify" empiricism so as to avoid the Humean conclusions. In their efforts they were stimulated and encouraged by those who followed in Hume's footsteps. John Stuart Mill, who sought to apply Hume's approach as rigidly as possible, stimulated them all to try to find the errors in the Humean doctrine. Sir William Hamilton, the Scottish Commonsense Realists, and the British empiricist Shadworth Hodgson all gave moral encouragement by their efforts to reform empiricism. But the efforts of the Scottish Realists and of Hodgson were not the source of the views of Peirce or James; they were rather accepted as encouragement so far as the pragmatists found their views to receive independent corroboration in the results of such men as Reid and Hodgson.

Taking advantage of the efforts of their predecessors in the history of philosophy, the pragmatists undertook a re-examination of this whole problem in the light of developments in scientific methodology. The result of this effort was American pragmatism.

Part 1

THE PRAGMATICISM OF CHARLES PEIRCE

2

Theory of Knowledge

Charles Sanders Peirce (1839–1914) was born in Cambridge, Massachusetts, the second son of Benjamin Peirce, Jr. and Sarah Hunt (Mills) Peirce. The family, on the father's side, was descended from John Pers, or Peirce, a weaver of Norwich, Norfolk County, England, who had come to Watertown, Massachusetts, by 1637.

The Peirce family had a long and close connection with Harvard University. Peirce's paternal grandfather, Benjamin Peirce, Sr. (1778–1831), was a member of the Massachusetts legislature and librarian of Harvard for the last five years of his life. Peirce's father, Benjamin Peirce, Jr. (1809–1880) graduated from Harvard in 1829 and taught mathematics and astronomy at that university for forty-nine years. Peirce's older brother, James Mills Peirce (1834–1906) graduated from Harvard in 1853 and was a member of the Harvard faculty from 1861 to his death in 1906. He taught mathematics, served as the first dean of the Harvard graduate school (1890–95) and was dean of the faculty of arts and sciences (1895–98).

Charles Peirce was a precocious child. He had little formal education in his early years although his father gave him a careful training in mathematics and philosophy. At eight Peirce began to study chemistry of his own accord and at twelve set up his own chemical laboratory. By the time he was thirteen he had made a careful study of Whateley's *Elements of Logic*. The father's mathematical tutelage consisted in giving the boy problems to be solved without giving him the theorems to solve them and encouraging Peirce to discover for himself the theorems which would solve the problems.

Peirce graduated from Harvard in 1859 with a very low scholastic record—he ranked seventy-first in a class of ninety-one. The informality of his early education seems to have given him an independence of thought which ill fitted the rigid system found at Harvard in the days prior to the introduction of the elective system.

In 1861 Peirce joined the staff of the United States Coast and Geodetic Survey, with which he served in varying capacities until 1891. Although Peirce's own interests were more in the direction of philosophy and logic, his father wanted him to be a scientist. In 1862 he received an M.A. from Harvard, and in 1863 an Sc.B. in chemistry, *summa cum laude*. This completed his formal education. In addition to his work with the Coast Survey he served as an assistant at the Harvard Observatory from 1869 to 1872, and from 1872 to 1875 he there made the series of astronomical observations contained in *Photometric Researches* (1878), which was the only book he ever published. In 1875 he was sent to Paris as the first American delegate to the International Geodetic Conference, where he read a paper which made an important contribution to the determination of the gravitational constant.

Peirce's academic connections were not extensive. In all he taught a period of only eight years—and that conjointly with his work for the Coast Survey. In 1864–65 he lectured at Harvard on the philosophy of science, gave the university lectures in philosophy there in 1869–70, and in 1870–71 was the university lecturer on logic. He gave scattered lectures at various institutions in and around Boston for the remainder of his life, but his only other formal academic connection was with Johns Hopkins University where he was a lecturer in logic from 1879 to 1884.[1]

Although Peirce was anxious for an academic appointment, and although William James sought vigorously to obtain one for him, all efforts were in vain. Part of the difficulties were personal and part social. Although Peirce appears to have been an inspiring teacher, he refused to take seriously even the few rigors of academic life. He met his classes irregularly and failed to keep appointments. That he could be ill-tempered and perverse is evident in his writings. In 1863 he married Harriet M. Fay, a prominent and respected member of Boston society. In 1883 he divorced her on the grounds that she had deserted him in 1876. Peirce then married a Madame Pourtalais (Juliette Froissy), who seems to have been an excellent wife for him for the rest of his life. However, Peirce's divorce from his first wife was undoubtedly a significant factor in his inability to secure academic tenure.

In 1887 he inherited some money and bought a house in Milford, Pennsylvania, where he and his wife lived the rest of their lives. Peirce's chief source of income during this period was what little he was able to earn writing book reviews for such journals as *Nation, The North American Review,* and *Popular Science Monthly,* the latter being a somewhat more technical journal then than it now is. He also wrote many definitions for Baldwin's *Dictionary of Philosophy and Psychology.* He published only a few articles although he wrote a great deal, and his work did not become widely known until the publication of his collected papers in the 1930s.

Poor and forgotten, he died of cancer in 1914. Only William

---

[1] An excellent account of Peirce's association with Johns Hopkins may be found in the article, by Max H. Fisch and Jackson I. Cope, titled "Peirce at Johns Hopkins University," in the volume *Studies in the Philosophy of Charles Sanders Peirce,* edited by Philip P. Wiener and Frederick H. Young (Cambridge: Harvard University Press, 1952).

James did what he could to make Peirce's final years easier.

Indirectly through James and Dewey, the work of Peirce exercised a continuing influence on American philosophy, although there was but little of his own work available to American philosophers until 1931. On Peirce's death, his unpublished manuscripts were purchased from his widow by Harvard University. After several years of sorting and classifying, the bulk of the manuscripts were printed by Harvard University Press from 1931 to 1935 in six volumes titled *The Collected Papers of Charles S. Peirce,* under the joint editorship of Charles Hartshorne and Paul Weiss. Two subsequent volumes, edited by Arthur W. Burks, appeared in 1958.

A collection of Peirce's published papers under the title of *Chance, Love and Logic,* edited by Morris Cohen with an introduction by John Dewey, had been published by Harcourt, Brace in 1923 and had stimulated curiosity about Peirce's views. Since the publication of *The Collected Papers,* a number of books have been published about Peirce, and interest in his philosophy is increasing.

This interest has been brought into focus by a basic controversy that has developed in contemporary philosophy. The controversy is that between the logical positivists on the one hand and those philosophers who believe in the possibility of metaphysics on the other. If the positivists are right, the metaphysicians are talking nonsense. If the metaphysicians are right, the positivists are merely developing a special kind of technical virtuosity in a very narrow field only remotely related to true philosophy.

For the most part the offensive has been largely in the hands of the positivists. The tremendous strides made by avowed positivists, and by those closely related to them philosophically, in the fields of symbolic logic and the study of formal language systems, have been such as to place their opponents, at least momentarily, somewhat in awe of them. The efforts of the metaphysicians on their own behalf sometimes seem so feeble that a disinterested observer might almost think that the positivists were beating a straw man.

The kind of approach to certain basic philosophical problems currently used by positivists finds its nearest correlate, in American philosophy, in pragmatism; and of all pragmatists it is most akin to much of the work done by Peirce. The most noticeable characteristics of positivism are its emphasis upon scientific methodology in epistemology, its study of language systems and its development of formal logic, with a closely allied interest in mathematics. All of these trends of thought are basic to the work done by Peirce. Peirce was a scientist in his own right and was thoroughly imbued with the empirical approach to knowledge. In the study of language systems he was a pioneer in the development of the theory of signs. In symbolic logic he did a great deal of work which indicated an extensive interest in the subject far in advance of his own day. Peirce was introduced to mathematics by his father, and Peirce himself did original work in this field. This kinship of interests with positivism indicates that Peirce would be sympathetic toward the logical and empirical emphases in the program of contemporary positivism.

But this represents only one side of Peirce's philosophical interests. He was an extremely serious student of the history of philosophy and of the works of the major philosophers. He read much in both ancient and medieval philosophy in the original and was a keen student of such moderns as Berkeley and Kant. The result of this aspect of his thought was the production of a metaphysical system quite as abstruse and certainly as ambitious in its scope as that of Kant or Alfred North Whitehead. Although clearly an avowed empiricist, Peirce would not have shared with the positivists the opinion that empiricism denies the possibility of metaphysics.

In metaphysics Peirce subscribes to a version of what he

calls metaphysical realism or scholastic realism, out of which he develops pragmatism. Scholastic realism was a position developed by certain medieval scholastic philosophers to deal with the problem of the nature of universals. Peirce tells us that, "Before we treat of the evidences of pragmaticism,[2] it will be needful to weigh the pros and cons of scholastic realism. For pragmaticism could scarcely have entered a head that was not already convinced that there are real generals" (5.503).

Scholastic philosophy is sometimes looked upon as a dry and rather dusty desert extending from St. Augustine to Descartes. Peirce believed that the scholastic controversy over the status of universals had a vital contribution to make to language problems. Bertrand Russell, in commenting on Peirce's interest in this problem, says, "I think Peirce was right in regarding the realist-nominalist controversy as one which is still undecided and which is as important now as at any other time."[3]

John of Salisbury (1117–1180) upon revisiting the university he had attended as a young man, and finding the students still debating the problem of nominalism versus realism, is reported to have commented, "One never gets away from this question. The world has grown old discussing it, and it has taken more time than the Caesars consumed in conquering and governing the world. . . . From whatever point a discussion starts it is always led back and attached to that."

To understand Peirce it is necessary to begin with a brief survey of this rather technical philosophical problem and, in particular, to see something of the solution to it in the form of the realism advocated by Duns Scotus, one of the great

---

[2] "Pragmaticism" was the name Peirce gave to his own version of pragmatism in order to distinguish it from the version of James.

[3] In the foreword to James Feibleman, *An Introduction to Peirce's Philosophy* (New York: Harper, 1946), p. xv.

medieval philosophers, for if frequency of reference is any standard, Duns Scotus was certainly one of the most persistent influences on the development of Peirce's metaphysics.

THE PROBLEM OF UNIVERSALS

The problem of universals is stated by DeWulf as follows:

The problem of universals is the problem of the correspondence of our intellectual concepts to things existing outside our intellect. Whereas external objects are determinate individuals, formally exclusive of all multiplicity, our concepts or mental representations offer us the realities independent of all particular determination; they are abstract and universal. The question, therefore, is to discover to what extent the concepts of the mind correspond to the things they represent; how the flower we conceive represents the flower existing in nature; in a word whether our ideas are faithful and have an objective reality.[4]

It is important to notice carefully what the problem is here because it is not what the problem of the reality of universals is sometimes held to be. In the above definition, DeWulf states the problem twice, using practically the same words each time: "the problem of the *correspondence* of our intellectual *concepts* to *things* existing outside our intellect"; "the question, therefore, is to discover to what extent the *concepts* of the mind *correspond* to the *things* they represent" (italics added). To a modern philosopher this sounds more like the problem of truth than of reality. Be that as it may, this was the problem that the medievals were trying to solve when they were dealing with the problem of the reality of universals. The controversy over realism was not a controversy as to whether or not there were Platonic entities. The problem was whether or not the concepts of the mind corresponded to anything in the external

---

[4] M. DeWulf, "Nominalism, Realism and Conceptualism," *Catholic Encyclopedia*, XI (1909).

world. If so, the concepts were held to be real; if not, they were mere figments of the human imagination. Of course, one answer to this would be to assert that there were Platonic entities. Suppose one took this position; then he was called a realist. But he was called a realist not because he believed there were real Platonic entities, although this was true, too, but because he believed the universals in the mind were real, i.e., corresponded to something in reality. As Peirce says, some of the realists may have believed that there were real Platonic entities, but their realism (in the medieval sense) did not consist in that, but only in their believing that the mental entity was real, i.e., corresponded to an extra-mental entity.

There were four answers given to this problem during the Middle Ages. The first was extreme realism, or Platonism. According to this view there are universal entities existing in an extra-physical realm. The ideas in the mind correspond to these entities. The objects in the physical world reveal them. Thus there are universal entities both within and without the mind. Therefore, the mental entities are real.

At the opposite extreme from this view is nominalism. Nominalism models the idea on the thing. Since the thing is particular, the idea is particular. There are no general ideas because there are no general things. What are called general ideas, or concepts, are merely names, *nomina,* or even noises, *flatus vocis.* Thus there are no universal entities either within or without the mind. Therefore, universal entities are not real, in fact they are not even fictions, for there are no such things even within the mind.

A mediating view between these two extremes was conceptualism. On this view the mind experienced only particulars but by a process of comparison attained generalized concepts. These mental entities are compounds of particular experiences. Thus there are universal entities within the mind, but none without the mind. Therefore, the mental entities are not real.

The fourth position with regard to this problem was called moderate realism. This position was in the current of the Aristotelian answer to the problem. Following a suggestion made by Avicenna, the Arabian commentator on Aristotle, this position was developed in the works of Albert the Great, Thomas Aquinas, and Duns Scotus. As the moderate realists set the problem it was this: All knowledge is in terms of concepts. If these concepts correspond to something that is to be found in reality they are real and man's knowledge has a foundation in fact; if they do not correspond to anything in reality they are not real and man's knowledge is of mere figments of his own imagination.

The moderate realists rejected all of the solutions suggested above. They rejected extreme realism because of the objections Aristotle made against Plato. They rejected nominalism because on that view science was not possible. Since science, and knowledge generally, was of the nature of concepts or general formulae, if, as the nominalists held, man had no general ideas but only particular experiences and general names, and if there was nothing in reality corresponding to these general names, then the general names were names of mere fictions and all science was fictitious. From this point of view conceptualism was but a form of nominalism. The conceptualists did not go so far as to say that man had no general concepts, just names, but they held that the concepts did not correspond to anything in reality. In man's mind there were concepts, in the world there were particulars; this being so, the concepts were but fictions.

As their solution to the problem, the moderate realists held that each external object has an essential nature, or an essence. This essence *qua* essence is neither universal nor particular, it just is. It is neutral. It cannot exist in a separate realm by itself, but it can exist either in an object or in a mind. When it exists in an object it appears as a universal; but in neither case is it either particular or universal in itself.

It is obvious that if the moderate realists could successfully meet the difficulties which this position itself would produce, they would then have a solution for their problem. For then the concept would be real, that is, would not be a fiction of the imagination but would correspond to something which really existed in the external world. Because they adopted this solution to the problem these men were realists, but because they did not take the extreme view of the Platonists, that the universal existed out of any mind or any object, they were moderate realists.

PEIRCE'S SOLUTION

Even from the slight examination of the controversy given above it is possible to see that the basic problem involved was the same problem as that which is at the heart of contemporary discussions of theories of meaning. Man has certain ideas. If these ideas are meaningful (in the medieval terminology, real) they must ultimately refer to something in the external world. Any idea that does not refer to some external entity is meaningless (fictional in medieval terminology). On this view any one who held that a given concept was real had to state what particular it referred to; if he could not indicate such a particular the concept was a fiction.

That Peirce saw the issue in this light may be seen from his statement of the medieval problem: "The question . . . is whether *man, horse,* and other names of natural classes, correspond with anything . . . independent of our thought" (8.12). The moderate realist position, that the referent of a concept is to be found in the experience of a particular, gave Peirce the orientation from which grew the pragmatic position that the ultimate meaning of an idea is to be found in particular experiences. To show the similarities between these views in more detail we must examine Peirce's position.

The three basic concepts in Peirce's epistemology are what he calls firstness, secondness, and thirdness. These are terms that Peirce uses in a categorial rather than a substantive sense, and which therefore have different referents in logic, metaphysics, epistemology, and so on. He describes them variously as three modes of reality (6.342), three categories of being (1.417), or three universes of experience (5.455). As they appear in his epistemology they are closely analogous to some of the basic concepts of scholasticism. For our present purposes we need only discuss firstness and thirdness. A firstness is an idea (6.455)—not an actual idea but only the possibility of an actual idea. For this reason Peirce often calls it a possibility (1.25). It is not an hypostatization such as Plato's forms are, but neither is it an existent thought in some mind. One might argue that it is therefore a nothing. A firstness is between a mere nothing and an existent thing. The difference between a firstness and nothing is that it is possible for a firstness to become actual whereas nothing cannot. Nothing is defined by Peirce as the self-contradictory (6.352), so that a possibility is not a nothing, i.e., is not self-contradictory. Because it is not, it is possible that it could become actual. In this way it is more than a nothing but less than an actual thought. A firstness is something that *can* enter a mind, but considered in its state as a pure firstness it is only the possibility of an idea, not an actual idea.

What Peirce is seeking to describe here is a realm analogous to Platonic ideas (6.452) or unactualized scholastic essences (1.432, 6.337), although he is apparently striving to avoid hypostatizing either firsts or the realm of firstness. The similarity of firstness with the medieval view of unrealized essences may be seen by comparing firstness with Minges's statement of Scotus's opinion on unrealized essences. "Scotus . . . does not attribute to the universals or abstract essences . . . an existence of their own, independent of the individual beings in which they are realized. . . . In the state of mere ideality or possibility before their realization, things have an essence, an ideal conceivable being, but not an actual one." [5]

In his discussion of actually existing objects Peirce analyzes an existent object into qualities and matter (1.527). The qualities are firstnesses which have become embodied (1.527). But as such they are still not actualized ideas; they only become actualized when they are experienced by some mind (1.422, 1.25). When an object is experienced, the qualities produce in the mind a percept. Peirce uses the latter term in a sense analogous to contemporary usage of sense-percept, sense-datum, or sense-image. The percept is the resultant of a psychological process of sensation which is subconscious in its operation (5.182). The percept appears in consciousness as a kind of image (5.115) or feeling (5.116).

Both Peirce and the moderate realists subscribe to the Aristotelian doctrine of immediate perception. "The realist will hold that the very same objects which are immediately present in our minds in experience really exist just as they are experienced out of the mind; that is, he will maintain a doctrine of immediate perception" (8.16). The object is exactly as it is perceived, or the perception is exactly like the object. Because of this doctrine of immediate perception, Peirce tells us, "The percept is the reality" (5.568), i.e., the percept is an actualization of what is a potentiality in the object.

A thirdness is a meaning, a general concept (1.339). Peirce's metaphysical realism consists in his view that the generals [6]

---

[5] Parthenius Minges, "Duns Scotus," *Catholic Encyclopedia*, V (1909).

[6] The term "generals" is used by Peirce where the scholastics used "universals." See 2.367, where the "not" is obviously a typographical error for "now."

which go to make up meanings are real. That is, they have a real external counterpart. His position is that every thirdness must refer to an object to be meaningful (real). Or, every idea must refer to some percept. Stated in detail, his position is as follows: A percept rises to consciousness as a concept by the application to the percept of attention, or "the power of abstraction" (5.295). "By the force of attention, an emphasis is put upon one of the objective elements of consciousness" (5.295). That is, the entire percept, as such, does not rise to consciousness, but attention, like a searchlight, plays over first one part of the percept and then another part, abstracting various elements from the percept and bringing them to the level of consciousness. Thus, in any judgment about a percept there are at least two abstracted concepts—the subject and the predicate. Consider the perceptual judgment, "This stove is black." On the basis of this judgment we make the abstraction of "blackness"; that is, we consider blackness in itself. This blackness as considered in itself is not a fiction; it is not a product of my imagination. It is real. It has an external counterpart, namely the blackness that is in the stove. All that is meant by saying that blackness is real is that there is something which has blackness in it; that is, something which is black. Since this is so, blackness is not a fiction but a reality. "It is perfectly true that all white things have whiteness in them, for that is only saying, in another form of words, that all white things are white; but since it is true that real things possess whiteness, whiteness is real" (8.14).

Furthermore, if it is also possible to abstract blackness from the perceptual judgment, "This chair is black," then blackness is found in both the stove and the chair. But the fact that blackness is found in two different objects shows that blackness is indeterminate with regard to what it is predicated of. Since it is indeterminate in this respect, it is general. Hence, blackness is a real general.

A final point is that if blackness is found in two objects, it is not that the *same* blackness is found in both of them but that blackness *as* found in both of them is the same. "This was one of the points brought out in the controversy in reference to the nature of universals. As Sir William Hamilton says, not even the humanity of Leibniz belongs to Newton, but a different humanity. It is only by abstraction, by an oversight, that two things can be said to have common characters" (2.415).

Thus, to assert that all men are mortal is not to assert that the same mortality belongs to all men, but to assert that the mortality that belongs to each man is similar to the mortality that belongs to each of his fellow men. It is only when we speak loosely and treat concepts as abstractions, or pure firstnesses with no reference to their exemplification, that we identify the mortality of A with that of B. When we express ourselves more rigorously we cannot say that the mortality of A is identical with the mortality of B, but only that the mortality of A is similar to the mortality of B.

I should like to demonstrate Peirce's position by two other examples taken from one of his early (1868) articles. In speaking of triangularity, Peirce says, "The nominalists, I suspect, confound together thinking a triangle without thinking that it is either equilateral, isosceles, or scalene, and thinking a triangle without thinking whether it is equilateral, isosceles, or scalene" (5.301).

That is, the nominalists are right in holding that whenever we think of a triangle we must think of one which is equilateral, isosceles, or scalene. But they are wrong in holding that this is all we can do. By abstraction we can abstract the general concept of triangularity from the percept of any particular triangle, and think of it without thinking whether it is equilateral, isosceles, or scalene.

This point is stated more fully in a second example referring to the general concept "man":

Scholastic realism is usually set down as a belief in metaphysical fictions. But, in fact, a realist is simply one who knows no more recondite reality than that which is represented in a true representation [i.e., a percept]. Since, therefore, the word "man" is true of something, that which "man" means is real. The nominalist must admit that man is truly applicable to something; but he believes that there is beneath this a thing in itself, an incognizable reality. His is the metaphysical figment.[7] . . . The great argument for nominalism is that there is no man unless there is some particular man. That, however, does not affect the realism of Scotus; for although there is no man of whom all further determination can be denied, yet there is a man, abstraction being made of all further determination. There is a real difference between man irrespective of what the other determinations may be, and man with this or that particular series of determinations, although undoubtedly this difference is only relative to the mind and not *in re*. Such is the position of Scotus. Occam's great objection is, there can be no real distinction which is not *in re*, in the thing-in-itself; but this begs the question for it is itself based only on the notion that reality is something independent of representative relation [i.e., of what is given in the percept] (5.312).

The point of this last sentence is that when Scotus makes the distinction between manness and a man, Occam says that this is not a real distinction. This means that the two entities "manness" and "a man" cannot exist separately; therefore, says Occam, any such distinction is fictitious. But this begs the question, for it assumes that for manness to be real in Scotus's sense, it would have to be something that could exist separately, that is, outside of any man.

[7] Peirce means here that the nominalist denies that the percept and the reality are identical. The nominalist introduces an unknowable *ding-an-sich* as the cause of the percept.

Consider the general concept of manness as rational animality. This concept is real if there is something in the physical world which corresponds to it. The nominalists object that there is not. They say, there is this man and that man, but there is no manness, no rational animality. The Scotists (and Peirce) answer: 1) You admit that there is a man; 2) any man has the following characteristics: (a) generic: animality, (b) specific: rationality, (c) other individuating and particularizing determinations which make him *this* man; 3) but since *every* man exemplifies the generic and specific qualities, i.e., rational-animality, there is something in the world which exemplifies rational-animality, and since a concept is real if it is exemplified in the real world, this concept is a real concept. Although manness is not exemplified by itself with no particularizing determinations, it is exemplified in every man. To see it, all we need do is to ignore the particularizing features. What is left is manness.

It is perhaps worthwhile to point out that this is not conceptualism. According to conceptualism, we form abstract concepts by abstracting from a number of different objects, no one of which completely exemplifies the concept. Thus the concept of chairness is obtained, according to this view, by examining a number of different chairs and abstracting one feature from this chair, another feature from that chair, another from a third, etc.; by combining these ideas in our mind we formulate a conception of chairness which is not completely exemplified anywhere in the world and is therefore only a convenient fiction, a mnemonic aid for summarizing a group of experiences. According to the moderate realists, it is not necessary to experience a number of chairs to form the concept; it may be formed by experiencing only one chair.

Peirce's early view on the reality of generals is thus seen to come down to a pure Scotism. Scotus tells us that the species "man" is real because it may be found in any man by making a formal distinction (a distinction made in the mind but based on the object) between the species in any man and his other characteristics. Peirce tells us that the species "man" is real because it may be found in any man by abstraction, by separating it from his particularizing characteristics. Obviously these two views come to the same thing.

THE ORIENTATION TOWARD PRAGMATISM

With the above statement of Peirce's realism as a background it is not difficult to see what he means by saying that pragmatism "could scarcely have entered a head that was not already convinced that there are real generals" (5.503). Pragmatism is a method for defining general concepts (5.8). If one is a nominalist and believes that there is no such thing as "triangularity" anywhere—that triangularity is only a fiction— then there is no place that he can look to see what triangularity really is. But if he is a realist and believes that triangularity may be found in any triangle, then he knows how to define it; it may be defined as part of what one will experience when one examines a triangle.

It is at this point that we must get a firm grasp on the elusive doctrine of immediate perception.[8] Triangularity may be defined as a part of the experience of a triangle because "the percept is the reality" (5.568). "The experience of a triangle" and "a triangle" are epistemologically identical. Therefore, if we list all of the possible experiences one might have of a triangle, these experiences *are* the triangles.

Now how would we go about it if we wanted to list these experiences? We could just state the bald list of experiences, but the list by itself might not suffice to enable the individual for whose benefit the definition is being made actually to obtain those precise experiences. To insure that he would have

[8] See p. 30.

the proper experiences, perhaps the best approach would be to prescribe for him a certain action such that, if he accomplished it, he would then be confronted by the required experience. Such a prescription would be a plan or a guide for action. One who performed the prescribed action would have the requisite experience and would then know—by experience of it—the property being defined. Of course, such a plan for action would necessarily be complex, but if it is sufficiently detailed so as actually to give a perceptual acquaintance with the property being defined, then it would serve as a definition. Peirce gives an example of this procedure:

If you look into a textbook of chemistry for a definition of *lithium*, you may be told that it is that element whose atomic weight is 7 very nearly. But if the author has a more logical mind he will tell you that if you search among minerals that are vitreous, translucent, grey or white, very hard, brittle, and insoluble, for one which imparts a crimson tinge to an unluminous flame, this mineral being triturated with lime or witherite rats-bane, and then fused, can be partly dissolved in muriatic acid; and if this solution be evaporated, and the residue be extracted with sulphuric acid, and duly purified, it can be converted by ordinary methods into a chloride, which being obtained in the solid state, fused, and electrolyzed with half a dozen powerful cells, will yield a globule of a pinkish silvery metal that will float on gasolene; and the material of *that* is a specimen of lithium. The peculiarity of this definition—or rather this precept that is more serviceable than a definition—is that it tells you what the word lithium denotes by prescribing what you are to *do* in order to gain a perceptual acquaintance with the object of the word (2.330).

One might generalize this approach by holding that a concept may be defined by prescribing that: If you act in a certain manner, then you will have certain experiences, and the sum of the ideas resulting from these experiences constitutes the meaning of the concept being defined. The development of this thesis leads to Peirce's version of pragmatism.

Such a theory of meaning can only be accepted if one believes that concepts are real, that is, if he believes that the concepts have a real external counterpart. If he believes this, and wants to know where to look for this counterpart, then a pragmatic definition will give him a practical guide for actions that will result in an experience of the counterpart. But if he does not believe that concepts are real, then when he follows out the pragmatic definition he will not believe that what he experiences will be the external counterpart, or the referent of the concept, for he does not believe that the concept has any referent. In short, to accept pragmatism is to accept metaphysical realism with reference to concepts.

As Peirce says (1.27), the realist-nominalist controversy is a question to which only two answers are possible: yes or no. If one admits that concepts are general ideas and then asks, is there anything in reality that stands in a one-to-one relation to the concept, an affirmative answer is only possible on a realist position; a negative answer relegates concepts to the realm of fictions. It follows from this that pragmatism could not be accepted by anyone who does not also accept metaphysical realism, and that the former could scarcely have entered the head of anyone who did not already understand the latter (5.503).

THE STRUCTURE OF IDEAS

Thus far in our discussion of Peirce's philosophy we have concerned ourselves primarily with the relation of the idea to the object and with a description of the process by which the idea gets into the mind. We have now to ask what an idea is when it is in a mind and then to ask what the relation may be between ideas and conduct. The first problem is the problem of the meaning of meaning; the second problem leads into pragmatism as a theory of definition.

What is the meaning of meaning? That is, what do we mean (denote, intend, refer to) by the sign "meaning"? Peirce tells us that pragmatism "is a method for ascertaining the real meaning of any concept, doctrine, proposition, word, or other sign" (5.6). If pragmatism is a method for ascertaining meanings, then the problem of what a meaning may be is an important problem for the pragmatist.

In reference to meaning, Peirce says: "The object of a sign is one thing; its meaning is another. Its object is the thing or occasion, however indefinite, to which it is to be applied. Its meaning is the idea which it attaches to that object, whether by way of mere supposition, or as a command, or as an assertion" (5.6).

If a meaning is an idea, then we can begin our inquiry by investigating the problem of what an idea is. There are two ways of examining ideas. We may consider them epistemologically, in which case we analyze their formal structure (are ideas simples or complexes? etc.); or we may consider them psychologically, in which case we would discuss their material nature (what is the psychological or physiological analogue of the epistemological entity "idea"?).

Peirce's epistemological analysis of an idea is the whole basis of his pragmatism. He begins by asking how many kinds of ideas there may be and he finds that there are three (5.7). The first kind is an idea of a percept or sense-datum in itself, without relation to anything else, for example, the idea of redness. In Peircean terminology, this is the idea of a "firstness." In the second place, there are ideas of acting or being acted upon. This involves two objects, that which acts and that which is acted upon. Hence this is an idea of a "secondness." This kind of idea cannot be reduced simply to two ideas of firstness. The idea of billiard ball A acting upon billiard ball B is not the same as the idea of billiard ball A plus the idea of billiard ball B. The third kind of idea is the idea of a sign, which is the

idea of a "communication conveyed by one person to another
(or to himself at a later time) in regard to a certain object
well known to both" (5.7). A sign relation cannot be completely reduced to a mere combination of the first two types of
ideas. The signification by A that B is related to C cannot be
reduced simply to A plus B plus C. It is something more than
its constituents; it is the assertion of a relation between them.

According to Peirce, these three kinds of ideas have two important characteristics: 1) They cannot be reduced to one
another (1.343, 1.345, 5.469); 2) All complex ideas may be
reduced to combinations of these three (1.347, 3.420, 5.469).

Peirce calls these types of ideas the "indecomposable concepts" (5.5). He often compares them to atomic elements in
chemistry, since elements cannot be reduced to one another
but all other chemical substances are compounds of them. For
pragmatism the vital importance of these indecomposable concepts may be seen by continuing the analogy with chemistry.
Just as a chemical compound may be defined by stating the
atomic elements which go to make it up and by indicating
the relation between them, so a complex idea may be defined
by stating the indecomposable concepts which go to make it
up and by indicating the relations between them.

The doctrine of pragmatism thus has an architectonic construction (5.5). Having made his analysis and found three types
of indecomposable concepts, Peirce then proceeded to construct the pragmatic method as a procedure for discovering
the exact indecomposable concepts of any particular complex
idea (5.5).

He calls this analysis of indecomposable concepts "The
Kernel of Pragmatism" (5.464) and "The Bedrock beneath
Pragmaticism" (4.562). He enunciates it at great length in
what he titles a "Prolegomena to an Apology for Pragmaticism"
(4.530ff.). He worked out the position in terms of a system
of "existential graphs" which he called his "chef d'oeuvre"

(4.347*ff.*). He holds that the nature of these concepts is demonstrated in logic where he argues that monadic, dyadic, and
triadic relations cannot be reduced to one another, but any
higher order relation can be reduced to a combination of these
(3.421). He says, "Such, at least, is the doctrine I have been
teaching for twenty-five years, and which if deeply pondered
will be found to enwrap an entire philosophy" (3.422). He
considered this the fount and origin of all his thought. "The
little that I have contributed to pragmatism (or, for that matter, to any other department of philosophy), has been entirely
the fruit of this outgrowth from formal logic, and is worth
much more than the small sum total of the rest of my work, as
time will show" (5.469).

An idea of a firstness is an idea of a perception; an idea of
a secondness is an idea of acting or being acted upon; since
in the case of human experiences this always involves an act
of will, Peirce calls it an idea of a volition. So a firstness is an
idea of a perception, a secondness an idea of a volition (5.7).
These are both simple ideas. The idea of a perception is simply
the idea of a perception, and the idea of a volition is simply that
and nothing else. An idea of a thirdness, or a sign, however, has
a more complex structure. A thirdness relates some two other
objects by means of a third. Thus a sign signifies to some individual, A, that some property, B, belongs to some object, C.
So that a sign can be explicated in terms of its three elements
and the relations between them. This may appear to be a contradiction of our statement above, that these three kinds of
ideas cannot be reduced to one another. The analogy with
chemistry may be helpful again. We say that the nature of
water can be explicated by the expression H_2O. Actually this
is not the case if we read this to mean that water can be expressed as two volumes of hydrogen plus one volume of oxygen. For it is possible to have two volumes of hydrogen and
one volume of oxygen without having water. What is needed

is that we have two volumes of hydrogen and one volume of oxygen in a specific relation to one another. Accordingly, a full statement of what water is would involve these two elements plus a statement of the relation between them. Similarly here we cannot reduce a thirdness simply to firsts and seconds, but we can explicate the meaning of a third by indicating the firsts and seconds that are involved in it plus a statement of the relation between them.

Consider as an instance of a thirdness the case of a driver approaching an intersection at the corner of which there is a sign which contains the word "stop." This sign signifies to the driver, A, that the property of stopping, B, is applicable to the intersection, C.

This example has the merit of illustrating that a thirdness is not always just a relation among simple ideas (firsts and seconds). One, or more, of the elements related may itself be a thirdness. Thus A is a firstness, the driver's awareness or perception of himself. C is a firstness, the driver's awareness or perception of the intersection. But B (stopping) is a thirdness. Every thirdness can be reduced to its elements, so, we may ask, what are the elements involved here? To stop, B, means that the driver must have the volitional experience, D (a secondness), of willing to act by stepping on his brake pedal, and then have this followed by the perception, E (a firstness), of being at rest. Thus B relates D to E. If either D or E were a thirdness, a complete explication of the meaning of the stop sign would involve a further reduction to firsts and seconds.

Thus the bottom meaning of a sign will always be stated in terms of ideas of perception and/or ideas of volition. That is, every thirdness denotes some combination of firsts and seconds. "Now the bottom meaning of a sign cannot be the idea of a sign, since that latter sign must itself have a meaning which would thereby become the meaning of the original sign. We may therefore conclude that the ultimate meaning of any sign consists either in an idea predominantly of feeling or in one predominantly of acting and being acted on" (5.7).

There is a certain looseness in the above discussion in the use of the terms "idea" and "sign" which we need to clarify here. The ideas of a first, a second, and a third are all ideas and hence are really signs. However, Peirce considers pragmatism to be concerned primarily with explicating the meaning of thirds, and hence often refers to them as if they were the only kind of sign. He speaks a little more precisely in 5.8, where he singles thirds out by giving them the name "intellectual concepts." He says, "But pragmatism does not undertake to say in what the meaning of all signs consist, but merely to lay down a method of determining the meanings of intellectual concepts, that is, of those upon which reasonings may turn."

Thus pragmatism is concerned primarily with explicating the meaning of thirds, and the position, in general, is that all ideas of the third type (intellectual concepts) may be analyzed into ideas of the first type (ideas of perception) and ideas of the second type (ideas of volition), in certain relations to one another.

THE PRAGMATIC MAXIM

We must now see a little more precisely what an intellectual concept is. According to Peirce (5.8), intellectual concepts are "those upon which reasonings may turn" and reasoning "turns upon precise necessary reasoning." As an example of necessary reasoning we are referred to mathematics. Peirce here quotes his father's definition of mathematics as "the science which draws necessary conclusions." That is, mathematics shows what theorems follow, logically and necessarily, if one performs the customary operations on the postulates of a mathematical system. If such and such operations are performed, then such and such a result will ensue. Peirce goes on to argue that the reasonings of the scientists are of the same order as those of the mathematician although, due to physical factors that enter into scientific experiments, less certain (5.8).

He concludes, "Such reasonings and all reasonings turn upon the idea that if one exerts certain kinds of volition, one will undergo in return certain compulsory perceptions. Now this sort of consideration, namely that certain lines of conduct will entail certain kinds of inevitable experiences is what is called a 'practical consideration'" (5.9).

This definition of a practical consideration is of considerable importance. It is "the idea that if one exerts certain kinds of volition, one will undergo in return certain compulsory perceptions" or "that certain lines of conduct will entail certain kinds of inevitable experiences." Thus the idea of an intellectual concept resolves into an idea of an entailment relation between ideas of the first two types.

Some light may be cast upon this definition of a practical consideration by an examination of what Peirce calls a logical consequence. He distinguishes between an antecedent, a consequent, and a consequence:

> In the language of logic "consequence" does not mean that which follows, which is called the *consequent*, but means the fact that a consequent follows from an antecedent (4.435, n.1).

> It may be mentioned that Scotus . . . and the later scholastics usually dealt, not with the Syllogism, but with an inferential form called a consequence. The consequence has only one expressed premise, called the *antecedent*; its conclusion is called the *consequent*; and the proposition which asserts that in case the antecedent be true, the consequent is true, is called the consequence (4.45).

A logical consequence, then, is not the antecedent, nor the consequent, but the assertion that the consequent follows from the antecedent.

A practical consideration is quite similar to this. A practical consideration is the idea that "certain lines of conduct will entail certain kinds of inevitable experiences" (5.9). That is, a practical consideration is an idea that if one does a certain action, then he will have a certain perception. Just as a logical consequence has as constituent elements an antecedent and a consequent, although the consequence is neither of these but rather is the relation between them, so a practical consideration has as constituent elements an experience of action and an experience of perception, but the practical consideration is neither of these but is the relation between them. The meaning of the proposition "There is a bookcase in that room" is the practical consideration "If I go into that room, then I will see a bookcase." The practical consideration does not consist of the antecedent, my going into the room; nor of the consequent, my seeing the bookcase; but of the idea that the consequent follows upon the antecedent; that is, *if* I go into the room, *then* I will see the bookcase. A practical consideration is thus seen to be an idea of the general form, "If I conduct myself in manner *x*, then I will have experience *y*," which may be taken as equivalent to Peirce's version that "if one exerts certain kinds of volition, one will undergo in return certain compulsory perceptions" (5.9). Stated more generally, a practical consideration is an idea of an entailment relation which holds between an idea of volition and an idea of perception.

On this interpretation of a practical consideration, we can see at once what Peirce means by saying that intellectual concepts are those upon which reasonings turn. If we know that a certain concept is applicable to a certain object, we may immediately reason about it in a number of ways. We may reason that if we act toward the object in manner A, then we will have experience B; if we act toward it in manner C, then we will have experience D; etc. But if we interpret meaning, as is ordinarily done, as merely a list of certain properties of an object, then we have no basis for any reasonings. If by saying that an object is gold we mean merely yellowness, malleability, heaviness, etc., we cannot do any reasoning about such predicates. We can only reason about them when, implicitly or explicitly, we rephrase them as practical considerations: if I look at this object, then I will see yellowness; if I strike it, then I will experience malleability; if I lift it, then I will experience heaviness; etc. To express the same point in more technical terminology, logical reasoning cannot take place in a universe of discourse made up solely of terms; we must be given some relations between the terms before any reasoning can take place. Therefore, when Peirce holds that the meaning of an intellectual concept is the sort of idea upon which reasonings may turn, his position is that meanings consist of practical considerations, and upon these reasonings may turn, for they prescribe relations between terms.

In calling considerations of this sort "practical," Peirce means simply that they influence practice. Suppose that I believe that a concept is applicable to a given object, and I believe that one of the considerations which is true under these circumstances is that if I conduct myself in manner A, then I will have experience B. And suppose that I want to have experience B. My knowledge of the consideration, plus my desire for B, influences my practice so that I act in manner A. That is, from any consideration of the form "If I conduct myself in manner x, then I will have experience y" I may infer the practical dictum "If I want to have experience y, then I will conduct myself in manner x."

We may distinguish here two meanings of practical—a cognitive aspect and a purposive aspect. The cognitive aspect includes a knowledge of what the conceivable considerations are which might enter into a human experience; the purposive aspect includes the cognitive aspect plus the realization that if one has in mind the purpose of attaining the experience indicated in the cognitive consequent, he must perform the action indicated in the cognitive antecedent. Peirce calls the purposive aspect the "intellectual purport" of the concept. He tells us that the pragmatist "has always explicitly stated that the intellectual purport of a concept consists in the truth of certain conditional propositions [i.e., practical considerations] asserting that if the concept be applicable, and the utterer of the proposition or his fellow have a certain purpose in view he would act in a certain way (5.528).

This is due to the fact that if a concept is applicable, "it follows that the concept has a capability of having a bearing upon conduct; and this fact will lend it intellectual purport. For it cannot be denied that one, at least, of the functions of intelligence is to adapt conduct to circumstances, so as to subserve desire" (5.548).

The element of purpose, or intellectual purport, is basic to what Peirce meant by pragmatism. It was because of the importance he attached to the relation between meaning and purpose that he called his theory pragmatism. He tells us that he took the term from Kant (5.412). Kant uses the term "pragmatic" as a name for hypothetical imperatives having to do with "skill in the choice of means to one's own greatest well-being." [9] This certainly involves purpose. Peirce tells us: "Quite the most striking feature of the new theory was its recognition of an inseparable connection between rational cognition and rational purpose; and that consideration it was which determined the preference for the name pragmatism" (5.412).

But by 1905 Peirce felt that the name was attaining a usage so separated from the notion of purpose that he ought to give it up. "So then, the writer, finding his bantling 'pragmatism' so promoted, feels that it is time to kiss the child good-by and

[9] Immanuel Kant, *The Fundamental Principles of the Metaphysics of Ethics*, trans. Otto Manthey-Zorn (New York: Appleton-Century, 1938), pp. 32–33.

relinquish it to its higher destiny; while to serve the precise purpose of expressing the original definition, he begs to announce the birth of the word 'pragmaticism,' which is ugly enough to be safe from kidnappers" (5.414).

In pragmaticism—i.e., Peirce's version of pragmatism— what we have called the cognitive and the purposive aspect of meaning become identified. The cognitive aspect includes a knowledge of what the considerations are which might enter into a human experience. But how do we know whether a particular consideration is such that it might enter into human experience? We ask the question, is there any purpose a human being might have in mind which could be such that it would induce him to act in accord with this consideration? If so, it has cognitive meaning; if not, not. That is, only those considerations which have purposive bearing have cognitive meaning (5.428). From this point of view pragmatism is a method designed to discover those considerations which are such that they may have an influence upon human action. And these considerations it holds to be the meaning of the concept. Thus it is that Peirce comes to the maxim with which he closed his 1903 Harvard lectures on pragmatism: "The elements of every concept enter into logical thought at the gate of perception and make their exit at the gate of purposive action; and whatever cannot show its passports at both these two gates is to be arrested as unauthorized by reason" (5.212).

Those practical considerations which have a purposive bearing constitute the intellectual purport of a sign or other symbol, and it is the intellectual purport which pragmatism equates with the meaning and endeavors to define (5.438).

THE FORMULATION OF A PRAGMATIC DEFINITION

Keeping in mind the above analysis, let us now apply it to a concrete case. Let us consider the sign "tree" to see how this sign comes to take on a meaning and what the meaning may be, as an illustration of Peirce's analysis.

We may begin by asking what constitutes the definition of a term. The classical doctrine, going back to Aristotle, is that a definition must state the essential nature of the object being defined, so that "man" is defined as a rational animal. Presumably, however, an individual who asks what a man is, does not know the essential nature of man, so this definition may not be of much help. Accordingly, suppose that he then asks what a rational animal is. He will be told that it is a part of the class of sensitive, living things. If he asks what this is, he will be told that it is part of the class of animate bodies. If he asks as to this, he is advised that it is part of the class of corporeal substances. But if he now asks what this is he is told that this is inexplicable.

In speaking of this doctrine, Peirce says,

The doctrine then was . . . that there is no way of defining a term except by enumerating all its universal predicates, each of which is more abstracted and general than the term defined. So unless this process can go on endlessly, which was a doctrine little followed, the explication of a concept must stop at such ideas as Pure Being, Agency, Substance and the like which were held to be ideas so perfectly simple that no explanation whatever could be given of them (5.207; see also 5.500).

While every language system must have its primitive indefinables, it is certainly inconvenient to have these indefinables consist of ideas as abstract as pure being, agency, substance, etc. One might hope that a theory of definition could be found which would have as its indefinables some set of terms more concrete and more recognizable as a part of human experience than these abstractions. This is what Peirce was seeking for in formulating pragmatism, and he constructed the pragmatic maxim as an alternative to this method of definition (5.500).

An individual who finds the traditional theory of definition unsatisfactory may feel that there are other alternatives which offer a hope of success. For example, one might think that the meaning of a general term is a certain visual image, so that the meaning of treeness in a human mind is some visual image. But, aside from the arguments in favor of imageless thought, the term "tree" is applied to objects which give quite different visual images, e.g., a palm tree and a pine tree. Accordingly, it scarcely seems as though a meaning can be an image. Or one might think that the meaning of treeness is simply a certain set of words which comes into the mind when treeness is thought of. But this will not suffice either. For if one says that by treeness he means simply the word "tree," he is in the difficult position of holding that the French *arbre* and the German *baum* do not signify treeness.

If one undertakes to discover what treeness is, i.e., to discover the meaning of the word "tree," he will find that the meaning is limited in two ways. First of all, there should be nothing in a meaning that is not found in the object. For example, if no tree is edible, then edibility will not be any part of the definition of "tree." If, then, there will be nothing in the definition which is not found in the object, the definition is limited on one side by the object being defined. It is limited on the other side by the individual who is doing the defining. That is, if trees have properties which no individual ever knows anything about, such properties can never be part of what anyone means by a tree, for human meaning cannot transcend possible human experience. "It is precisely the pragmatists' contention that symbols, owing their origin (on one side) to human conventions, cannot transcend conceivable human occasions" (5.532). This is the aspect of pragmatism that was emphasized by William James and that produced the greatest controversy when pragmatism was first suggested. Today it is a truism in language theory.

Thus we find a definition limited on two sides. It is limited on one side by the object and on the other side by the individual who experiences the object. Meanings may change, because as more experiences are had of the object additional features of it may be discovered. The meaning of a term may thus change extensively throughout history. Witness the history of scientific terms such as time, space, atom, etc.

Within these limits, then, let us see how a meaning is formulated. Suppose we consider a child just learning to talk and becoming increasingly aware of the external world around him. Suppose some fine autumn day that his father takes him out for a walk. They climb a hill and at the top of the hill the child encounters an object which he touches and finds to occasion an experience of roughness. He says to his father, "What is that?" His father replies, "That is a tree." Thus the word "tree" now means to the child something such that if he touches it he will have an experience of roughness. The child leans against the tree to rest and finds that the tree supports him. He now adds to the meaning of "tree" the idea that a tree is an object such that if he leans against it he will have the experience of being supported. Suppose his father now cuts the tree down and takes part of it home and puts it in the fireplace, from which there presently comes warmth. The child's meaning of "tree" now grows to include the idea that a tree is an object such that if he cuts it down and puts it in the fireplace he will experience warmth. The next summer he learns that objects called trees are green in summer, that if one sits under them in summer he will feel cooler, etc., etc. Thus what the child means by a tree continues to grow as his experiences grow. When he gets to the point where he has had all of the commoner experiences of a tree, his meaning of "tree" will coincide with that held by most people, and he will have no difficulty knowing what they mean by "tree."

What the child knows, then, is that with reference to any

object, A, to which the term "tree" is applicable, there is a series of propositions such as the following which is true of this object:

1. If I act so as to touch A, then I will have the experience of roughness.

2. If I act so as to lean against A, then I will have the experience of being supported.

3. If I act so as to cut A down and put it in the fireplace, then I will have the experience of warmth.

4. If I act so as to sit under A in the summer time, then I will have the experience of feeling cooler.

And so on.

The sum of all such propositions constitutes what is meant by treeness. Each of these propositions represents an idea of a relation which holds between an idea of volition and an idea of perception. The sum of these ideas of relations between possible experiences constitutes the meaning of treeness. We may amplify this illustration of a pragmatic definition by referring to Peirce's original formulation of the pragmatic maxim: "Consider what effects, that might conceivably have practical bearings we conceive the object of our conception to have. Then our conception of these effects is the whole of our conception of the object" (5.402).

The "object of our conception" here is a tree. The effects "that might conceivably have practical bearings" are the practical considerations, "our conception of these effects" is the whole of our idea of a tree.

SOME THEORETICAL IMPLICATIONS

There are two possible misinterpretations to be avoided in understanding a definition such as that given above. Peirce holds that the meaning of a concept is analyzable into practical considerations. But a practical consideration may be thought of as having three parts: an antecedent, or idea of acting (a secondness); a consequent, or idea of perception (a firstness); and the practical consideration proper, or the idea of a relation between the antecedent and the consequent. On Peirce's view it is the sum of the practical considerations which constitute the meaning. But it is possible to misinterpret it so as to assert that it is the sum of the actions which constitutes the meaning or that it is the sum of the percepts which does so. Peirce rejects both of these alternatives (5.402, n.3). For him the units which go to make up meanings are ideas of the form, If I act in manner x, then I will have experience y.

Another point to be noted is that practical considerations are general propositions. They refer to all conceivable occasions of acting in way x. Accordingly the meaning of an idea cannot be stated completely in terms of any actual actions done in terms of these considerations; they refer to any conceivable, or possible, ways of acting in manner x, whether such actions actually do occur or not. The emphasis on conceivable experiences enables meanings to be general. If meanings included only the actual actions they would be applicable to only a finite number of instances, but since they include all conceivable actions of the sort x they are general; for "it is plain that no possible collection of single occasions of conduct can be, or adequately represent *all* conceivable occasions" (5.532).

We may now ask as to what the physiological or psychological analogue of a thought or idea may be. According to Peirce, the physiological counterpart of a thought is a habit (5.538). His interpretation of a thought as a habit is doubtless due to the following similarities between habits and thoughts:

1. Both habits and thoughts are general. Just as no finite number of applications of a concept can completely exhaust a meaning, so no finite number of actions can completely represent an habitual mode of behavior.

2. Both habits and thoughts are expressible only in terms of human behavior and experience.

3. The essence of both habits and thoughts is a relation. As the thought does not consist of the antecedent or the consequent but of the relation between them, so the habit does not consist of the stimulus or the response but of the relation between them.

4. Finally, both habits and thoughts are relevant to human purposes. When I have in mind certain purposes I have certain habitual ways of responding in order to attain them.

What we are trying to do when we ask what a man means by some term is to determine how he habitually acts toward an object to which he will apply the term. That is, we want to characterize a habit. A habit is a very tenuous thing but, since it is a way of acting, it may be characterized in two respects: it may be characterized in terms of when it causes us to act and how it causes us to act (5.400). As to the when, the stimulus to action is always derived from perception; as to the how, the end of all action is the attainment of some sensible result. "Thus we come down to what is tangible and practical, as the root of every real distinction of thought, no matter how subtle it may be; and there is no distinction of meaning so fine as to consist in anything but a possible difference of practice" (5.400).

Suppose that a man has an idea, or a habit, how can we discover what it is? If he has an idea of what treeness is, an habitual way of acting toward objects which he considers to be trees, and if I have an idea of treeness, how can we find out whether our ideas of treeness are the same? We are finally brought face to face with the problem a theory of meaning is intended to solve: How can we discover what different individuals mean by a given sign?

In speaking of pragmatism Peirce says that it is nothing but an application of the "older logical rule, 'By their fruits ye shall know them'" (5.465).

That is, the idea which a man may have is a private, personal thing not subject to public examination. Hence I cannot discover what his idea is by a direct examination of it. But if the situation is such that an idea bears certain fruits and the fruits are such that I can know them, then I can thus indirectly get to know what his idea is.

Peirce tells us, "Now the problem of what the 'meaning' of an intellectual concept is can only be solved by the study of the interpretants, or proper significate effects, of signs" (5.475).

But what are these interpretants or effects of signs? "The Immediate Object of all knowledge and all thought is, in the last analysis, the Percept. This doctrine in no wise conflicts with Pragmaticism, which holds that the Immediate Interpretant of all thought proper is Conduct. Nothing is more indispensable to a sound epistemology than a crystal-clear discrimination between the Object and Interpretant of knowledge" (4.539).

The immediate interpretant of an idea, then, is conduct. It would follow from this that if we wanted to see what an idea was, we would have to observe what conduct it gave rise to. But why is it the case that conduct serves as an interpretant for a thought? This is due to the analysis we made above of the structure of an idea. To return to our example of treeness, suppose I want to know if some individual has the same idea of treeness that I have. I observe how he acts toward an object which he calls a tree. Suppose that I see him in the summer and he is perspiring and as I watch him he goes over and stands under an object which he calls a tree; then I know that his idea of a tree agrees with mine to the extent that he believes that a tree is something such that if you stand under it in the summer you will feel cooler. Suppose he is tired and leans against it; then I know that he believes that a tree is an object such that if you lean against it, it will support you. Suppose that on a cold day I see him cut it down and put it in the fire; then I know he believes that a tree in the fireplace means warmth; and so on down the list of propositions which go to make up my idea of a tree. If I find that his actions indicate that he believes every one of the propositions that I believe, then he means the same thing by a tree that I mean.

From this situation, three important propositions follow:

1. If he always acts toward an object which he calls a "tree" just as I act toward an object which I call a "tree," then we mean the same thing by "tree."

2. If he acts differently in some respects than I do, then we have different meanings for "tree."

3. If he always acts the same way toward an object that I call a "tree" as I do, only he calls this object a "druid," then he means the same thing by a "druid" that I mean by a "tree."

These actions of his follow from, and hence are consequences of, the practical considerations which go to make up his idea. He believes the practical consideration that "If I stand under a tree on a hot day I will feel cooler." His action— standing under the tree—is a consequence of this practical belief, and hence is called a practical consequence.

Thus we come to a later (1905) statement of the pragmatic maxim: "In order to ascertain the meaning of an intellectual conception one should consider what practical consequences might conceivably result by necessity from the truth of that conception; and the sum of these consequences will constitute the entire meaning of the conception" (5.9).

SOME OBJECTIONS EXAMINED

Having attained an initial formulation of the pragmatic maxim, we may examine some objections that may be raised against it.

One such objection would raise the issue of whether the term "habit" properly describes an idea. Do we not seem to have ideas which are not habits? With reference to this objection I think Peirce would not deny this so far as firstnesses and secondnesses are concerned. That is, the term "redness," for example, may denote simply the idea of redness and nothing else. No habit need be involved. What I take Peirce to intend, however, is that all ideas of the third sort, all intellectual concepts, all ideas that influence practical behavior, that are guides to action, are habits. They prescribe ways in which we would respond, specific stimuli being presented.

A second objection might be raised: Does not the term "habit" properly refer only to a stimulus-response pattern that is established only after it has been repeated a number of times, so that the "habit" would be present only after the idea has led us to behave in the specified manner on a number of occasions? In reply to this objection, Peirce would simply deny that this is the case. For him a habit is a disposition, a tendency, to respond in a specified fashion. This tendency may be established even though the action has in fact never been performed. We may, in imagination, have rehearsed a certain situation and decided how we *would* act in response to a stimulus even though we may never have had occasion to actually so respond. In such a case he would say we would have a tendency to so respond, a habit would be formed, without our ever having so responded.

Peirce gives the following illustration of such a situation:

I well remember when I was a boy, and my brother Herbert, now our minister at Christiania, was scarce more than a child, one day, as the whole family were at table, some spirit from a "blazer," or "chafing-dish," dropped on the muslin dress of one of the ladies and was kindled; and how instantaneously he jumped up, and did the right thing, and how skilfully each motion was adapted to the purpose. I asked him afterward about it; and he told me that since Mrs. Longfellow's death, it was that he had often run over in imagination all the details of what ought to be done in such an emergency. It was a striking example of a real habit produced by exercises in the imagination (5.487n.; see also 5.538).

Dewey argues in a similar manner:

Repetition is in no sense the essence of habit. Tendency to repeat acts is an incident of many habits but not of all. A man with the habit of giving way to anger may show his habit by a murderous attack upon some one who has offended. His act is nonetheless due to habit because it occurs only once in his life. The essence of habit is an acquired predisposition to *ways* or modes of response (*Human Nature*, p. 42).

A third question that might be raised would deal with the propriety of equating a habit, which seems to be a physical (or physiological) entity, with an idea, which is a psychic (or psychological) entity. Although pragmatism is often accused of making this identity, I do not see that it in fact does do so. Peirce is quite insistent that so far as a habit is a way of behavior it is only the interpretant of an idea (4.539), not the idea itself. The actions performed are the "fruits" of an idea; by studying them we come to know the idea, but the idea is not itself a physical mode of behavior.[10]

We may therefore conclude that the pragmatic theory of meaning is the theory that the meaning of an idea may be explicated by describing the ways in which we would habitually act and the experiences we would habitually expect from any object to which we would apply this idea. Further, since the idea is represented in behavior by a habit, the ways in which people behave may be taken as cues to their ideas. By translating ideas into behavior, pragmatism reduces meanings to

[10] Objections might be raised at this point concerning the "mind-body" problem. I do not see that any of the pragmatists deal with this problem successfully. But then I do not see that anyone else has done so either. One might call to mind Ralph Barton Perry's dictum that an objection which applies equally to all philosophies cannot be held specifically against one philosophy.

something public and observable rather than private and personal.

Having seen how the pragmatic theory would be applied to determine the meaning of an idea of a concrete object like a tree, we may now turn to an examination of the way in which a pragmatist would deal with an abstract concept. We will use Peirce's analysis of the term "reality" for this purpose.

3

Theory of Reality

In defining what the real is, Peirce uses what appear to be two different definitions. The first of these is: "The real is that which is not whatever we happen to think it, but is unaffected by what we may think of it" (8.12; but see also 5.405, 5.430, 5.525, 5.565, 6.327, 6.349, 6.495).

In spite of the fact that Peirce wrote in 1909 that this was the sense in which he "always" used the word (6.327), it is also true that he usually coupled to it what looks like a second definition: "The opinion which is fated to be ultimately agreed to by all who investigate is what we mean by the truth, and the object represented in this opinion is the real" (5.407; see also 5.430, 5.311, 2.654).

I propose to begin with the first definition and show how the second is evolved out of it.

According to the first definition, the ultimate reality of the object does not depend upon its being observed, although, since it is unaffected by the act of being observed, if it is observed it will be the same for all observers.

That this is the interpretation Peirce wishes to place upon the term real may be seen from the following:

That is *real* which has such and such characters, whether anybody thinks it to have those characters or not (5.430).

If Man is the measure of things, as Protagoras said, then there is no complete reality (6.349).

I define the *real* as that which holds its characters on such a tenure that it makes not the slightest difference what any man or men may have thought them to be, or ever will have thought them to be (6.495).

Thus, the reality of the object remains unaffected by a change in percipients. It has its characters "whether anybody thinks it to have those characters or not." As we have already indicated, Peirce subscribes to a doctrine of immediate perception, i.e., he believes that when anyone perceives an object, he perceives it directly and immediately, exactly as it is. But if the characteristics of an object do not change with a change in percipients, and if each percipient perceives the object exactly as it is, it follows that the object will appear the same to every observer. Thus, from the first definition and the doctrine of immediate perception, we may formulate a criterion of reality: A real object is an object that appears the same to every observer.

In the first definition Peirce, in true scholastic style, is trying to distinguish the real from the fictional or, as he also calls it, a figment. He says that "the fictive is that whose characters depend upon what characters somebody attributes to it" (5.152; see also 5.405, 6.328, 6.453).

In this sense the content of a dream is fictitious in that the content could have been different than it was had it so been dreamt, although the fact of the dream is real. So also with a fictional character in a book. The author can give the character any characteristics he wishes, the character is dependent upon how the author thinks it, but once the character is created, e.g., Hamlet, it is a real character in so far as it has features, which do not change simply by virtue of the fact that you or I may think of them differently.

When Shakespeare wrote *Hamlet* he took something out of

his own imagination (largely) and gave it "a local habitation and a name." In creating his character Shakespeare could give him whatever disposition he wished—he could be bright, gay, stupid, or shrewd. But this is not the case with a reality. If I think of it as a creature of my own imagination and try to alter its characteristics, I find that I cannot, and this tells me that it is not a creature of my imagination but a real thing whose nature is independent of how I think it to be.

Once a character in fiction is created or once a dream is dreamt, it attains a status different from a figment and becomes a real mental entity. To distinguish objects of this sort from real external objects, Peirce calls them mental objects as distinguished from external objects (6.327). In this sense a tree is an external object whereas Hamlet is a mental object, although both are real.

But now the problem is, how am I to distinguish the external from the mental? That is, if I "see" something, how can I decide whether it is external or mental—whether it had its origin in some external object or is just a product of my imagination or of someone else's? For example, suppose that I think I see a little green man in the corner. How can I discover if there is a little green man there or if I only conjured him up? Peirce gives us three "tests of externality" (6.334; see also 8.149).

The easiest of these tests is to attempt to "suppress the apparition" by an effort of will. That is, I say to myself, the little green man is not really there, and I look more closely and try to convince myself that he is just an hallucination. If I succeed, this is the most conclusive of all tests to show that the apparition is mental. If I fail, I can resort to the second test. I call in other observers. If they do not see him, then he is not real, for the real is, by our first definition, such that it does not change if perceived by different people. If they do see him, however, and I am still sceptical of his existence, I may resort to the third test. I try to take a picture of the little man, I put a microphone in the corner to see if it records any noise, I shine a light on him to see if he throws a shadow, etc. If all three of these tests are positive, if I cannot suppress the perception of the little man, if other observers see him, and if physical apparatus records his presence, I have no choice but to believe that he is an external object. If one of them fails, however, I may doubt his externality.

According to Peirce, "The above tests critically applied, avail to separate apparitions into two discrete classes, with none of an intermediate character" (6.334). This is true providing we extend them to the unlimited community, a concept which we must now examine.

By applying the tests for externality we find what appear to be many real external objects in the world. We find houses and trees and people. Suppose I undertake to examine one of these objects critically to see what its real nature is. I make a careful study of it and obtain as complete an idea as possible of it. I list all its main characters and find that it has five: A, B, C, D, and E. I examine the object carefully and I am convinced that it really has all five of these characters. But this is not adequate to satisfy our first definition of reality, for according to it an object is real if its characters are unaffected by how *any* man observes them to be. Accordingly I call in another man. He studies the object. He applies the same techniques and conducts the same experiments that I have conducted, but he is unable to find that the object has character E. Assuming that he is a competent investigator and that his results are verified by other investigators, I know that character E cannot be real, for the real is by definition what is knowable to any man, and since character E is not knowable to the second observer it cannot be really present in the object but must be a mental, or subjective, element which I introduced into the object by virtue of some idiosyncrasy in me, not in the object. However, there may be some element among the four remaining characters which is really subjective and due to some idiosyncrasy common to both observers. But if so, they do not know the object as it really is. To find out if this is the case they call in a third observer. But for all they know there may be some subjective element common to the observations of all three of them. The only way that they can find this out is to call in a fourth observer. It is easy to see that this will be an infinite process. Therefore, according to our first definition, the only time we can know how something really is, independently of how you or I or any man may perceive it, is in that indefinite future when the object shall have been examined by an unlimited number of men. But this statement is our second definition of reality: "The opinion which is fated to be ultimately agreed to by all who investigate is what we mean by the truth, and the object represented in this opinion is the real" (5.407).

What is meant by saying that this opinion is fated? In a footnote to the second definition (5.407, n.1) Peirce tells us that "Fate means merely that which is sure to come true, and can nohow be avoided. . . . We are all fated to die." In another place he says that fate is just a kind of destiny and that everything may be said to be destined

which is sure to come about although there is no necessitating reason for it. Thus, a pair of dice, thrown often enough, will turn up sixes some time, although there is no necessity that they should. The probability that they will is 1: that is all. *Fate* is that special kind of *destiny* by which events are supposed to be brought about *under definite circumstances* which involve no necessitating cause for these occurrences (4.547, n.1; see also 7.334–35).

Something may be fated, or inevitable, without being predetermined. A situation is said to be predetermined if some person or some thing determines that it will happen before it happens by starting a particular causal chain which must necessarily produce the situation. Something is fated if it will come about regardless of any particular causal chain. Thus, as Peirce says, we are all fated to die. Regardless of what we may do to avoid it, we will all eventually die. So with throwing a pair of dice. One might throw a pair of dice for a long time without sixes coming up, but if he continues to throw long enough, sooner or later he will certainly throw sixes. Thus it is not pre-determined that the dice shall come up sixes, although it is inevitable that if thrown often enough they will eventually do so.[1]

The situation is similar in man's investigation of an external object. It is not predetermined that he shall come to a knowl-edge of its real nature; it is simply inevitable that he should eventually do so, provided he continues his investigation far enough. The reason that it is inevitable is that the method of observation, if it does not result in a knowledge of the real nature of the object during any finite period of time, is self-corrective and therefore must result in a knowledge of the real nature of the object over an infinite period of time. The method is self-corrective because, although one observer, or a large group of observers, may examine an object and come to a false conclusion about it, the object continually constrains each suc-cessive observer to see it as it really is, and if this process is continued over an infinite period of time the method will cor-rect the error, since, by continually referring back to the object, an infinite number of observers must sooner or later discover and remove any subjective elements in the conception of the object and eventually perceive the object as it really is.[2]

[1] Peirce says that the probability of the dice coming up sixes eventually is 1, but that there is no necessitating cause involved. To make these two propositions consistent he assumes a frequency theory of probability applied directly to laws, i.e., laws are of a statistical, not a universal, character. Peirce originated this view of law which implies a rejection of determinism. When Peirce says that the dice are not predetermined to come up sixes but will inevitably do so, he means that the law is not necessary but statistical, and that the probability is 1.

[2] For a modification of this position, see the discussion of tychism on p. 87.

This position does not imply that it is necessary to complete an infinite investigation to know the real object; it is necessary only to complete the infinite investigation to know *that* we know the real object. Any one man or any group of men may get to know the object without their knowledge containing any subjective elements whatever, but they can never know that their knowledge contains no subjective elements until the infinite investigation has been completed. "There is nothing, then, to prevent our knowing outward objects as they really are, and it is most likely that we do thus know them in numberless cases, although we can never be absolutely certain of doing so in any particular case" (5.311).

Now the fact that we cannot know that we know the real object until the infinite investigation has been completed means that we can never *know* that we know it, i.e., we can never know that our knowledge is certain. Peirce frankly recognizes that this is the case and calls his position Fallibilism for this reason (1.171*ff.*).

THE COMMUNITY OF OBSERVERS

At this point it is quite reasonable to ask why, if one cannot ever know that he has knowledge, he ought to bother to try to get knowledge. Peirce's answer is that we do not investigate for our own benefit, but we must identify our interests with the interests of the entire community of investigators (5.354, 2.654*ff.*). He holds that the method, and therefore the logic of scientific investigation, exemplifies a social principle. Man cannot attain any sure knowledge for himself. His knowledge has probability only in terms of the experiences of other investigators. Peirce holds to a frequency theory of probability, and must face the problem of how, on a frequency theory, a probability that refers to an infinite sequence can apply to a finite case. What does it mean, on a frequency theory, to tell a man about to undergo an operation that there are seven chances out of ten that he will survive? It certainly does not mean that he could die in ten ways but he will not die in seven of them, nor does it mean that if he has the operation ten times he will survive seven times. This prediction has meaning only when applied against the background of the social group. The prediction is that over an unlimited number of cases of this operation, seven out of ten people will survive. Thus, man has knowledge only as he sees himself as a member of a community of investigators (5.354*f.*).

In spite of the fact that knowledge may appear to us to be ultimately fated to come about, there is no guarantee that things are as they appear to us to be. Our method is based on certain assumptions: that knowledge of the universe is possible, and that investigation can succeed in giving us that knowledge. But there is no guarantee that such is the case. It is at best a hope.

Peirce recognizes this difficulty and admits frankly that all we can do is to "hope" that we will not be deceived—"the assumption that man . . . shall ever arrive at a state of information greater than some definite finite information, is entirely unsupported by reasons" (5.357). However, under these circumstances, "the only assumption upon which he can act rationally is the hope of success. So this sentiment is rigidly demanded by logic" (5.357). In 1899 (in almost the same words that William James used in justifying the will to believe in 1896) Peirce held that "the one unpardonable offence in reasoning" is to "block the way of inquiry" (1.135*f.*). But to say that you cannot hope to succeed *is* to block the way of inquiry, for to say that you cannot hope to succeed is to say that inquiry is futile, and if inquiry is futile, no one will investigate and, therefore, certainly no one will then ever attain any knowledge. Hence, the only possible position for any investigator, whether scientific or philosophical, is to hope that there is an attainable answer to his question. If there is, infinite investigation is sure to reveal it; if there is not, he is no worse off than he was before. Since every method of investigation must be based on this hope, reason demands it as the only possible basis of all investigation.

THE METHOD OF INVESTIGATION

Peirce discusses the problem of choosing a method of investigation in the article on "The Fixation of Belief" (5.358*ff.*). Here he examines the general problem of the purpose of inquiry and the methods for conducting it. He suggests that inquiry begins when we find ourselves in doubt as to how we should act. Doubt is a state of dissatisfaction and irritation, and we desire to pass from it to a state of belief. When belief is attained, inquiry ceases, and we are free to continue our actions. Thus the purpose of inquiry is to enable us to pass from a state of doubt to a state of belief.

To attain this purpose, we develop a method of inquiry built around a "guiding principle" or a habit of inference which experience has shown us will enable us to resolve our doubts. Such a guiding habit is sound if it enables us to discover a reliable plan for action, and not otherwise. Thus the question of the logical worth of such a principle is a matter of fact. Either it gives us such a plan or it does not. If not, then it is worthless and we change it. If it does, and enables us to pass from doubt to belief, we develop it and extend it to other fields.

Peirce suggests four guiding principles or methods which men have held. The first of these he calls the method of tenacity. On this method a man resolves his doubts by taking firm hold of a certain belief and refusing to doubt it. He ignores all evidence to the contrary and refuses to hear arguments on the other side. This method enables him to remain in a state of belief with no doubts. Peirce compares this to the method of the ostrich who is reputed to hide his head in the sand and say that there is no danger. This method may work in many cases, but sooner or later one will find that he holds a belief contrary to what others hold and he will begin to wonder whether they may not be as right as he. We all have the social impulse and wish to live with others so that, unless we elect to be hermits, we want a method which will enable us either to convince others to agree with us or ourselves to agree with them. The problem then is how to settle belief not in the individual alone but in the entire community. This problem cannot be settled by the method of tenacity.

The second method Peirce suggests is the method of authority. To settle opinion in the entire community, let some authority, some institution, be set up to declare what opinions men shall hold on all important subjects, and let all members of the community be forced to adhere to these beliefs. This method may lead to a consensus within the community, but sooner or later men will discover that other communities do not agree with them, and the question of who is right will again raise doubts, so that this method also appears unsatisfactory.

Peirce suggests as a third possibility the method of taste. To resolve our doubts between communities we may try to take as beliefs what men would like to believe, what appeals to their tastes, what would be approved by them if it were true. This emotional approach to truth is accepted by many. But, aside from the fact that different people will have different tastes, it will undoubtedly occur to some members of the community that what they would like to believe may not necessarily be in accord with the facts. And as soon as this occurs to them, they will begin to doubt their beliefs.

Thus we see that our method of inquiry will need to meet three requirements: It must be based on something outside of us if it is not to be simply a matter of taste; it must be public, for it is to produce a common belief for all, not just a belief for the individual; and it must give us reason to believe that it will enable us to formulate opinions which are in accord with the facts.

Peirce holds that the method of inquiry which satisfies these requirements is the method of science. The basic conception involved in this method is the conception of reality. Developing our method around the efforts to discover reality, or what is the case, satisfies our requirements: 1) The method is based on something external to us, something that is objective, namely, reality; 2) The method is public, not private; other individuals who do not accept the results of this method may perform the required investigation and come to the same results, so that if used the method should lead to a common belief; 3) The method gives us reason to believe that it will enable us to base our opinions on the facts, for, while the method is not infallible, it is, as we have seen, self-corrective, so that errors which do occur will be corrected by further investigation and we should eventually attain a knowledge of the facts.

The above discussion will serve to suggest some of the reasons why Peirce exhibits so much concern over making clear what is involved in the concept of reality and in trying to show how the real object determines our knowledge of it.

A PRAGMATIC DEFINITION

We are now in a position to apply the pragmatic maxim to the term "reality" and formulate a definition of it in somewhat the same fashion that we formulated a definition of the term "tree" in the previous chapter.

The pragmatic maxim tells us that the meaning of a term consists in the practical considerations which would be true of any object to which we would apply the term. Accordingly we must ask ourselves what practical consideration would be true of any object to which we would apply the term "real."

Suppose that I act toward an object in manner x and get experience y. To assert that the properties presented in that experience are real properties of that object is, on Peirce's analysis, simply to assert the practical consideration that "If any investigator acts toward this object in manner x, then he will have an experience of the sort y."

Certain features of this definition call for more explicit treatment. It will be observed in the first place that this makes reality a social concept, not a personal one. The real nature of any object must be determined by reference to the experiences of the community of investigators. In this respect this definition is nothing more nor less than a statement of what scientists mean by reality. Real attributes of any object— physical, biological, or social—are those attributes open to public inspection by the community of scientists. To say that I have discovered a new property of, say, protoplasm, is to describe an experiment (i.e., a certain manner of acting) which, if engaged in by any investigator, will lead to his having a certain experience (that of a previously unobserved property). To assert that I have discovered a new property of protoplasm which I cannot describe in such a way as to make its existence known to public verification by other scientists is, from the point of view of science, to talk nonsense.

A second aspect of this definition is that it defines reality in terms of human experiences. It accordingly rules out all discussion of realities that are not experienced in any way by human investigators. Any statements about "realities" that enter in no way into human experience are meaningless on this view. "Realities" outside the community of investigators, that is, objects not experienced by any investigators, or objects that exist prior to any investigation or after all investigation has ceased, and which do not in some way connect up with the experiences of the community of investigators, cannot be meaningfully discussed.

A third point, that would follow from the second, would be that the pragmatist cannot admit of any unknown or unknowable *ding-an-sich* as the real cause of knowledge. In other words, the pragmatist cannot hold that there is a real object that causes certain subjective human experiences (color, sound, odor, taste, etc.) and that we never know the object but only our subjective experiences of it. In other words, it would seem as though the pragmatist was required to be a phenomenalist of some variety. And yet all the pragmatists deny that they are phenomenalists. The justification they offer for this denial is the doctrine of immediate perception. This is the doctrine that when we experience an object we do not, as the phenomenalist would have it, "experience our experiences," but we experience the object as such. "But we have *direct experience of things in themselves.* Nothing can be more completely false than that we can experience only our own ideas. That is indeed without exaggeration the very epitome of *all* falsity (6.95)."

Not only does Peirce hold this view, but we shall see that James and Dewey do also. The chief difficulty with immediate perception is how to account for the error of illusion. For example, if we see a stick partly in water it appears bent at the surface of the water. And all observers see it as bent. The pragmatists hold that the error is one of judgment, not of perception. Dewey argues, for example, that we see something as bent. We infer it is the stick. But more careful analysis shows us that it is the light-wave, not the stick that is bent. The error is an error in judgment, not in perception. Peirce holds the same view (5.568). But this "solution" only throws us back on the difficulty we sought to evade. It tells us there is a stick in the water which no one "sees" (since what we see is the light-wave), and that stick is straight. This solution therefore requires us to talk about a stick that does not enter into the experience of any observer—a stick that cannot meaningfully be talked about by the pragmatist.

In the first chapter I suggested that pragmatism was an effort to re-examine traditional problems of meaning in the light of developments in scientific methodology. It is now possible to see how some of this is done in the pragmatic analysis of the concept of reality. In effect, what the pragmatic theory of meaning does in this case is to provide us with a clear formulation of what a scientist would mean by the term "reality." The advantages of the analysis are that it clarifies both the strengths and the weaknesses of the scientific concept. The danger is that one may become so enamored of the strengths that he ignores the weaknesses or so pleased to discover the weaknesses that he ignores the strengths.

Some of the difficulties may be summarized as follows. They are shared by both pragmatism and science: 1) The pragmatic theory of meaning which interprets ideas in terms of conduct fails to deal adequately with the mind-body problem, or the relation between ideas and physical behavior; 2) The pragmatic theory of reality which describes reality in terms of what is public and common in human experience neglects, by its emphasis on public knowledge, the possibility of private and personal knowledge limited to the experiences of a single individual or a select group of individuals; 3) By defining reality in terms of what is common to human experiences the pragmatist assumes the inter-subjectivity of knowledge—that is, he assumes that I can know that some other observer is in fact having the same experience I am having—although no techniques have as yet been formulated by which we can ascertain that the experiences of any two observers are in fact similar, much less identical; 4) Finally the pragmatist subscribes to a belief in a real world which is open to direct inspection by normal observers. His assertion of this is made in the face of a great deal of contrary evidence well known in the history of epistemology, and briefly suggested above by the reference to the problem of illusion.

While all these weaknesses are shared by both pragmatism and modern science, they may also both be credited with the same merit, namely, that in spite of their philosophical obtuseness toward some of the Gordian knots in philosophy, they have formulated a theory of meaning and a concept of reality which has allowed human knowledge to move forward in those areas where advances could be made rather than by stultifying progress on all fronts because of philosophical difficulties on some of them. I think the pragmatists would be satisfied with such an epitaph.

Such an attitude may be questionable philosophically. But there is also merit in the admonition that where you can't go over or under, go around. There can be little doubt in the mind of any careful student of pragmatism, and I believe there was little doubt in the minds of any of the pragmatists, that both the pragmatic method and the scientific method embodied serious difficulties which only the future could correct. Peirce advises us:

Thus, in brief, my philosophy may be described as the attempt of a physicist to make such conjecture as to the constitution of the universe as the methods of science may permit, with the aid of all that has been done by previous philosophers. I shall support my propositions by such arguments as I can. Demonstrative proof is not to be thought of. The demonstrations of the metaphysicians are all moonshine. The best that can be done is to supply a hypothesis, not devoid of all likelihood, in the general line of growth of scientific ideas, and capable of being verified or refuted by future observers (1.7).

4

The Reality of Laws

In the early 1870s (5.12), there met in Cambridge a group called "The Metaphysical Club,"[1] consisting, among others, of Peirce, William James, Chauncey Wright, and, the later Supreme Court justice, Oliver Wendell Holmes, Jr. It was these meetings that stimulated Peirce to the first formulation of pragmatism as it appeared in the 1877 and 1878 articles in the *Popular Science Monthly*.

Among the members of the Metaphysical Club was Francis E. Abbot, who exercised a greater influence on Peirce's thought than any other of his contemporaries. Abbot very likely influenced Peirce's thought at this early date, although the full impact of his influence does not appear until after the publication of Abbot's book *Scientific Theism* in 1885.[2]

In a letter to James in 1904, Peirce refers to "F. E. Abbot, one of the strongest thinkers I ever encountered" (*William*

[1] The name of this club seems to have survived only in the memory of Peirce. For a discussion of the club and its members see Philip P. Wiener, *Evolution and the Founders of Pragmatism*, Harvard University Press, Cambridge, 1949.

[2] This influence is more fully discussed in an unpublished Ph.D. dissertation by William Jerome Callaghan, "The Philosophy of Francis Ellingwood Abbot," Columbia University, 1959. See especially chapter V, "Scientific Theism."

James, II, 431). In 1903, in commenting on his own 1871 review of Fraser's *Berkeley* (8.7*ff.*), Peirce wrote,

In that paper I acknowledged that the tendency of science has been toward nominalism; but the late Dr. Francis Ellingwood Abbot in the very remarkable introduction to his book entitled "Scientific Theism," showed on the contrary, quite conclusively, that science has always been at heart realistic, and always must be so; and upon comparing his writings with mine, it is easily seen that these features of nominalism which I pointed out in science are merely superficial and transient (1.20).

In 1893 Peirce wrote that he "entirely approved" Abbot's position (4.51), and in 1898 said that Abbot "has so clearly and with such admirable simplicity shown that modern science is realistic that it is perhaps injudicious for me to attempt to add anything upon the subject" (4.1).

This praise is especially significant since Peirce rarely spoke well of the philosophical efforts of his contemporaries. Much as he liked James personally, he was highly critical of his philosophical writings, as well as those of other leading philosophers of the day.

Peirce's thought prior to the meetings of the Metaphysical Club is concerned primarily with the reality of general concepts in so far as they refer to particular objects. The articles on pragmatism which appeared in 1877 and 1878 reveal a shift toward a concern with the nature of scientific laws. The increasing interest in this problem was probably due in large part to Abbot's influence on the discussions of the Metaphysical Club. It would seem significant that Peirce's next period of philosophical activity after Abbot's book appeared in 1885 is characterized by a predominant interest in the problem of laws. He did a series of five articles for the *Monist* during the years 1891–93 in which he set forth in detail his realistic position on scientific law. These articles appear as Chapters 1, 2, 5, 9, and 11 of Book I, Volume VI, of the *Collected Papers.*

They represent his final great creative period. In his first period, the late 1860s, he worked out his views on the reality of those concepts that refer to particular objects; in the late 1870s, he enunciated his pragmatism; in the early 1890s, he developed his views on the reality of those concepts that refer to scientific laws. Although the bulk of his writing comes after 1899, he is by then concerned primarily with explicating, defending, and reorganizing his earlier views.

REALISM, NOMINALISM AND LAWS

To review briefly, we have seen that to be a metaphysical (or scholastic) realist is to hold that ideas are real, and by this is meant not that the ideas *per se* are real ideas (for on this basis all ideas are real) but rather that they are ideas of real things, so that to be a realist is to hold that the object of a general idea is a real thing. To be a nominalist is to hold that general ideas are not real in this sense, that is, to hold that there is nothing in nature that corresponds to a general idea. Peirce answers this objection as far as concepts of objects are concerned by resort to a moderate realism in which he holds that the object of a general concept such as man exists in the world as embodied in any particular man. In dealing with scientific laws he develops a similar view. In connection with scientific laws the problem is formulated as follows: We have in our minds certain general concepts which we term "laws of science." The question Peirce is concerned with is the question of what there is in the external world that corresponds to these concepts. His metaphysical realism commits him to the view that unless there is something real of a general nature in the external world that corresponds to the general concepts in our minds which we call "scientific laws," then the laws are fictions. A nominalistic position on this issue would be the denial of anything real in the external world of a general nature. The nominalist would hold that there are only particular, individual events which we lump together, for convenience, under a general concept—the generality being a property only of our concept, not of the external world.

As his opponents, the nominalists of this controversy, Peirce singles out the followers of Hume and Mill. According to this school of thought, as Peirce explicates it, that in nature which corresponds to the concept of a law of science in the mind is a certain observed or observable regularity or uniformity in the behavior of particular objects. Thus, corresponding to the concept of the law of gravitation, there is only a certain uniformity as to how objects have behaved in the past, are behaving now, and will behave in the future. Outside of this uniformity, according to the nominalists, there is nothing else. To assume that in addition to the uniformity there is a force which is responsible for and determines the uniformity is to talk of a fiction. Thus Peirce says, "Leibnitz was a professed nominalist. For him, a law was nothing more than a regularity, a regularity nothing less than a law" (6.273). To reduce the law to the uniformity is to be a nominalist (6.99). Peirce explicates the nominalistic position to be "that the facts are, in themselves, entirely disconnected, and that it is the mind alone which unites them. One stone dropping to the earth has no real connection with another stone dropping to the earth" (6.99). It is the question of the reality of the connection between the events which divides the nominalist from the realist. Both agree that the events are real; the nominalist, however, holds that there is in nature nothing corresponding to any connection between them, each event being a particular, isolated feature of the universe. This emphasis on the particular, coupled to the assertion that the connection between particulars is a result purely of the action of the mind, characterized medieval nominalism and gives Peirce his basis for using the term in the discussion on laws.

In arguing against the nominalistic position, Peirce holds that the position is unphilosophical and unscientific. It is unphilosophical because the function of philosophy is to explain experience, and to say of any experience that it is inexplicable is philosophically unjustifiable. Particularly is this true of experiences of uniformities. "Uniformities are precisely the sort of facts that need to be accounted for. That a pitched coin should sometimes turn up heads and sometimes tails calls for no particular explanation; but if it shows heads every time, we wish to know how this result has been brought about. Law is *par excellence* the thing that wants a reason" (6.12).

Nominalism is an unscientific position because whether or not the business of philosophy is explanation, certainly the business of science is prediction. On nominalistic grounds a scientist may make a prediction, but he has no more reason to think that it is true than that it is false. Since the nominalist denies any real connection between events of the past and events of the future—each event being entirely separate from all others—the past is no guide to the future and the nominalist has no basis whatever for making predictions (6.99).

On this analysis of nominalism and realism, it is immediately obvious that Peirce (and Abbot) are correct in holding that science is not nominalistic but is realistic. For scientists do believe that the past is a guide to the future and do believe that they have a basis for making predictions. Such being the case, scientists are realists. This argument, of course, does not prove that there are real laws, but it does indicate that the philosophical basis of science is realistic, not nominalistic. Even this is no new discovery, since philosophers generally recognize a difference between what is philosophically demonstrable about the nature of scientific laws and what the scientist actually thinks about them when he is engaged in scientific activities.

Abbot, in the preface to *Scientific Theism*, sets forth the basic tenets of a scientific realism to be: 1) There are real objective relations existing between things; 2) These relations are known by the perceiving mind.[3]

These are the basic tenets of any scientific realism.[4] Peirce attempts to prove the position by concentrating on the second point. On his theory of reality all that is meant by asserting that there are real, objective relations (point 1) is that there are relations which are perceived by everyone (point 2). For this reason he sets out to prove point 2; if this can be shown, point 1 is true by the definition of reality.

THE PERCEPTION OF GENERALITY

He first undertakes to show that perception involves generality. As an example of the direct perception of generality, he offers the following:

A line abuts upon an ordinary point of another line forming two angles. The sum of the angles is proved by Legendre to be equal to the sum of two right angles by erecting a perpendicular to the second line in the plane of the two and through the point of abuttal. This perpendicular must lie in the one angle or the other. The pupil is supposed to *see* that. He sees it only in a special case, but he is supposed to perceive that it will be so in any case. The more careful logician may demonstrate that it must fall in one angle or the other; but this demonstration will only consist in substituting a different diagram in place of Legendre's figure. But in any case, either in the new diagram or else, and more usually, in passing from one diagram to the other, the interpreter of the argu-

[3] Abbot, *Scientific Theism*, pp. ixf.
[4] See also Alfred North Whitehead, *Process and Reality*, (New York: Macmillan, 1929), pp. 265–66.

mentation will be supposed to *see* something, which will present this little difficulty for the theory of vision, that it is of a *general nature* (5.148).

In a psychological sense I am willing to take the word of the psychologist if he says that such a general truth cannot be *perceived*. But what better can we do in logic? (5.164).[5]

For this and similar reasons, Peirce denies that all experience is experience of particulars. He holds that perception contains a general element, that is, we perceive general relations as well as particulars. Generality "pours in upon us through every avenue of sense" (5.157). While some medieval nominalists may have denied that we experience relations, Peirce is wrong if he means to imply that Hume and Mill and their followers do so. They would certainly admit, for example, that we experience a contiguity in time and space between a stone being released and the same stone falling. This relation of contiguity is experienced under other circumstances also, and therefore may be said to be general. But this does not suffice to overthrow modern nominalism (as distinguished from medieval nominalism). The question at issue is not whether we experience relations but whether any of these relations are of a necessary character, so that if I experience A and B in the relation R, it follows necessarily that whenever A occurs in the relation R, B will follow? To take an example: I release a stone in a gravitational field and it falls. Suppose that at the next moment after I release it I also sneeze. There are at

⁵ This argument is analogous to the argument Bertrand Russell uses for believing in the reality of universals. In 1912 Russell wrote, "The relation of resemblance, therefore, must be a true universal. And having been forced to admit this universal, we find that it is no longer worthwhile to invent difficult and unplausible theories to avoid the admission of such universals as whiteness and triangularity." *Problems of Philosophy* (London: Oxford University Press, [1912], p. 151.) As late as 1943 Russell held the same position. See Russell's "Reply to Criticisms" in Paul A. Schlipp, *The Philosophy of Bertrand Russell* (Evanston, Ill.: The Library of Living Philosophers, Inc., 1946), p. 688.

least two relations observed, or experienced, between A, the stone being released, and B, its striking the ground. One is the relation of falling, the other the relation of the experimenter sneezing. Now the question is, which, if either, of these relations expresses a law? That is, is either of them a necessary relation? Will a stone being released always result in the stone falling and/or in the experimenter sneezing before the stone strikes the ground? Or is one or both of these relations an accidental relation not due to any law of nature? Whitehead takes a possible way out of this difficulty by holding that we actually experience the causal relation and thus know by experience that some relations are necessary and some are accidental.[6]

Peirce takes a more devious path. According to his view we do not know which relations are necessary by virtue of any direct experience of a causal relation. He holds that man, by virtue of being a part of nature, has a natural affinity for the basic principles which operate in nature, so that he does not learn by experience which relations are necessary but is somehow in tune with the infinite and has an instinct which guides him toward selecting the necessary relations. The instinct is not infallible and, in dealing with complicated relations, it may be quite misleading, but still it provides him with a sense of recognition, when he experiences some relations, that they are more likely to turn out to be necessary relations than are certain others which he also experiences.

How is it that man ever came by any correct theories about nature? We know by induction that man has correct theories; for they produce predictions that are fulfilled. But by what process of thought were they ever brought to his mind? A chemist notices a surprising phenomenon. Now if he has a high admiration of Mill's *Logic,* as many chemists have, he will remember that Mill tells him that he must work on the principle that, under precisely the

---

[6] Whitehead, *Process and Reality,* pp. 265–66.

same circumstances, like phenomena are produced. Why does he then not note that this phenomenon was produced on such a day of the week, the planets presenting a certain configuration, his daughter having on a blue dress, he having dreamed of a white horse the night before, the milkman having been late that morning, and so on? The answer will be that in early days chemists did use to attend to some such circumstances, but that they have learned better. How have they learned this? By an induction. Very well, that induction must have been based upon a theory which the induction verified. How was it that man was ever led to entertain that true theory? You cannot say that it happened by chance, because the possible theories, if not strictly innumerable, at any rate exceed a trillion—or the third power of a million; and therefore the chances are too overwhelmingly against the single true theory in the twenty or thirty thousand years during which man has been a thinking animal, ever having come into any man's head. Besides, you cannot seriously think that every little chicken, that is hatched, has to rummage through all possible theories until it lights upon the good idea of picking up something and eating it. On the contrary, you think the chicken has an innate idea of doing this; that is to say, that it can think of this, but has no faculty of thinking anything else. The chicken you say pecks by instinct. But if you are going to think every poor chicken endowed with an innate tendency toward a positive truth, why should you think that to man alone this gift is denied? If you carefully consider with an unbiased mind all the circumstances of the early history of science and all the other facts bearing on the question, which are far too various to be specifically alluded to in this lecture, I am quite sure that you must be brought to acknowledge that man's mind has a natural adaptation to imagining correct theories about forces, without some glimmer of which he could not form social ties and consequently could not reproduce his kind. In short, the instincts conducive to assimilation of food, and the instincts conducive to reproduction, must have involved from the beginning certain tendencies to think truly about physics, on the one hand, and about psychics, on the other. It is somehow more than a mere figure of speech to say that nature fecundates the mind of man with ideas which, when those ideas grow up, will resemble their father, Nature (5.591).

It is of interest to find that this doctrine is not peculiar to realistic metaphysicians alone. Hans Reichenbach, in speaking of Einstein's discovery of the Principle of Equivalence, says:

From the standpoint of logic, one cannot here speak of an inference, for this far-reaching assumption cannot be logically demonstrated by means of the scantily available facts. Rather we have here a typical procedure in physics, that of the formation of a hypothesis. . . . There seems to exist something like an instinct for the hidden intentions of nature; and whoever possesses this instinct, takes the spade to the right place where gold is hidden, and thus arrives at deep scientific insights. It must be said that Einstein possesses this instinct to the highest degree.[7]

Bertrand Russell also seems to be convinced that there is some justification for this view. He says of Peirce:

He holds—and I confess that an examination of scientific inference has made me feel the force of this view—that man is adapted, by his congenital constitution, to the apprehension of natural laws which cannot be proved by experience, although experience is in conformity with them. "The chicken you say pecks by instinct. But if you are going to think every poor chicken endowed with an innate tendency towards a positive truth, why should you think that to man alone this gift is denied?" This is an important question to which I do not know the answer.[8]

This is certainly an important question and it is not an easy one to answer. Modern psychology is not in a position to give us any very satisfactory answer to the question of what an instinct is, much less the question of what instincts we have and what their powers and reliability may be. I do not see that there is any scientifically rigorous basis upon which

[7] Hans Reichenbach, *From Copernicus to Einstein* (New York: Philosophical Library, 1942), p. 94.
[8] In Feibleman, *An Introduction to Peirce's Philosophy*, p. xvi.

to accept or reject this theory. In these circumstances one can only proceed with caution. Among those philosophers who have studied the methods and techniques of science, the names of Peirce and Reichenbach and Russell must stand high. With this array of authority it seems necessary to admit that there is, at least, nothing obviously false about the view and that it is acceptable as a basis for development.

But having conceded this much to Peirce, it is difficult, in the light of the increased complexity of science since his day, to share his enthusiasm for man's ability for instinctive comprehension. He tells us that "it cannot any longer be denied that the human intellect is peculiarly adapted to the comprehension of the laws and facts of nature" (2.750). If the human intellect is "adapted" to an understanding of relativity physics and quantum mechanics, it is certainly an odd kind of adaptation.[9] Peirce bases his reasons on the success of Galilean mechanics as a development of our instinctive ideas of space, time, and force (2.753). He tells us that "man has thus far not attained to any knowledge that is not in a wide sense mechanical or anthropological in its nature, and it may be reasonably presumed that he never will" (2.753). It is difficult to see how relativity physics can be said to be mechanical or anthropological in even the widest sense of these terms.

THE METAPHYSICS OF SCIENTIFIC LAW

We may turn now to a related, but somewhat different, question. If we do experience necessary relations, what is

[9] The mathematical complexity of the theory of relativity, for example, was such that Einstein is reported to have said when he announced it that probably no more than a dozen men in the world would understand it. The deep cleavage among contemporary physicists as to the exact meaning of the Principle of Indeterminism in Quantum Mechanics would suggest that the human intellect is not too well adapted to an understanding of this principle.

there in the universe that corresponds to these experiences? This question takes us into the metaphysics of the *Monist* articles. By way of an introduction to the problem of these articles, it may be helpful to point out that it will not do for the realist to describe a necessary relation simply as a relation that always occurs. It might always occur by accident. This is nominalism. It is not just that the relation always occurs, but that it necessarily always occurs; the law describes an active general principle which makes the relation occur. Furthermore, a real law refers not simply to those regularities which have occurred or will occur, but to instances which do not actually occur, but might have occurred.

No collection of facts can constitute a law; for the law goes beyond any accomplished facts and determines how facts that *may be*, but all of which never can have happened, shall be characterized. There is no objection to saying that a law is a general fact, provided it be understood that the general has an admixture of potentiality, so that no congeries of actions here and now can ever make a general fact (1.420).

The realist must hold that the law is real even when no instances of it are being exemplified. The law of the nominalist, the uniformity, is completely exemplified in the instances. In order that there be any difference between these two views, the realist must show a meaningful way of talking about a law which is not being exemplified. For the realist there must be an entity in the universe which is an actual regularity when the law is being exemplified but that is a potential regularity when the law is not being exemplified. This is the problem that Peirce takes up in the *Monist* articles of 1892 and 1893. In these articles he develops his three basic doctrines of tychism, synechism, and agapasm. I shall discuss them in the order named.

The second of Peirce's five papers in the *Monist* is titled, "The Doctrine of Necessity Examined" (6.35*f*.). He here deals with the mechanical determinism of classical physics, according to which "every single fact in the universe is precisely determined by law" (6.36). Although Peirce believes in the reality of law, and accordingly that there is an element of law in the universe, he denies that the law is absolute. His argument is based upon the fact of growth and of increasing complexity among evolved forms of life.

Question any science which deals with the course of time. Consider the life of an individual animal or plant, or of a mind. Glance at the history of states, of institutions, of language, of ideas. Examine the successions of forms shown by paleontology, the history of the globe as set forth in geology, of what the astronomer is able to make out concerning the changes in the stellar systems. Everywhere the main fact is growth and increasing complexity. Death and corruption are mere accidents or secondary phenomena. Among some of the lower organisms, it is a moot point with biologists whether there be anything which ought to be called death. Races, at any rate, do not die out except under unfavorable circumstances. From these broad and ubiquitous facts we may fairly infer, by the most unexceptionable logic, that there is probably in nature some agency by which the complexity and diversity of things can be increased; and that consequently the rule of mechanical necessity meets in some way with interference (6.58).

The argument here is that the fact of growth and increasing variety in the universe is opposed to the philosophy that everything comes about by law; mere mechanical functioning could not cause diversification. This argument is not very sound. The universe could be a machine of such a sort that it exhibited increasing complexity as time progressed. Peirce fails to meet this answer squarely. In talking of growth he says, "Though it may possibly be an affair of mechanism perhaps, [it] certainly presents all the appearance of increasing diversification" (6.64). This is too weak. If the fact of growth "may possibly . . . perhaps" be explained mechanically, then it will not suffice to overthrow the mechanical philosophy.

Nevertheless, Peirce uses growth as a basis for introducing an element of absolute chance in the universe. This he calls tychism. He characterizes the operation of chance not as a variety of irregularity occurring outside of the realm of law, but as "a violation of law, or lawlessness" (6.602). Chance does not operate in one realm and law in another, but rather they both operate in the same realm so that the laws are not absolutely rigid but exhibit some minute deviations.

This element of chance in the universe necessitated a change in Peirce's early view that the community of investigators was "fated" (5.407) to come to some final conclusion about the nature of any object or the answer to any question. In 1893, in a controversy with Paul Carus over necessity and chance, Peirce admits (6.602) that his early view of chance was not that it violated law but that it was merely due to our ignorance, but he describes this as "a transitional belief which I have now passed through" (6.602). In 1893 he writes:

We cannot be quite sure that the community ever will settle down to an unalterable conclusion upon any given question. Even if they do so for the most part, we have no reason to think the unanimity will be quite complete, nor can we rationally presume any overwhelming consensus of opinion will be reached upon every question. All that we are entitled to assume is in the form of a hope that such conclusion may be substantially reached concerning the particular questions with which our inquiries are busied (6.610).

While Peirce still holds that the general truths which will be known by the ultimate community are "objectively real," he denies that they will be "strictly universal, exact and certain" (6.610). This view is a considerable modification of the theory that we must come to an absolute piece of knowledge if we only continue our investigations long enough.

In the third article of the *Monist* series, Peirce introduces his doctrine of synechism, or continuity in the universe. This article is titled, "The Law of Mind," and in it Peirce states synechism as it applies to ideas: "There is but one law of mind, namely, that ideas tend to spread continuously and to affect certain others which stand to them in a peculiar relation of affectibility. In this spreading they lose intensity, and especially the power of affecting others, but gain generality and become welded with other ideas" (6.104).

Peirce gives as an example of this law (6.136) an experience which he had many years previously of seeing a cardinal dressed in his robes. While his recollection of the color of the cardinal's cloak has lost some of its intensity, so that the memory of it is not as vivid as it was immediately after he had seen it, the idea of the color has "spread," that is, when he thinks of that color now he also thinks of experiences he has had since then with other colors; the idea has lost some of its intensity but has become generalized by association with experiences of other colors. "The one primary and fundamental law of mental action consists in a tendency to generalization. Feeling tends to spread; connections between feelings awaken feelings; neighboring feelings become assimilated" (6.21).

This principle, according to Peirce, makes the history of thought, whether individual or communal, to consist of a continuum of feelings or ideas becoming always more generalized. This is called the doctrine of synechism.

On the basis of this association of ideas Peirce explains habits. "Habit is that specialization of the law of mind whereby a general idea gains the power of exciting reactions" (6.145). "By induction, a habit becomes established. Certain sensations, all involving one general idea, are followed each by the same reaction; and an association becomes established, whereby that general idea gets to be followed uniformly by that reaction" (6.145).

By means of habit intellectual ability is explained: "Intellectual power is nothing but facility in taking habits and in following them in cases essentially analogous to, but in nonessentials widely remote from, the normal cases of connections of feelings under which those habits are formed" (6.20).

Finally Peirce unites synechism with tychism to avoid any strict behavioristic conclusion to his psychology.

But no mental action seems to be necessary or invariable in its character. In whatever manner the mind has reacted under a given sensation, in that manner it is more likely to react again; were this, however, an absolute necessity, habits would become wooden and ineradicable and, no room being left for the formation of new habits, intellectual life would come to a speedy close. Thus, the uncertainty of the mental law is no mere defect of it, but is on the contrary of its essence. The truth is, the mind is not subject to law in the same rigid sense that matter is. It only experiences gentle forces which merely render it more likely to act in a given way than it otherwise would be. There always remains a certain amount of arbitrary spontaneity in its action, without which it would be dead (6.148).

The psychology set forth here seems to be innocuous enough. A contemporary psychologist might choose to speak in terms of conditioned reflexes or patterns of behavior, but, taken as a description of mental processes, Peirce's view seems unobjectionable.

In the last article in the *Monist* series, "Evolutionary Love" (6.287f.), Peirce sets forth the doctrine of agapasm. He distinguishes three modes of evolution (6.302): Darwinism, or evolution by fortuitous variation, which he calls tychasm; evolution by an inward principle of mechanical necessity, which he calls anancasm; and evolution by creative love, or agapasm. It is easy enough to dismiss Peirce's preference for the latter of these interpretations as being due to the influence of the nineteenth-century conception of evolution as progress. However, this explanation may be too simple. At the least it must be recognized that Peirce sees clearly that such a view is contrary to Darwinism. That is, he does not identify Darwinian evolution with evolution as progress, as most of his contemporaries tended to do. He sees that they are two different things. And he admits that his preference for agapasm is based largely on a "passionate predilection for it" (6.295). He sees, also, that there is no scientific basis for preferring the latter, and that basing the preference on emotional grounds "will probably shock my scientific brethren" (6.295). His position is analogous to that of Plato in the *Symposium*, who holds that the motivating force in the world is love, and to that of Whitehead's doctrine of God as creativity. It would hardly seem reasonable to accuse Plato or Whitehead of being under the influence of the nineteenth-century concept of evolution as progress. And since Peirce does not confuse Darwinian evolution with progress, but clearly recognizes that they are two different views, his acceptance of the latter ought not to be dismissed lightly as being due to the influence of his age, but deserves the respect due to a philosopher who sees the alternatives clearly and selects one of them.

But having said this much about Peirce's choice, there seems to be nothing more to say. One who comes prepared to hear his arguments finds that there are none. True, he suggests a continuity in the development of thought and an evolution in scientific concepts due to the influence of the work of one man upon the thought of another (6.315), but these could be equally well explained on Darwinian views. His view really seems to come down to that of William James in "The Will to Believe," that where we have to make a choice and have no empirical evidence to guide us we must resort to our own preferences in the matter.

He holds that agapasm evidences itself primarily in the fact that an idea tends to associate itself with some ideas and dissociate itself from certain others. This fact is ascribed to a "sympathy" or a feeling of one idea for another.

The agapastic development of thought is the adoption of certain
mental tendencies, not altogether heedlessly, as in tychasm, nor
quite blindly by the mere force of circumstances or of logic, as in
anancasm, but by an immediate attraction for the idea itself, whose
nature is divined before the mind possesses it, by the power of
sympathy, that is by virtue of the continuity of mind (6.307).

PEIRCE'S COSMOGONY

We are now in a position to synthesize Peirce's metaphysics.
We have examined somewhat the basic concepts of it: firstness, secondness, thirdness, tychism, synechism, and agapasm.
In the first *Monist* article Peirce suggests briefly how these
various concepts will be combined (6.33). A more detailed exposition is set forth in the draft of a book, which Peirce intended to complete although he never did, written about 1890
and titled, "A Guess at the Riddle" (1.354*ff*.). In 1.409 to
1.417 he sets forth a rather grandiose cosmological scheme
intended to picture the history of the cosmos from its beginning to its end. On the order of Plato's *Timaeus*, the scheme
is an interesting example of such metaphysical speculation. I
shall here indicate only the general outlines of the view.

Peirce refers to the whole cosmological question as the riddle
of the sphinx. What he here suggests is explicitly labeled a
"guess" (1.410). Accordingly we may expect that he will go
beyond the limits of what can, at least for the present, be
verified. He suggests that in the beginning there were only
firsts—unpersonalized experiences. This was complete chaos.
There were no actually existing entities and no order. But
there was secondness, or brute force, and thirdness, or the
tendency to take habits. The secondness, exerting brute, unreasonable force on the firsts, gave some of them existence.
Some of these existents were repeated and, by the tendency

to habit-taking, tended to perpetuate themselves. As more existents developed, more habits developed. The firsts were mere possibilities of experience and hence feelings or ideas. But as more habits were developed the existents became more and more subject to habit. i.e., law, and lost the freedom and spontaneity of their firstness and became matter—"mind hidebound with habits" (6.158). As the universe develops, these habits will become more and more binding so that what began as complete indeterminacy will end in complete determinacy. The habits which in the beginning had no existence at all will in the end have complete control of the universe. These habits or laws are thus forms which are working their way out in the universe. Chance, in interfering with the present operation of law, represents what is still left of the complete indeterminacy with which the world began. As the habits become more and more rigid, chance will disappear until in the infinite future it will not exist. But the laws, or habits, tend to merge and generalize into one another and to unite the various events which they control. This makes for increased relations between events and, finally, a complete continuum in which everything is united to everything else. But this final stage is not to be deplored since regularity and order provide evidence of rationality in the universe, and a completely ordered universe is a completely reasonable one. Therefore, the process represents reason working its way out in the world.

In a book review in 1893, Peirce indicates man's place in this scheme of things:

Having once surrendered to the power of nature, and having allowed the futile ego in some measure to dissolve, man at once finds himself in synectic union with the circumambient non-ego and partakes of its triumph. On the simple condition of obedience to the laws of nature, he can satisfy many of his selfish desires; a further surrender will bring him the higher delight of realizing to some ex-

tent his ideas; a still further surrender confers upon him the function of cooperating with nature and the course of things to grow
new ideas and institutions. . . . The whole fact of reality, with the
relation of the ego to the non-ego is not described until the individual Will is recognized as merging into the environing non-ego,
as the individual instant of time merges into its past and future.[10]

This final resolution of everything into one, will be God.
"Every reality, then, is a Self, and the selves are intimately
connected, as if they formed a continuum. Each one is . . .
a quasi-map of the entire field of all the selves, which organic
aggregate is itself a Self, the Absolute Idea of Hegel. So far
as a philosophical conception can be identified with God it is
God." [11]

The universe is God's purpose working itself out in the
world. "The universe is a vast representamen, a great symbol
of God's purpose, working out its conclusions in living realities" (5.119). Finally, this purpose is to infuse everything
with reason, "that Reasonableness for the sake of which the
Heavens and the Earth have been created" (2.122).

It is very difficult to know what to say about all this. In
Peirce's own day, when transcendentalism was in its flower,
speculation of this sort was doubtless looked upon more
favorably than it is in our own more positivistic era. About
all that can be said today is that this sort of description of the
world may have some truth in it, but there is little evidence
that such is the case. At the basis of the entire view is objective idealism. Peirce's argument may be set forth thus:

1. Ideas found in the human mind exhibit two primary
characteristics: They tend to merge with other ideas in such
a way as to lose their individual identity and to become
generalized, and they tend to form habits.

[10] *Nation*, LVII (1893), 251–52.   [11] *Nation*, LXXV (1902), 95.

2. External so-called physical objects are qualitatively of the same nature as the ideas found in the human mind—matter is "mind hide-bound with habits" (6.158).

3. Therefore, analogously, physical objects tend to merge with other physical objects (i.e., form communities, nations, and institutions) in such a way as to lose their individual identity and to become generalized, and they tend to form habits (laws).

The psychology suggested in the first step seems satisfactory, but it is difficult to say as much for the philosophy of the second step. Peirce's acceptance of objective idealism is in accord with a dominant tendency in late nineteenth century philosophy. Most of his contemporaries were idealists because of the difficulties posed by Cartesian dualism. In the first of the *Monist* articles he tells us that "the old dualistic notion of mind and matter, so prominent in Cartesianism, as two radically different kinds of substance, will hardly find defenders today. Rejecting this, we are driven to some form of hylopathy, otherwise called monism. . . . The one intelligible theory of the universe is that of objective idealism, that matter is effete mind, inveterate habits becoming physical laws" (6.24–25).

However, the temper of the times has changed so much that in contemporary philosophy one would be hard put to find very many philosophers who would care to subscribe to an objective idealism.

LAW AS HABIT

We began our inquiry into Peirce's cosmology in an effort to find an answer to the problem of what external entity a realist could hold to be the physical counterpart of the idea of a law at a time when the law was not active. Peirce's answer is that a law is a habit, and a real habit is something "which really *would* produce effects, under circumstances that may not happen to get actualized" (6.485). For example, suppose that it is a habit of mine to comb my hair with my right hand. For the nominalist the habit is real only at the times when I am actually combing my hair. That is, the habit is reduced to a series of individual events which exhibit a uniformity, and it is meaningless to talk about the habit being real at a time when I did not comb my hair. For the realist this is not the case. Even though I did not comb my hair at, say, moment A, still it is meaningful to say that if I had combed it at moment A, I would have combed it with my right hand since I have a real habit, a real potentiality, which really would produce effects under circumstances that did not happen to get realized. To deal with this question, we need to decide whether a potentiality can be discussed meaningfully. To this problem we shall presently address ourselves. But, even if we can successfully meet this difficulty, does this give us any help in establishing the reality of laws as Peirce describes them? Even if there are real mental habits, or patterns of reaction, there can only be real physical habits, or laws, if the physical is basically psychical and thus of such a nature as to partake of the mental phenomenon of habit-taking. It is difficult to see that Peirce is able to prove that the physical is basically psychical, and with the rejection of this view we must also reject his view that laws are of the nature of habits.

PRAGMATISM AND POTENTIALITY

To return to our previous point, we have seen that the realist's view involves an element of potentiality not found in the nominalistic view. Since, on pragmatic grounds two theories mean the same thing if they issue in the same consequences, the realist must find some difference between his view and that of the nominalist if he is to avoid the conclusion that the two views are really one and that the dispute is only terminological. Both views admit the reality of actually observed objects and of connections that actually do occur in the universe. The difference is that the realist claims that in addition to the actual there is also the potential. On this view an object is real at times when it is not actually being observed, although it is only a real potentiality; i.e., it is a reality which prescribes how an actual occurrence would be experienced if it were realized. Also a law is real at times when it is not operative; so that a law is not merely a sum of those connections which do occur but a prescription stating how connections would have occurred that did not actually occur. In other words, to talk about the unobserved nature of either an object or a law is to talk about their nature as potentialities. If the realistic position is to be tenable at all the realist must find some meaningful way of discussing potentiality. The crucial question, then, for a pragmatist who wishes to be a realist, is this: Does the pragmatic theory of meaning permit the use of the concept of potentiality?

Pragmatism is an experiential or psychological meaning theory. It does not rest its criterion of meaning on logical or formal grounds—a proposition is not meaningful simply because it has a certain syntactical structure—but on psychological grounds. Pragmatism undertakes to explicate the psychological or cognitive content of a sentence in terms of volitions and sense-experiences, so that to say that a proposition (or a concept) is meaningless for a pragmatist is to say that it cannot be expressed in terms of psychological experiences. The primitive elements of the pragmatic criterion include experiences of volition and perception with the assertion of a relation holding between them. Obviously experiences of volition and of perception are psychological. This is also true of the relation—the practical consideration. In the case of a stipulated definition the practical consideration expresses my psychological resolve to use the word only as defined. In the case of asserting that the concept applies, i.e., that some proposition concerning it is true, the consideration expresses a psychological belief on my part that I may expect experiences of the sort described by the consequent if I act in the manner prescribed by the antecedent. Thus, in terms of pragmatism, a meaningless proposition is not merely formally meaningless but psychologically meaningless.

It would seem as though the formulation of the pragmatic criterion in psychological terms would make it extremely difficult for the pragmatist to ascribe meaning to the concept of potentiality. For the primitive elements of the meaning would have to be psychological experiences of volition and perception and they would, further, have to be experiences of the object or law in question at times when it was not being experienced. And this is obviously impossible. For example, the pragmatist can ascribe meaning to the idea of a law by telling me what experiences may be expected at times when I actually experience the law, but if he is to describe to me the meaning of a "potential" law, he must not use experiences referring to the law as actualized in experience but must explain its nature at times when it is unexperienced, and the terms used to describe the unexperienced law are only meaningful psychologically if stated in terms of experiences. But what experiences can state an "un-experience"? In short, the meaning of an actualized, or experienced, law can be expressed in terms of experiences, but no experiences are adequate to describe a potential, or unexperienced law. The same objection is true of the concept of an object as a potential entity.

Peirce admits that the potential cannot be described in terms of the actual. He says that the nominalistic error "lies in holding that the potential, or possible, is nothing but what the actual makes it to be" (1.422). But if the potential is more than the actual, since all my experiences are only of the actual,

I cannot describe the more-than in terms of experiences.
Peirce's answer to those who deny the potential is:

The refutation of the position consists in showing that nobody does,
or can, in the light of good sense, consistently retain it. . . . It is
impossible to hold consistently that a quality only exists when it
actually inheres in a body [i.e., is perceived to inhere]. If that were
so, nothing but individual facts would be true. Laws would be fictions; and in fact, the nominalist does object to the word "law,"
and prefers "uniformity" to express his conviction that so far as the
law expresses what only *might* happen but does not, it is nugatory.
. . . But I confess I do not take pains to answer a doctrine so
monstrous, and just at present out of vogue (1.422).

Calling a doctrine "monstrous" sounds suspiciously like a
last resort for a philosopher. I would agree with Peirce that
"nobody does or can, in the light of good sense," be a complete nominalist. On the other hand, pragmatism by limiting
meaning to actualized experiences makes realism as applied
to laws meaningless. The realist believes that there are real
potentialities in the world, but pragmatism makes it impossible for him to have a meaningful concept of potentiality.

This argument does not, however, point out anything new.
Pragmatism is an experiential theory of meaning. So far as it
is such, it must ultimately meet the issue which Hume stated
so definitively for empiricism. To the extent that it departs
from Hume's position by admitting potentialities as real features of the universe, it manages to avoid his difficulties but it
does not solve them.

Finally, an experiential theory of meaning faces the difficulties of explaining how, if we only experience actualities,
we ever formulated the concept of a potentiality, and why, if
it is but a fiction of our imagination, it works so successfully.
Of course, these objections cannot be held against pragmatism in particular, for they apply equally against any empirical theory of meaning. But they do stand as problems still

to be solved. The problem of the meaning of potentiality remains as perhaps the most important problem facing philosophy today. A pragmatic statement of the meaning of potentiality would require a statement of the psychological content of the concept as well as an indication of what there was in the external world which corresponds to it. Hume's analysis of causation has shown that any solution of the latter problem must be circular. Any solution of the former probably would be also, since any statement of the psychological concept of potentiality would consist of general propositions of the form "if I act in manner x then I will have experiences of the sort y," and any general proposition must contain potentiality; so that any definition of potentiality must involve potentiality and hence would be circular.

More briefly, the issue is this. No complete description of reality can be made simply by using actualities. A complete description of the world involves potentialities as well as actualities. But 1) all that we experience are actualities, and 2) a potentiality cannot be reduced to actualities. Accordingly, no empirical theory of meaning can completely describe the world. This impasse the pragmatists share with the rest of modern empirical philosophers.

We may conclude the discussion of Peirce with a brief summary of his metaphysics. We began with a statement of his metaphysical realism. We found this view to be related to the position of those scholastics known as moderate realists. The position of the moderate realists involved two denials, one aimed at the extreme realists and the other at the nominalists. The moderate realists denied that there were any platonic hypostatizations existing in a separate realm. This differentiated them from the extreme realists. They also denied that all of man's ideas were determinate particular ideas; he had general ideas. This differentiated them from the nominalists. But to be a realist was to affirm that man's ideas had an external counterpart. To satisfy the need to give man's knowledge a realistic basis without resorting to the reification of the Platonists, the positive position of the moderate realists involved two points: 1) that all of man's experience was of particular objects, but 2) that each particular object had the possibility of a universal. From these two points they argued that the general concept in the mind was the realization of the potentiality found in the particular object. Thus, the general concept was real, for it had an external counterpart in a real potentiality found in the particular.

These two points were of great importance for Peirce's thought. The first set the framework for pragmatism. Scotus and Aquinas held, in effect, that general concepts, or abstract terms, were only meaningful so far as they referred to concrete particulars. This view is a basic thesis in modern language theory: the abstract is only meaningful so far as it may be expressed in terms of the concrete particular. In the development of pragmatism, Peirce widened the scope of this formula to cover propositions as well, and argued that all signs are meaningful only so far as they refer to concrete particulars. On the other hand, while derived from scholastic realism, Peirce's pragmatism adds a new and vital element to the view by insisting that meanings refer not to concrete objects, as the scholastics held, but to experiences of objects. It is this shift in emphasis that limits meaningfulness to human experience, which gave pragmatism a vitality of its own that imparted a fresh impetus to American philosophy.

But it was precisely this shift in emphasis that made Peirce's pragmatism inconsistent with his metaphysics. He developed his metaphysics out of the second point in the scholastic position—that each particular object had the potentiality of becoming a universal. The scholastics had dealt only with the denotation of concepts relating to objects. The problem of law was not an important one in their discussions. Peirce, however, had to face the realists' problem both as it applied to objects and as it applied to laws. He used the same procedure in both cases. He held that general concepts of objects were real because there were in the universe particular objects which had a potentiality of becoming actualized in an unlimited number of experiences and hence were real generals, and that general concepts of laws were real because there were in the universe real laws which had a potentiality of acting in an unlimited number of cases and hence were also real generals.

On Peirce's view, there are two senses of reality, one of which is independent of any observer and the other of which is dependent upon an observer. The latter sense is consistent with his pragmatism for it can be explicated in terms of human experiences, but the former sense requires that objects and laws which are unobserved have a reality at the times when they are unobserved. This type of reality is a mere potential reality and Peirce seems to think that it can be adequately defined in terms of pragmatism by holding that to say an object has a potential reality is merely to say that if experienced it will produce an experience of a certain sort. It seems to me that this definition of potentiality is untenable, since it requires us to assert nothing that cannot be equally well asserted by one who denies that there is any potential reality and admits only actualized realities to be meaningful. If the pragmatist is to make potential realities meaningful, he must define the meaning of an unobserved entity, but since his theory of meaning admits only experiences as meaningful he is prohibited from ascribing any meaning to unexperienced objects and unexperienced laws.

I conclude, therefore, that Peirce's metaphysics is incompatible with his pragmatism. The metaphysics requires that it be meaningful to refer to unobservable objects and laws. The pragmatism makes any such reference impossible.

THE INFLUENCE OF PEIRCE

Although Peirce published but very little during his life-time, he was very fortunate in having been able through that little and through personal contact to have exercised an in-fluence on the leading philosophers of his day. William James dedicated his first book in philosophy—*The Will to Believe,* in 1896—to Peirce with these words: "To My Old Friend, Charles Sanders Peirce, To whose philosophic comradeship in old times and to whose writings in more recent years I owe more incitement and help than I can express or repay." This was written before James launched pragmatism and is not due to any sense of a connection with Peirce on that ground. Although James was one of the warmest personalities in American philosophy, there were others to whom he could have dedicated his first book, and his dedicating it to Peirce was more than a mere act of comradeship.

The publication of Josiah Royce's *The World and the In-dividual* (1899–1901) brought Royce into close contact with Peirce. As a result of these contacts, Royce stated in the pref-ace of his *The Problem of Christianity* (1913), "As to certain metaphysical opinions which are stated, in outline, in the second volume of this book, I now owe much more to our great and unduly neglected American logician, Mr. Charles Peirce, than I do to the common tradition of recent idealism, and certainly very much more than I have ever owed, at any point of my own philosophical development, to the doctrines which, with technical accuracy, can be justly attributed to Hegel." [12]

Morton G. White gives 1903 as the year that Dewey broke from Hegelianism.[13] In 1903 Dewey wrote to James: "I must

[12] Josiah Royce, *The Problem of Christianity* (New York: Macmillan, 1913), I, xi. See also Royce's *War and Insurance,* p. 50.

[13] Morton G. White, *The Origin of Dewey's Instrumentalism* (New York: Columbia University Press, 1943), p. 148.

say, however, that I can see how far I have moved along when I find how much I get out of Peirce this year, and how easily I understand him, when a few years ago he was mostly a sealed book to me, aside from occasional inspirations" (*William James*, II, 523). In his *Logic: The Theory of Inquiry* (1947), Dewey says in a footnote: "The readers who are acquainted with the logical writings of Peirce will note my great indebtedness to him in the general position taken" (*Logic*, p. 9, n.1).

I do not wish to imply that James or Dewey were slavish followers or mere interpreters of Peirce. Quite the contrary; each of them had developed a position of his own, but each of them did receive stimulus and encouragement from Peirce and felt an intellectual obligation which I think has been underestimated. What Peirce's pragmatic method did do was to provide a crystallization of some definite tendencies in the thought of James and Dewey and to provide them with a rallying point and a sense of a common conviction, which enabled them to enter the philosophic lists with a united front.

Part II

THE PRAGMATISM OF WILLIAM JAMES

5

Philosophy of Religion

William James (1842–1910) was the son of Henry James, Sr., and Mary James. His paternal grandfather emigrated to this country from Ireland in 1798 at the age of eighteen years. By judicious investment in the Erie Canal, he amassed a fortune of three million dollars and became one of the wealthiest men in America. He was a staunch Presbyterian, and in those days this meant a thorough-going Calvinist. When he died he sought to provide for the spiritual as well as the material well-being of his descendants by stipulating that his wealth should be held in a trust fund until his youngest grandchild came of age. His intent was to make adequate provision for the welfare of his descendants without exposing them to the temptations of great wealth while they were young. The result was that for two generations the members of the James family were free to engage in whatever pursuits they wished without too much concern for money.

Henry James, Sr. attended Princeton Theological Seminary for two and a half years before he rebelled against its puritanism. He spent the remainder of his life as a writer and lecturer, and described his profession as that of a "student." His literary friendships with such men as Emerson and Oliver Wendell Holmes, Sr., and his fascination with such esoteric intellectual movements as Swedenborgianism and Fourierism provided an intellectual environment for his children that stimulated and encouraged philosophical open-mindedness.

The bare facts of William James's life are simply told. He was born in New York City on January 11, 1842. His father had his own ideas about the education of his children and they attended several schools both here and abroad. Most of the period from thirteen to eighteen years of age William was at school abroad. He there acquired that cosmopolitan touch and fluency in French and German which were to remain with him all his life.

William went through a period when he thought he was to be a painter, but after a year's serious effort decided he could not excel in this field. In 1861 he entered the Lawrence Scientific School at Harvard. In 1864 the family moved to Boston, and William entered the Harvard Medical School. His most influential teachers here were Charles W. Eliot and Louis Agassiz. In 1865–66 he accompanied Agassiz on an expedition up the Amazon. The years 1867 and 1868 were spent mainly studying in Europe, and in 1869 he received his M.D. from Harvard. The next three years were a period of ill health and mental depression, which we will discuss briefly presently, and in 1878 he became an instructor in anatomy and physiology at Harvard. In 1875 he began teaching the first courses in psychology ever offered in this country. In 1879 he began teaching philosophy, and in 1880 he became an assistant professor of philosophy. In 1890 he published his two-volume *Principles of Psychology*, which long remained the standard work in this country on that subject.

After this time his interest switched almost entirely to philosophy. In 1896 he completed his first collection of philosophical writings, *The Will to Believe and Other Essays*.[1]

---

[1] There is some difficulty as to the proper date for the material in this volume. The title lecture, "The Will to Believe," was first given in 1895.

In 1898 he suffered an injury to his heart, while hiking in the mountains, that was to lead to his death in 1910. In spite of his poor health, the next twelve years were to be his most fruitful period. In 1901–02 he gave the Gifford Lectures at Edinburgh, which were published in 1902 as *The Varieties of Religious Experience*. In 1907 he published *Pragmatism*, which grew out of a series of lectures given the previous year at the Lowell Institute and at Columbia. In 1909 he published *A Pluralistic Universe*, the Hibbert Lectures given at Oxford in 1908–09, and also in 1909 he published *The Meaning of Truth*. He died at Chocorua, New Hampshire, on August 26, 1910. Posthumous publications were *Some Problems of Philosophy*, 1911; *Memories and Studies*, 1911; *Essays in Radical Empiricism*, 1912; and *Collected Essays and Reveiws*, 1920.

This skeletal collection of facts can give no idea of the warmth and richness of the personality of William James. The reader who may be interested in pursuing James's life in more detail is referred to the monumental two-volume study done by Ralph Barton Perry in 1935 titled *The Thought and Character of William James* [2] and to the collection, *The Letters of William James*, edited by his son Henry James.

The member of his family who appears to have been most influential in William James's development was his father, Henry James, Sr. William James was always very close to his three brothers and his sister—particularly to his brother Henry James, Jr., the novelist—but William was the oldest child and seems to have gone his own way in his intellectual development as far as his brothers and sister were concerned.

The copyright date of the volume was 1896. The first edition was published in 1897. Since the chief value of the date, in this case, is to show at what point in the author's intellectual career the material passed out of his control so far as changes are concerned, I have used the date 1896 throughout this study.

[2] The present author, as must anyone who writes on William James, acknowledges his indebtedness to Perry's superb scholarship.

The influence of his father seems to have been exercised in two ways. Henry James, Sr. embodied those traits of personality that we have learned to associate with the Irish people. He was a man with a vast capacity for friendship and a compassionate tenderness toward those whom he took to be his friends. This genius for loving his fellow man is well revealed in the letters of the elder James. The extent to which William inherited this outgoing personality may be seen by comparing his letters with those of his father. Without looking at the signature it is often difficult to tell whether father or son wrote the letter, so similar were they in the warmth of their feelings. This warmth is reflected in the literary style of both of them. Here is no pedantry nor any cold logic divorced from the world of human affairs. Both of them felt too keenly the worth and weight of humanity to be able to soar for long in the clear blue empyrean enjoyed by some philosophers. William James threatened all his life to do a "serious" philosophical treatise rather than a popular one, but his love of mankind was too great. This trait was of great importance, however, for it gave James's writings a warmth of appeal that made them popular and spread pragmatism to an audience that Peirce and Dewey could never touch. There is little doubt that the respect given philosophy in contemporary America is due in no small part to the effect of William James's Irish personality on the American mind of the turn of the century.

The chief influence of the elder James on his son was intellectual, although more in the way of posing a problem than in solving it. The basic motivation for a man's whole intellectual effort may often come from some personal conflict which he must find a way to resolve. This was the case with both father and son, and the conflict was the same in both cases. When this warm Irish personality plunged into the cold sea of Calvinistic fatalism, there was bound to be some steam generated. New England puritanism was never the same again after the impact of the humanism of William James, but neither of the Jameses was ever able to throw off completely the religious influence of his background. They modified it, although in some form it was always with them. Both of them went through what was once called a nervous breakdown as a result of this intense emotional conflict, and both only came out of this mood when they found a solution to the problem.

We have autobiographical passages in which each of these men describes his traumatic experience. The elder James spent most of his life as a writer and student on religious matters. In 1844, when he was thirty-three years old, he had been studying the book of Genesis for several years in connection with his thesis that the book was not a natural history but a spiritual history of man, and had come to what he considered a very satisfactory stage in his work; he was cheerful and in good health and spirits when he had the experience described below:

One day, however, towards the close of May, having eaten a comfortable dinner, I remained sitting at the table after the family had dispersed, idly gazing at the embers in the grate, thinking of nothing, and feeling only the exhilaration incident to a good digestion, when suddenly—in a lightning-flash as it were—'fear came upon me, and trembling, which made all my bones to shake.' To all appearance it was a perfectly insane and abject terror, without ostensible cause, and only to be accounted for, to my perplexed imagination, by some damned shape squatting invisible to me within the precincts of the room and raying out from his fetid personality influences fatal to life. The thing had not lasted ten seconds before I felt myself a wreck; that is, reduced from a state of firm, vigorous, joyful manhood to one of almost helpless infancy. The only self-control I was capable of exerting was to keep my seat. I felt the greatest desire to run incontinently to the foot of the stairs and shout for help to my wife,—to run to the roadside even, and appeal to the public to protect me; but by an immense effort

I controlled these frenzied impulses, and determined not to budge from my chair till I had recovered my lost self-possession. This purpose I held to for a good long hour, as I reckoned time, beat upon meanwhile by an ever-growing tempest of doubt, anxiety, and despair, with absolutely no relief from any truth I had ever encountered save a most pale and distant glimmer of the divine existence, when I resolved to abandon the vain struggle, and communicate without more ado what seemed my sudden burden of inmost, implacable unrest to my wife.

Now, to make a long story short, this ghastly condition of mind continued with me, with gradually lengthening intervals of relief, for two years, and even longer.[3]

James was to find his way out of this slough of despondency only some years later when he discovered the writings of Swedenborg. He developed a position which he was with difficulty able to explain to others. In speaking of his father's position, William James gives us advice which might apply as well to the writings of William James himself:

Do not *squeeze* the terms of the logic too hard! And if you are a positivist, do not be too prompt to throw the book down with an ejaculation of disgust at Alexandrian theosophizing, and of wonder that such brain-spinning should find a printer at the present day. My father's own disgust at any abstract statement of his system could hardly be excelled by that of the most positivistic reader. I will not say that the logical relations of its terms were with him a mere afterthought; they were more organic than that. But the core and centre of the thing in him was always instinct and attitude, something realized at a stroke, and felt like a fire in his breast; and all attempts at articulate verbal formulations of it were make-shifts of a more or less desperately impotent kind. This is why he despised every formulation he made as soon as it was uttered, and set himself to the Sisyphus-labor of producing a new one that should be less irrelevant. I remember hearing him groan, when

[3] *The Literary Remains of the Late Henry James,* edited with an Introduction by William James (Boston: Osgood, 1885), pp. 59–60.

struggling in this way, "Oh, that I might thunder it out in a single interjection that would tell the *whole* of it, and never speak a word again!" But he paid his tribute to necessity; and few writers in the end were more prolix than he.[4]

The elder James's solution to his problem was too complex to be treated here. Essentially it involved man's salvation through a denial of his selfhood as an individual and his identification of himself with God, who was to be found not apart from, but in the rest of, creation. In his own words:

My being lies utterly outside of my*self*, lies in utterly forgetting my*self*, lies in utterly unlearning and disusing all its elaborately petty schemes and dodges now grown so transparent that a child is not deceived by them; lies, in fact, *in honestly identifying myself with others*. I know it will never be possible for me to do this perfectly,—that is, attain to self-extinction,—because being created, I can never hope actually to become Divine; but at all events I shall become through eternal years more and more intimately one in nature, and I hope in spirit, with a being who *is* thoroughly destitute of this finiting principle,—that is, a being who is without selfhood save in His creatures.[5]

We can best complete this bare outline of an extremely rich personality by quoting a description of him by one of his contemporaries:

Henry James, the elder, was a person of delightful eccentricity, and a humorist of the first water. When in his grotesque moods, he maintained that, to a right-minded man, a crowded Cambridge horse-car "was the nearest approach to heaven upon earth!" What was the precise nature of his philosophy, I never fully understood, but he professed to be a Swedenborgian, and carried on a correspondence full of droll incidents with anxious inquirers, in various parts of the country. Asking him one day about one of these, he replied instantly, "Oh, a devil of a woman!" to my great astonishment as I was not then thoroughly familiar with his ways. One

[4] *Literary Remains*, pp. 15–16.   [5] *Literary Remains*, p. 75.

of his most amusing experiences was that the other Swedenborgians repudiated all religious connection with him, so that the sect to which he belonged, and of which he was the head, may be said to have consisted of himself alone. He was a writer of extraordinary vigor and picturesqueness, and I suppose there was not in his day a more formidable master of English style.

His son, the author, then a youth of nineteen or twenty, was just beginning to try his literary wings. There could not be a more entertaining treat than a dinner at the James house, when all the young people were at home. They were full of stories of the oddest kind, and discussed questions of morals or taste or literature with a vociferous vigor so great as sometimes to lead the young men to leave their seats and gesticulate on the floor. I remember, in some of these heated discussions, it was not unusual for the sons to invoke humorous curses on their parent, one of which was, that "his mashed potatoes might always have lumps in them!" [6]

In this atmosphere William James grew up. His father's struggle with the New England conscience had been primarily a struggle between an orthodox religion and an unorthodox one. In William's day the same struggle was to appear in the different guise of science versus religion. James, as a young man, became quite interested in science—particularly in physiology and psychology—and seems to have come quite early to a realization that the crux of the issue was whether man was the mere machine that science made him out to be or whether he had a free will and could of his own volition do the good.

James's study of science led him further and further toward the mechanistic view, but his religious inclinations were so opposed to the direction his beliefs were taking that finally, when he was about thirty years old, he had an experience analogous to his father's which he described as follows:

[6] *Life and Letters of Edwin Lawrence Godkin,* edited by Rollo Ogden (New York: Macmillan, 1907), II, 117–18.

I went one evening into a dressing-room in the twilight to procure some article that was there, when suddenly there fell upon me without any warning, just as if it came out of the darkness, a horrible fear of my own existence. Simultaneously there arose in my mind the image of an epileptic patient whom I had seen in the asylum, a black-haired youth with greenish skin, entirely idiotic, who used to sit all day on one of the benches, or rather shelves against the wall, with his knees drawn up against his chin, and the coarse gray undershirt, which was his only garment, drawn over them inclosing his entire figure. He sat there like a sort of sculptured Egyptian cat or Peruvian mummy, moving nothing but his black eyes and looking absolutely non-human. This image and my fear entered into a species of combination with each other. *That shape am I,* I felt potentially. Nothing that I possess can defend me against that fate, if the hour for it should strike for me as it struck for him. There was such a horror of him, and such a perception of my own merely momentary discrepancy from him, that it was as if something hitherto solid within my breast gave way entirely, and I became a mass of quivering fear. After this the universe was changed for me altogether. I awoke morning after morning with a horrible dread at the pit of my stomach, and with a sense of the insecurity of life that I never knew before, and that I have never felt since. It was like a revelation; and although the immediate feelings passed away, the experience has made me sympathetic with the morbid feelings of others ever since. It gradually faded, but for months I was unable to go out into the dark alone.

In general I dreaded to be left alone. I remember wondering how other people could live, how I myself had ever lived, so unconscious of that pit of insecurity beneath the surface of life. . . . I have always thought that this experience of melancholia of mine had a religious bearing (*Varieties,* pp. 160–61).[7]

That James's struggle was mechanism versus free will may be seen by his identifying himself with the idiot who had no

[7] That James is here describing his own experience (which, in a footnote to page 158 he compares with that of his father) we are assured by his son. See *Letters,* I, 145.

mind of his own and was but a machine, and by the fact that he only begins to get out of his despondency when he is convinced by a French philosopher that the will is free. He wrote in one of his notebooks:

I think that yesterday was a crisis in my life. I finished the first part of Renouvier's second "Essais" and see no reason why his definition of Free Will—'the sustaining of a thought *because I choose to* when I might have other thoughts'—need be the definition of an illusion. At any rate, I will assume for the present—until next year —that it is no illusion. My first act of free will shall be to believe in free will (*Letters*, I, 47).

James told his father that his depression was largely overcome as a result of this discussion of Renouvier's (*Letters*, I, 169–70).

The struggle with the free will problem was only one thread in a larger pattern of James's concern over the mechanistic-theistic controversy. It will serve, however, to illustrate the kind of mental depression James fell into and to indicate why his philosophy was oriented toward discovering a method that would enable him to avoid the horns of his dilemma.

THE PROBLEM

Peirce did not look upon pragmatism as a method for solving problems, but as a method for eliminating pseudo-problems. He wrote to James: "after all pragmatism solves no real problems. It only shows that supposed problems are not real problems. But when one comes to such questions as immortality, the nature of the connections of mind and matter . . . we are left completely in the dark. The effect of pragmatism here is simply to open our minds to receiving any evidence, not to furnish evidence" (*William James*, II, 430).

It was this invitation for an opening of the mind that first interested James in pragmatism. James had the problem which gnawed unceasingly at his intellectual vitals—is there a God or is the world merely a fortuitous concourse of atoms? He sought for many years to use pragmatism as a means of clearing the way for what appealed to him as a satisfactory solution to this problem. In the lecture in which he first announced pragmatism, James sought to apply it to this problem; in his book on pragmatism he sought to apply it to this problem; and in the volume on which he was working at the time of his death James is still concerned with the relation of pragmatism to this issue.

In 1880, in the first of his writings oriented primarily toward philosophy, "The Sentiment of Rationality," James stated clearly not only the problem but the haunting emotional connotations which it had for him.

A philosophy may be unimpeachable in other respects, but either of two defects will be fatal to its universal acceptance. First, its ultimate principle must not be one that essentially baffles and disappoints our dearest desires and most cherished powers. . . .

But a second and worse defect in a philosophy than that of contradicting our active propensities is to give them no object whatever to press against. A philosophy whose principle is so incommensurate with our most intimate powers as to deny them all relevancy in universal affairs, as to annihilate their motives at one blow, will be even more unpopular than pessimism. Better face the enemy than the eternal Void! This is why materialism will always fail of universal adoption, however well it may fuse things into an atomistic unity, however clearly it may prophesy the future eternity. For materialism denies reality to the objects of almost all the impulses which we most cherish. The real *meaning* of the impulses, it says, is something which has no emotional interest for us whatever. . . . Any philosophy which annihilates the validity of the reference by explaining away its objects or translating them into terms of no emotional pertinency, leaves the mind with little to care or act for. This is the opposite condition from that of nightmare, but when actually brought home to consciousness it produces a kindred horror. In nightmare we have motives to act, but no power; here we have powers, but no motives. A nameless *unheimlichkeit* comes over us at the thought of there being nothing eternal in our final purposes, in the objects of those loves and aspirations which are our deepest energies. . . . Small as we are, minute as is the point by which the cosmos impinges upon each one of us, each one desires to feel that his reaction at that point is congruous with the demands of the vast whole,—that he balances the latter, so to speak, and is able to do what it expects of him (*Will to Believe,* pp. 82–84).

In 1896, in his famous essay on "The Will to Believe," James argues the same issue. Two years later, in 1898, in a lecture before the Philosophical Union at the University of California, James returns to this theme, and here makes his first written reference to pragmatism as a method which opens the way to a possible solution of this problem. In the opening chapters of his book on pragmatism in 1907, James elaborates the same argument he used in the 1898 paper. In the first chapter of the book he makes his famous distinction between the tender-minded and the tough-minded thinker. He assigns them these characteristics: [8]

The Tender-Minded	*The Tough-Minded*
Rationalistic (going by "principles")	Empiricist (going by "facts")
Intellectualistic	Sensationalistic
Idealistic	Materialistic
Optimistic	Pessimistic
Religious	Irreligious
Free-willist	Fatalistic
Monistic	Pluralistic
Dogmatical	Sceptical

It requires no great perspicacity to perceive that we have here the theist and the materialist. At the end of the first

[8] *Pragmatism,* p. 12.

lecture, having made this distinction, James says: "I offer the oddly-named thing pragmatism as a philosophy that can satisfy both kinds of demands. It can remain religious like the rationalisms, but at the same time, like the empiricisms, it can preserve the richest intimacy with facts" (*Pragmatism*, pp. 32–33). In his next chapter he says, "The pragmatistic philosophy . . . neither begins nor ends by turning positive religious reconstructions out of doors—it treats them cordially as well. I hope I may lead you to find it just the mediating way of thinking that you require" (*Pragmatism*, p. 40).

THE METHOD

Both in the California address and in his book on pragmatism, James begins his argument by a reference to the concluding pages of the first volume of Herbert Spencer's *Psychology*, wherein Spencer argues that matter and mind are ultimately reducible to the same thing. James takes this view to imply that mind and matter, and hence the universe which is composed of them, have a common origin which may be called indiscriminately either God (mind) or matter. James says that this position is tenable with regard to the past, for since the world is what it is and was made by whatever made it, to call that maker God or matter is only to give two different names to one entity. So that if we consider only the past, God and matter are terms which really mean the same thing. James holds, however, that the pragmatic method is a method of defining terms by looking to the future rather than the past, and he argues against the view that God and matter mean the same thing, as follows:

1. If the actions which we prepare and the experiences which we expect from the application of two different terms are different, then the terms have a different meaning.

2. While it is true that looking backward gives us no dif-

ference between God and matter, looking forward does do
so. The future actions and the expected future experiences of
the man who believes in God are quite different from those
of the man who believes only in matter.

3. Therefore on the pragmatic view the term "God" and
the term "matter" have different meanings.

I think James is quite right here and that there is, on the
pragmatic view, a real difference between these two concepts. If I believe in God, I act in a certain manner and expect that I will, as a result of these actions, have certain future experiences. If I believe only in matter, then I act in a
quite different manner and expect quite different experiences.
The crucial question, however, is this: When am I *justified*
in applying one or the other of these concepts to the universe?

Let us investigate this question by first examining a similar,
but simpler, problem. Suppose a Mr. A and a Mr. B to be
arguing about whether a certain object is really a tree. Mr. A
says that it is and Mr. B says that it is not, that it is only a
cleverly constructed papier-mâché substitute. Mr. B proposes
to settle the question by cutting the tree down and examining
its innards. But Mr. A, firmly believing that the object is a
real tree, says he does not wish to destroy it by cutting it
down. He suggests, instead, that they wait until autumn to see
if the leaves change color, and that they watch it in the spring
to see if the seeds dropped by it produce seedlings. Mr. B
agrees that these two consequences are scarcely to be expected of an ersatz tree, and he will accept them as deciding
factors.

All during the summer Mr. A, believing that the tree is real,
goes out conscientiously and waters the tree and fertilizes it.
But Mr. B sedulously avoids doing any such thing since he
believes the object not to be a real tree. Mr. A's positive actions contrast sharply with Mr. B's negative actions. Clearly

Mr. A believes the tree to be real while Mr. B believes it to be ersatz. It is also clear that Mr. A does not mean the same thing by a real tree that Mr. B means by an ersatz tree. Each of them has a different belief and, on the basis of the available evidence, each is entitled to his belief. But the crucial question is when is the belief of one of them *justified?* When is A's belief more than a mere hope on his part, when does it become a solid reality, in short, a truth? His belief becomes a truth when in addition to his ways of acting he finds that he gets in return certain experiences. When the leaves do turn and the seedlings do sprout from the ground, then his belief, his faith, is justified. It is no longer merely something which he is entitled to believe; it is something he is justified in believing.

That is, we need to distinguish here the consequences of Mr. A's believing this object to be a tree (these consequences being certain actions on his part) from the consequences of the object really being a tree so that his belief is true (these consequences consisting in certain experiences which he has irrespective of his wishes, e.g., the leaves changing color whether or not he wishes them to do so).

So, in the case of the materialist and the theist, we must carefully distinguish the consequences which follow from Mr. A believing in theism and Mr. B believing in materialism, from the consequences which would follow from either of these beliefs being true. A and B are both entitled to their beliefs. The belief of either may, however, only be justified in this life when we see whether the extinction of the universe is announced by Gabriel's trumpet or the inexorable functioning of the Second Law of Thermodynamics.

The confusion between the consequences of a proposition as believed by us, and the consequences of the same proposition as true was a confusion James seemed to make whenever he talked about religion. He seemed to make it in "The Will to Believe," in the California address, and in the book on pragmatism. In the latter he rejects pessimism, the doctrine that the world is necessarily becoming worse, as too tough-minded; and optimism, the view that the world is necessarily becoming better, as too tender-minded. He offers, as a mediating view, meliorism—the doctrine that the world is not necessarily becoming better nor necessarily becoming worse, but rather that what the world will become is still an open question and that the direction of the outcome depends in part upon our efforts. If we seek to make the world better, it may become so; if we do not, it will probably become worse. He argues that we are entitled to believe in meliorism—that is, he shows that there is no evidence which disproves meliorism —and he shows that meliorism does not mean the same thing as materialism. It is partly to make this latter point that he introduces the notion of a "moral holiday." To show that the belief of the meliorist (or any other theist) has different consequences in terms of action than does the belief of the materialist, he suggests that one who believes that the control of the universe is, at least partly, in higher hands than ours, does not need to fight ceaselessly against evil, but may on occasion rest from the struggle and take a holiday from moral strife, confident that the ills of the world are still being combatted by other powers.

James argues, then, that since there is no evidence disproving meliorism and since it has different consequences in the way of action, and hence a different meaning, than materialism, we are entitled to believe it if we wish. It is this entitlement which gives us the right to believe. And it is this right to believe which James advocated under the unfortunate title of the "will to believe." In the essay on the will to believe—which he later admitted he should have called the right to believe [9]—James goes on, however, to argue not only

[9] *William James*, II, 245, 488.

that we have the right to believe, but that by willing to believe something we may actually aid in bringing it about. This is the doctrine which Peirce described in a letter to James as "the kind of expression which hurts a serious philosopher very much."

The whole issue hurt James in one sense and helped him in another. It made him the object of a virulent attack. He says that some of his opponents pretended to misread the title "The Will to Believe" as the will to deceive and the will to make-believe. On the other hand, because he was the center of this controversy, James's espousal of pragmatism pulled pragmatism into the limelight and made it an object of study in a way which it might never otherwise have been.

Under the barrage of criticism to which his attempt to support religion was subjected, James, ordinarily one of the best-tempered of men, gave way to an ill-natured exasperation. In the preface to *The Meaning of Truth,* he said he had offered the olive branch of the concept of a moral holiday to the theists and it had been rejected, "so all that I can do is to apologize and take my offering back. The absolute is true in *no* way then, and least of all, by the verdict of the critics, in the way which I assigned" (*Meaning of Truth,* p. x).

The real confusion which James was accused of making in all of his religious philosophizing, however, was the confusion we have examined above between the consequences of a proposition as believed by us and the consequences of a proposition as true. It was A. O. Lovejoy, in a letter acknowledging receipt of a copy of James's *Pragmatism,* who finally brought this difficulty home to James. In reply, James wrote:

But when it comes to your distinction between two meanings . . . of pragmatism, I have frankly to cry *peccavi*—you convict me of real sin. Consequences of true ideas *per se,* and consequences of ideas *qua believed by us,* are logically different consequences, and the whole "will to believe" business has got to be re-edited with explicit uses made of the distinction. I have been careless here, and I hope that you, in your article, will spread out the matter at the length it deserves. Failure to do it on my part has been a misdemeanor (*William James*, II, 481).

THE RIGHT TO BELIEVE

We have come now to a difficult point in the exposition of James's religious philosophy. The above analysis represents a possible interpretation of James's position and a common criticism of it. The validity of the criticism would appear to be established in the only way that is usually accepted as conclusively establishing the soundness of a criticism—the philosopher concerned accepting it himself. The difficulty is that a careful reading of James's argument will show that he did not make the confusion of which he was accused and to which he confesses. That he was not as convinced of the validity of the criticism as his letter to Lovejoy would seem to imply is suggested by the fact that James continued to use the same argument in a syllabus in his courses in philosophy and marked the syllabus for inclusion in the last book on philosophy that he was writing at the time of his death.[10]

We can best understand the argument of the essay titled "The Will to Believe" if we think of it as an essay on the right to believe. James admits that it should be so titled and, in fact, the essay is an attempt to justify our right to believe if we wish to do so. The argument is divided into two parts. The first part begins with an examination of possible ways of reacting toward hypotheses which are offered for our belief. We always have the option to accept or reject an hypothesis, and in deciding which to do we must consider the relation of the hypothesis to us. Is the hypothesis a living hypothesis for us, or is it a dead one? That is, does it strike a spark of interest

[10] *Problems*, Appendix, p. 221*ff*. and footnote thereto.

and kindle a fire in us so that we feel we would like to know whether it is true, or is it for us a dead hypothesis which stimulates no intellectual curiosity? James says that for most of us the hypothesis that Christianity is true would be a living hypothesis, whereas the hypothesis that Zoroastrianism is true is a dead hypothesis.

Secondly, the hypothesis may be forced or avoidable. If forced, we cannot evade a decision; if avoidable, we can. James suggests that if someone says to you, "When you go out either take your umbrella or leave it here," you can avoid the selection of an alternative by staying in the house and thus not going out. But if I say to you, "Accept this truth, or go without it," there is no middle ground where you may stand—a decision is forced from you. The agnostic makes his rejection of the truth as firmly as does the sceptic. In dealing with the agnostic, James makes a useful distinction between two values to be kept in mind in seeking truth. One thing we expect as the result of truth is to avoid error. A man who knows how to travel from one town to another will avoid the error of ending up in some other town. A second thing we expect is to know the truth, i.e., we not only expect negatively to avoid doing what is wrong but positively to succeed in doing what is right. These two values do not always go together, and the position of the agnostic is a case in point. By refusing to believe anything, he suceeds in attaining the first value— he avoids making a mistake. But by the fact that he refuses to believe anything, he thereby forfeits the second value; he will never know the truth. The man who believes takes a chance; he may make a mistake, but if there is a truth, he, at least, has the possibility of knowing it. If there is no truth, or if he believes a falsehood, he suffers what the agnostic avoids; he makes a mistake. But the view of the believer is subject to correction by the facts, and he may eventually attain the truth. The position of the agnostic, however, is irrational, for by refusing to believe anything he makes investigation impossible and thus blocks the road to inquiry. By this failure he loses the possibility of ever attaining the truth. Agnosticism is, then, an impossible position, philosophically, because it blocks the road to inquiry. Accordingly, one must either believe the religious hypothesis to be true or believe it to be false; he cannot be a thoroughgoing agnostic except at the price of stultifying inquiry. If all men were agnostics, no inquiry at all would take place and no new knowledge would be attained except as it might haphazardly drift into our experience. It is only by tentatively accepting an hypothesis, projecting it into experience, examining the results, formulating a revised hypothesis, projecting it into experience, etc., that knowledge may be obtained systematically.

Finally, the hypothesis may be momentous or trivial. If it is momentous, it is a chance that comes but rarely, and to reject it may be to miss an opportunity that may not present itself again—for example, the offer to accompany an expedition to the North Pole. On the other hand, an offer to go down to the corner for a cup of coffee is a trivial option since if one rejects it now he may take it up again in a few minutes.

If an hypothesis is dead or avoidable or trivial, we may without compunction refuse to exercise our option; we may make no decision at all on the hypothesis, or, if we make one it may be merely an offhand opinion. However, if the hypothesis is for us living, forced, and momentous, we have no choice; we can do nothing but elect to exercise our option. We must decide either to accept the hypothesis or reject it.

According to James, the religious hypothesis is for us living, forced, and momentous. Accordingly, we must make a decision as to whether we will accept it or reject it. When we must make such a decision, we may make it in one of two ways. We may make it upon grounds of reason or grounds of emotion. James feels that we should try reason first. But, in the case of the religious hypothesis, reason fails us. It is unable to make a decision. There are no rational grounds, i.e., no convincing arguments, for deciding either for or against the hypothesis. When we must make a decision, and we cannot make it on rational grounds, we are free to make it upon emotional grounds. If there is no better rational basis for accepting an hypothesis than for rejecting it, we have a right to do as we wish, to believe as we desire, providing we recognize that our decision is purely an emotional one. Thus the man who believes solely because he wants to, has a right to do so on those grounds. Thus is the *right* to believe vindicated. One may reject the truth of any of James's premises if he wishes, but the argument is a valid one and cannot be dismissed on purely logical grounds. James here commits no error of argument.

The second part of the argument for the right to believe appeals to a rather peculiar situation but a sound one. Here James seems to suggest that believing that something is true may make it true when it is not. This notion that wishing may make it so seems at first glance a most tender-minded and unphilosophical position reaching back almost to a childlike faith in the efficacy of desire. However, James's argument is not as naive as it appears to be. There are some special cases where things only happen when we do believe them to be true. James gives three illustrations in his writings. He asks us to consider the case of a mountain climber who has to jump across a chasm which is just at the extreme limit of his ability. If he believes that it is true that he can make the jump successfully, this belief will steady his nerves and he will succeed. If he seriously doubts that he can make the jump, the doubts may disturb him to the point where he will fail. Thus believing it was true that he could jump the chasm made it true that he could. That is, believing in it made it so, where otherwise it might not have been.

A second illustration refers to friendship. If the first time you meet a man you treat him as if he were your friend, when actually he is not, you may succeed in making him so. Whereas if you treated him with suspicion and required him to prove his friendship before you would believe it, he would never become your friend. Thus believing that he is your friend makes it become true that he is, where without the belief he would not be. A quite similar illustration is given by James in the case of the young man who believes that a young lady must love him. She does not, but he so firmly believes that she does that his belief touches her so deeply as to make her love him. Thus by believing he made it so.

The situations referred to above are all rather unusual. But with reference to them it does appear plausible to assert that believing in the truth of a proposition may, in some cases, make it so. James, in a typical metaphor, suggests that faith must sometimes run before the fact. The question then is whether the religious situation is analogous to the above situations. Is there anything about it that is such that it can only become true if we believe it? James thinks that there is. We must call to mind here that James believes in a melioristic universe. That is, he believes that the universe is not in its own right doomed to either success or failure; it may become better, but only if we aid it in doing so. For James the religious hypothesis implies the belief that the universe is in a state of flux; it is possible for it to pass from more evil to more good. The perfect universe, the completely good universe, exists only in the future and may be attained only by our efforts, but if we do not believe that we can make the universe better we will not try; therefore the success of the religious hypothesis depends upon our believing it true.

One need not accept the above analysis of what religion is, but if he does accept it—as James does—then it certainly entitles one to the right to believe, and since one who rejects it cannot deny but that it might be true, he cannot conscientiously object to the right of another to believe if he wishes.

We have seen that James has been accused of confusing the consequences of ideas as true with the consequences of ideas as believed by us. The former of these implies an external object which determines my actions—for the idea to be true there must be an external object corresponding to it which will determine my actions in certain respects. The latter implies an internal belief which determines my actions. If I believe in God, then I act in a certain way. This action may prove that I believe in God and show what I mean by God. But for God to be real, i.e., to be an object independent of my idea of him, I must have experiences which I do not cause, but which are externally caused rather than internally.

James does not fail to see this difference. His contention is, however, that the internal belief may produce the external object. Ordinarily we require the internal belief to follow the discovery of the external object. It is because this happens so consistently that we forget the exceptions. James's view is that this is an exception and that here the external object can only follow on the internal belief.

James is not trying to prove that God exists or that religion is true; he is only trying to prove that we have a right to believe that God exists and to act as though religion were true. The argument rests on two points: 1) We cannot decide the religious option on intellectual grounds but we must decide it; therefore we have a right to decide it on emotional grounds, and if our preference is to believe, then we have a right to believe; 2) since religion might be such that it cannot become true unless we believe it, we have a right to believe it, and to act accordingly.

It seems to me that when put in the above fashion James's defense of the right to believe is a valiant one and deserves a better treatment than it ordinarily gets.

THE SOLUTION

James's solution to his problem comes finally in the form of a religious metaphysics. The influences which directed him toward his final view are many. Almost every philosopher he studied seriously contributed to his thinking, either through suggesting ideas to him, or by objections to his views which irritated him to the point where he overcame them.

The metaphysical view that James finally came to is very similar to that of Peirce. The concepts of novelty and continuous growth are basic to the thought of both philosophers. James all through his philosophic career fought the view, dominant in Europe and America of his day, of a universe in which novelty and continuous growth were looked upon as illusions due to the finiteness of the human intellect. He devoted a major portion of each of his books on philosophy to attacking this view, which he called variously "the block-universe," "Monism" or "absolutism."

Monism—to use the term James used most often—was primarily an intellectualization of the traditional mystic view that all is one. Everything is one with God. It is one in being created by God, one in being used by him for his purposes, and one in ultimately returning to him. The intellectualization of this concept de-anthropomorphizes the notion of God and calls him the Absolute. Under the Absolute, everything—past, present, and future—is reduced to one in that it is all known to the Absolute. There is no novelty for him nor any change. The past, the present, and the future are for him one—the all. The view was developed in a more subtle fashion through the doctrine of internal relations. According to this doctrine, everything is related by its nature to everything else to form a unity such that any change in one part would mean a change in the other parts. For example, the parts of a watch are related by internal relations. Any change in one part would affect the other parts so that they would be unable to function prop-

erly. Hence, the parts of a watch may be said to form a unity
or to be one.

The opposite of this view was the doctrine of external relations. According to this view, some things may be related in
such ways that they are—so to speak—not related, i.e., a
change in one of them does not affect the others. Thus an
apple hanging from a tree might be said to be externally
related to our watch—if the apple falls from the tree no
change occurs in the watch.

The monistic position is that everything is related to everything else by internal relations. Thus all is one—we have a
genuine *uni*verse. Where we find only external relations we
have not looked closely enough. Further examination will
reveal internal relations.

In opposition to this monistic block-universe presided over
by an Absolute, James advocated a pluriverse, or pluralistic
universe—a universe that was not one but many. In his book
The Pluralistic Universe, James says: "Pragmatically interpreted, pluralism or the doctrine that it is many means only
that the sundry parts of reality *may be externally related.*
Everything you can think of, however vast or inclusive, has
on the pluralistic view a genuinely 'external' environment of
some sort or amount. Things are 'with' one another in many
ways, but nothing includes everything, or dominates over
everything" (p. 321).

Starting with a universe of many things, James unites them
in a fashion very reminiscent of Peirce: "The essence of my
contention is that in a world where connections are not
logically necessary, they may nevertheless adventitiously
'*come.*' Series of independent origin and purpose may in-
osculate by 'chance-encounter,' and thereafter mingle their
causalities and combine their effects" (*William James,* II,
382n.).

Thus, out of this many, James sees the universe as evolving
toward a possible unity. Things are not one now, but they

appear to be coming to be more so, and in the ultimate climax of the process may attain unity.

First there is solar, and then there is geological evolution, processes accurately describable as integrations in the mechanical sense, namely, as decrease in bulk, or growth in hardness. Then life appears; and after that neither integration of matter nor dissipation of motion plays any part whatever. The result of life, however, is to fill the world more and more and more with things displaying *organic unity.* By this is meant any arrangement of which one part helps to keep the other parts in existence. Some organic unities are material—a sea-urchin, for example, a department store, a civil service, or an ecclesiastical organization. Some are mental, as a "science," a code of laws, or an educational programme. But whether they be material or mental products, organic unities must accumulate; for every old one tends to conserve itself, and if successful new ones arise they also "come to stay" (*Memories,* pp. 135–36).

Into the primeval beginnings of this scheme James introduces consciousness. "If evolution is to work smoothly, consciousness in some shape must have been present at the very origin of things" (*Principles,* I, 149). As the evolutionary process develops we find not only human consciousness but "if evolution, Gods may be one of the results" (*William James,* II, 444).

James believes that by use of the empirical method we can discover facts of human experience that will show that there is a larger consciousness out beyond ours with which we can, upon occasion, have contact. In the *Varieties of Religious Experience* he undertakes to collect as many of these experiences as possible. In the *Pluralistic Universe* he summarizes the conclusions he reached in the *Varieties* as follows:

The believer finds that the tenderer parts of his personal life are continuous with a *more* of the same quality which is operative in the universe outside of him and which he can keep in working touch with, and in a fashion get on board of and save himself, when all his lower being has gone to pieces in the wreck. In a word, the believer is continuous, to his own consciousness, at any rate, with a wider self from which saving experiences flow in (p. 307).

The drift of all the evidence we have seems to me to sweep us very strongly towards the belief in some form of superhuman life with which we may, unknown to ourselves, be co-conscious. We may be in the universe as dogs and cats are in our libraries, seeing the books and hearing the conversation, but having no inkling of the meaning of it all (p. 309).

The line of least resistance, then, as it seems to me, both in theology and in philosophy, is to accept, along with the superhuman consciousness, the notion that it is not all-embracing, the notion, in other words, that there is a God, but that he is finite, either in power or in knowledge, or in both at once (p. 311).

The notion of a finite God is not new in philosophy. Plato's God, for instance, is limited in power. He tries to impose the forms completely on the receptacle but is unable to overcome the passivity of the receptacle which fails to cooperate. Leibniz held that God created the best of all possible worlds, implying thereby that there were worlds it was impossible for God to create. James's view is that God is either not omniscient or not omnipotent or both. It is this which accounts for evils such as pain, disease, and natural catastrophes in the world. If God knows how to eliminate these evils he lacks the power to execute his knowledge, or, if he has the power, he lacks the knowledge of how to do it.

This brings us to the melioristic universe. The universe is not necessarily getting better nor necessarily worse. But it has the potentialities for getting better. These potentialities may not get realized because God is finite; he is limited either in knowledge or in abilities. But it is possible—although not guaranteed—that they may become realized if man works together with God to try to make a better universe. The success of the whole depends upon us both. "He helps us and we help him" (*William James*, II, 443).

God is thus not the all of the absolutist; he is a part of the universe and we are another part. This view of God gives James a position which offers relief at the points where the traditional view of God pinched the most. It allows him to explain the existence of evil in a way that neither discredits the goodness of God—by imputing to God a foreknowledge of our plight coupled with an almost callous disregard for it—nor the intelligence of man—by holding that the problem of evil is a mystery beyond human comprehension. Although the view makes God considerably less than the absolute all, it compensates by making man's efforts worth something in the scale of the universe. New England Puritanism succeeded in making God everything by making man nothing. James seeks to strike a more perceptive balance. In doing so, he reflects two of the most ingrained beliefs of the American tradition—that each individual has an intrinsic worth and that his efforts do count for something in the scheme of things.

6

Pragmatism

We have seen that Peirce announced his pragmatism in the essay "How To Make Our Ideas Clear" in 1878. But pragmatism as a philosophical movement was not launched until twenty years later when William James gave his lecture "Philosophical Conceptions and Practical Results," on August 26, 1898, before the Philosophical Union of the University of California.[1] The original appearance of this address did not suffice, however, to make pragmatism known to the philosophical world. When the address was reprinted in a revised form in 1904, some further interest developed, but the movement did not become of dominant concern to philosophers until after the publication of James's book *Pragmatism* in 1907.

In the original California article, James admits his indebtedness to Peirce:

I will seek to define with you merely what seems to be the most likely direction in which to start upon the trail of truth. Years ago this direction was given to me by an American philosopher whose

---

[1] This essay has had a varied printing history. It first appeared in *The University of California Chronicle* (1898), I, 289–309. It was reprinted in James's *Collected Essays and Reviews*, 406–37, and the bulk of the article appears in Anderson and Fisch, *Philosophy in America*, 526–41. It appeared in a revised form in *The Journal of Philosophy, Psychology and Scientific Method* (1904), I, 673–87.

home is in the East, and whose published works, few as they are and scattered, are no fit expression of his powers. I refer to Mr. Charles S. Peirce, with whose very existence as a philosopher I dare say many of you are unacquainted. He is one of the most original of contemporary thinkers; and the principle of practicalism—or pragmatism, as he called it, when I first heard him enunciate it at Cambridge in the early '70's—is the clue or compass by following which I find myself more and more confirmed in believing we may keep our feet upon the proper trail (*Essays*, p. 410).

This reference to Peirce's method is not a belated recognition by James, nor did he pull it out of the blue for use in this lecture. He had recognized the importance of the method as soon as Peirce's article was published. In 1881—three years after Peirce's article appeared and seventeen years before James espoused pragmatism—in an address titled "Reflex Action and Theism," James said: "Indeed, it may be said that if two apparently different definitions of the reality before us should have identical consequences, these two definitions would really be identical definitions, made delusively to appear different merely by the different verbiage in which they are expressed" (*Will to Believe*, p. 124).

In a footnote to this sentence James adds, "See the admirably original 'Illustrations of the Logic of Science,' by C. S. Peirce, especially the second paper, 'How to make our Thoughts [sic] clear,' in the Popular Science Monthly for January, 1878."

Even prior to this acknowledgment James had been using the pragmatic approach. In 1879 he wrote, "No abstract concept can be a valid substitute for a concrete reality" (*Will to Believe*, p. 70), and in 1880 he said, "We are acquainted with a thing as soon as we have learned how to behave toward it, or how to meet the behavior which we expect from it" (*Will to Believe*, p. 85).

However, even in 1878 Peirce's pragmatism did not introduce an entirely new element in James's thought. The pragmatism fell on a fertile ground, a soil that had been prepared by James's contacts with the scientific approach of Agassiz. James wrote of Agassiz: "We cannot all escape from being abstractionists. I myself, for instance, have never been able to escape; but the years I spent with Agassiz so taught me the difference between all possible abstractionists and all livers in the light of the world's concrete fulness, that I have never been able to forget it" (*Memories*, p. 14). And as early as 1865 he said in reference to Agassiz, "No one sees farther into a generalization than his own knowledge of details extends" (*William James*, II, 2).

In addition to the scientific influence of such men as Agassiz and Chauncey Wright and the suggestions from Peirce, James was also led into his pragmatism by his study of the British empiricists. He often refers to Berkeley's treatment of substance as an example of the pragmatic method. However, about the same time that Peirce's article appeared, James was studying Locke's *Essay Concerning Human Understanding*, and Locke seems to have fertilized the empirical seed bed from which pragmatism sprouted.

In the margin of his copy of Locke, James wrote: "Terminates is an important word in Locke. Practical experience is a certain particular sensation in a particular place and time. . . . Sensation ought to be the *terminus a quo* and *ad quem* of all philosophy" (*William James*, I, 548). The last sentence of this note contains the familiar formula with which James in later years was so often to characterize the pragmatic method.

In 1890, in his *Principles of Psychology*, James again refers to Locke's position that all our ideas must ultimately terminate in sensations, and then goes on to a paragraph from which almost everything that he later says about pragmatism may be deduced.

A blind man may know all *about* the sky's blueness, and I may know all *about* your toothache, conceptually; tracing their causes from the primeval chaos, and their consequences to the crack of doom. But as long as he has not felt the blueness, nor I the toothache, our knowledge, wide as it is, of these realities, will be hollow and inadequate. Somebody must *feel* blueness, somebody must *have* toothache, to make human knowledge of these matters real. Conceptual systems which neither began nor left off in sensations would be like bridges without piers. Systems about fact must plunge themselves into sensation as bridges plunge their piers into the rock. Sensations are the stable rock, the *terminus a quo* and the *terminus ad quem* of thought. To find such termini is our aim with all our theories—to conceive first when and where a certain sensation may be had, and then to have it. Finding it stops discussion. Failure to find it kills the false conceit of knowledge. Only when you deduce a possible sensation for me from your theory, and give it to me when and where your theory requires, do I begin to be sure that your thought has anything to do with truth (*Principles*, II, 7).

That James was conscious of the background that the British empiricists provided for his thinking is shown by his reference, in his California address, to pragmatism as being in the tradition of "the great English way of investigating a conception" (*Essays*, pp. 410, 434, 437).

This reference also indicates that James was aware from the beginning that pragmatism was essentially a theory of meaning. Pragmatists of all stripes sooner or later relate meaning to a habit of action. But there are, in the main, three possible emphases which may result from this relation. In the first place it is possible to emphasize the habit prior to its acting; the emphasis here is upon the habit as a potentiality, as a piece of knowledge, as an idea of a habit. In the second place, it is possible to take the other extreme and to emphasize not the habit but the results of it; the emphasis here is upon the issue of the habit, on the particular, discrete actions. Finally, it is possible to mediate between these two extremes and to emphasize the habit as a way of acting; the emphasis here is upon the active, the functional, the dynamic. The first of these, the habit as a thought, gives the pragmatism of Peirce; the second, the habit as a source of individual acts, gives the pragmatism of James; the third, the habit as a means to an end, the pragmatism of Dewey.

We have seen how the emphasis in Peirce is upon the potential aspect of the habit. It was the desire to emphasize this aspect of his theory that led him to adopt the term "pragmaticist" as a means of distinguishing his work from that of the other pragmatists. "To say that I hold that the import, or adequate ultimate interpretation of a concept is contained, not in any deed or deeds that ever will be done, but in a habit of conduct, or general moral determination of whatever procedure there *may come to be,* is no more than to say that I am a *pragmaticist*" (5.504).

Peirce did not think of the pragmatic maxim as being nearly as rigorously tied down to the practical as it is generally thought to be. "If pragmatism is the doctrine that every conception is a conception of conceivable practical effects, it makes conception reach far beyond the practical. It allows any flight of imagination, provided this imagination ultimately alights upon a possible practical effect; and thus many hypotheses may seem at first glance to be excluded by the pragmatical maxim that are not really so excluded" (5.196).

James, however, did not take such a liberal interpretation of what was meant by practical. He interpreted the pragmatic maxim in a way which accentuated the practical effects, the particular actions which resulted from the habit. Peirce would not follow him here. He wrote that James "pushed this method to such extremes as must tend to give us pause" (5.3). In speaking of his 1878 essays, Peirce wrote that James had pressed them "further than the tether of their author would reach" (5.358n.).

Peirce expressed this difference in emphasis between his

pragmatism and that of James in a letter to Christine Ladd-Franklin. Peirce says:

Although James called himself a pragmatist, and no doubt he derived his ideas on the subject from me, yet there is a most essential difference between his pragmatism and mine. My point is that the meaning of a *concept* . . . lies in the manner in which it could *conceivably* modify purposive action, and *in this alone.* James, on the contrary, whose natural turn of mind is away from generals, and who is besides so soaked in ultra-sensationalistic psychology that like most modern psychologists he has almost lost the power of regarding matters from the logical point of view, in defining pragmatism, speaks of it as referring ideas to *experiences,* meaning evidently the sensational side of experience, while I regard concepts as affairs of habit or disposition, and of how we should react.[2]

Dewey has also recognized this difference between Peirce and James. He says:

William James alluded to the development which he gave to Peirce's expression of the principle. In one sense one can say that he enlarged the bearing of the principle by the substitution of particular consequences for the general rule or method applicable to future experience. But in another sense this substitution limited the application of the principle since it destroyed the importance attached by Peirce to the greatest possible application of the rule, or the habit of conduct—its extension to universality. That is to say, William James was more of a nominalist than Peirce (*Philosophy and Civilization,* p. 18).

Although there was this difference in emphasis between James and Peirce, the difference was only one of emphasis. When we come to examine James's pragmatism we will see that in all essential respects he is in agreement with Peirce.

[2] Christine Ladd-Franklin, "Charles S. Pierce at the Johns Hopkins," *Journal of Philosophy, Psychology and Scientific Method,* XII (1916), 718.

James, with his predominant interest in psychology, could hardly be expected to subscribe to a philosophical view about the meaning of ideas that was contradictory to or had no connection with his psychological views. As a matter of fact, long before James espoused pragmatism as a philosophical view he held to the psychological base upon which his pragmatism was built.

In 1881, in the lecture titled "Reflex Action and Theism," James states his view at some length.

In a general way, all educated people know what reflex action means.

It means that the acts we perform are always the result of outward discharges from the nervous centres, and that these outward discharges are themselves the result of impressions from the external world, carried in along one or another of our sensory nerves. Applied at first to only a portion of our acts, this conception has ended by being generalized more and more, so that now most physiologists tell us that every action whatever, even the most deliberately weighed and calculated, does, so far as its organic conditions go, follow the reflex type. There is not one which cannot be remotely, if not immediately, traced to an origin in some incoming impression of sense. There is no impression of sense which, unless inhibited by some other stronger one, does not immediately or remotely express itself in action of some kind. *There is no one of those complicated performances in the convolutions of the brain to which our trains of thought correspond, which is not a mere middle term interposed between an incoming sensation that arouses it and an outgoing discharge of some sort,* inhibitory if not exciting, to which itself gives rise. The structural unit of the nervous system is in fact a triad, neither of whose elements has any independent existence. The sensory impression exists only for the sake of awaking the central process of reflection, and the central process of reflection exists only for the sake of calling forth the final act. All action is thus re-action upon the outer world; and the middle stage of consideration or contemplation or thinking is only a place of transit, the bottom of a loop, both of whose ends have their point of application in the outer world. If it should ever have no roots in the outer world, if it should ever happen that it led to no active measures, it would fail of its essential function, and would have to be considered either pathological or abortive. *The current of life which runs in at our eyes or ears is meant to run out at our hands, feet, or lips.* The only use of the thoughts it occasions while inside is to determine its direction to whichever of these organs shall, on the whole, under the circumstances actually present, act in the way most propitious to our welfare.

The willing [acting] department of our nature, in short, dominates both the conceiving department and the feeling [perceiving] department; or in plainer English, perception and thinking are only there for behavior's sake.

I am sure I am not wrong in stating this result as one of the fundamental conclusions to which the entire drift of modern physiological investigation sweeps us. If asked what great contribution physiology has made to psychology of late years, I am sure every competent authority will reply that her influence has in no way been so weighty as in the copious illustration, verification, and consolidation of this broad, general point of view (*Will to Believe,* pp. 113–14; my italics—ECM).

Ten years later, in his *Psychology* James asserts the same principle in the early pages of his work. "It will be safe to lay down the general law that *no mental modification ever occurs which is not accompanied or followed by a bodily change*" (*Principles,* I, 5).

The same position is reiterated with amplification in the second volume:

Every impression which impinges on the incoming nerves produces some discharge down the outgoing ones, whether we be aware of it or not. Using sweeping terms and ignoring exceptions, *we might say that every possible feeling produces a movement of the entire organism, and of each and all of its parts.* What happens patently when an explosion or a flash of lightning startles us, or when we are tickled, happens latently with every sensation we receive. The only reason why we do not feel the startle or tickle in the case of insignificant sensations is partly its very small amount, partly our obtuseness (*Principles*, II, 372).

It is because the idea always runs out into an action that we can discover its meaning. The idea itself is inaccessible to observation, but the actions which follow from it are public and observable. From these we may infer what the idea is. If two ideas produce the same actions, they are the same idea; if they produce different actions, they are different ideas. If a supposed idea produces no actions, it is not an idea. The actions need not be either overt or obvious or immediate. They may be covert, disguised, and long delayed, but wherever we can trace a chain of actions back to its idea we know the meaning of the idea. Whenever we want to discover the meaning of an idea we have only to try to discover what modes of activity it might conceivably lead us to—that is, what practical consequences might flow from it.

RADICAL EMPIRICISM AND PRAGMATISM

James was, of course, an empiricist in his epistemology. But his empiricism differed in two important respects from that of those empiricists who preceded him. The first difference is usually brought out by classifying James as a normative empiricist and those who preceded him as genetic empiricists. The genetic empiricist is concerned with the genesis of ideas. He holds that all ideas are derived from experience, and thus is an empiricist. But his primary concern is with the psychological origin of our thoughts. The emphasis on psychogenesis leads him to analyze ideas by tracing them back to their source. He is oriented toward the past.

The normative empiricist, on the other hand, is not particularly concerned with where ideas may come from. One place is as good as another. He is interested in where the ideas lead to. For him an idea has the normative function of acting as a control for and a guide to future action. He does not trace ideas back to their cause but forward into their effects. For him the meaning and value of an idea is a function not of where it comes from but of where it will go to. In contrast to the genetic empiricist, the normative empiricist is oriented toward the future. As early as 1875, James was writing: "The truth of a thing or idea is its meanings, or its destiny, that which grows out of it. This would be a doctrine reversing the opinion of the empiricists that the meaning of an idea is that which it has grown from" (*William James,* II, 450).

The second way in which James's empiricism differed from earlier empiricism is indicated by the fact that he calls it a "radical" empiricism. British empiricism, particularly as found in Hume, was atomistic. Everything was "loose and separate" —dissociated from everything else. In order to bring conjunctive relations back into the world, philosophy after Hume had taken the Kantian direction and introduced them *a priori* as the forms of understanding. James was never tempted by the Kantian solution. He refused to accept the verdict that empiricism had failed with Hume. He held, instead, that the only trouble with Hume was that he had not gone far enough, he was not a "radical" empiricist. Hume had found disjunctions in experience. Had he looked further he would have found conjunctions as well.

To be radical, an empiricism must neither admit into its constructions any element that is not directly experienced, nor exclude from them any element that is directly experienced. For such a philosophy the relations that connect experiences must themselves be experienced relations, *and any kind of relation experienced must be accounted as "real" as anything else in the system (Radical Empiricism,* p. 42).

The conjunctions are as primordial elements of "fact" as are the distinctions and disjunctions (*Radical Empiricism,* p. 95).

Radical empiricism takes conjunctive relations at their face value, holding them to be as real as the terms united by them. The world it represents as a collection, some parts of which are conjunctively and others disjunctively related (*Radical Empiricism,* p. 107).

James's argument is that we actually do experience relations. When we hear two knocks at the door we experience the second knock as related to the first knock, otherwise we would not realize it was a second knock. "When I see a thing M, with L to the left of it and N to the right of it, I see it *as* one M; and if you tell me I have had to 'take' it twice, I reply that if I 'took' it a thousand times I should still see it as a unit" (*Radical Empiricism,* p. 105).

It is doubtful whether Hume would have disagreed with James on relations of this type. In the main, James's opponents are the associationist psychologists of his day and the followers of John Stuart Mill.

Aside from the above two points, James is definitely in the empiricist tradition: "Nothing shall be admitted as a fact . . . except what can be experienced at some definite time by some experient. . . . Everything real must be experienceable somewhere, and every kind of thing experienced must be somewhere real" (*Radical Empiricism,* p. 160). James is here concerned with placing himself squarely outside the tradition of a speculative metaphysics.

James's pragmatism follows naturally from his radical empiricism. He sometimes talks as though the two doctrines are quite separate. Although it might be possible to hold one without the other, in James's case the pragmatism comes out of the radical empiricism.

The basic aspects of the radical empiricism are expressed summarily by James as follows:

Radical empiricism consists first of a postulate, next of a statement of fact, and finally of a generalized conclusion.

The postulate is that the only things that shall be debatable among philosophers shall be things definable in terms drawn from experience. . . .

The statement of fact is that the relations between things, conjunctive as well as disjunctive, are just as much matters of direct particular experience, neither more nor less so, than the things themselves.

The generalized conclusion is that therefore the parts of experience hold together from next to next by relations that are themselves parts of experience (*Meaning of Truth,* pp. xii–xiii).

The "postulate" above states James's empiricism. The only meaning that my idea of an object can have must be something relevant to my experiences of the object. What is there, then, relevant to my experiences of the object that could constitute what it means to me? Obviously its relations to me, either directly, or indirectly through other objects. I experience these relations—which, according to the "statement of fact" above are as real as the object itself. When I know the object, *what* I know are its relations to me. The object then is what it is "known-as"—a term James often uses which he obtained from Shadworth Hodgson, the British empiricist. These relations are each of them matters of sensation. I *perceive* that the object is related to me in this or that fashion. Since each of these relations is a sensible reality, and since the sum of these relations is the meaning of the object for me, each part of the meaning of the object is such that it can terminate in a sensation.

As a name for these sensations in which the parts of the meaning terminate, James selects the phrase "practical consequences." In one sense the choice of this term was unfortunate. Although James did not intend to eliminate theoretical functions from meanings by using the term practical, many philosophers—not unnaturally—so interpreted him. What he was trying to eliminate was speculative or metaphysical meaning which issued in no experiential relation to any object at all. He was perfectly willing to include theoretical meaning provided it was a theory that eventually led to a sense-experience. He says:

One can easily get into a verbal mess at this point, and my own experience with "pragmatism" makes me shrink from the dangers that lie in the word "practical," . . . I am quite willing . . . to ascribe a primarily theoretical function to our intellect, provided you on your part then agree to discriminate "theoretic" or scientific knowledge from the deeper "speculative" knowledge aspired to by most philosophers (*Pluralistic Universe,* p. 249).

James recognizes that the relations between a perceiver and an object are generally asymmetrical—either the object is acting on the perceiver or the perceiver is acting on the object. There are two general classes of effects which result from these relations: sensations—where the object is acting on us; and reactions—where we are acting on the object. In terms of these effects James states his version of pragmatism as follows:

To attain perfect clearness in our thought of an object, then, we need only consider what conceivable effects of a practical kind the object may involve—what sensations we are to expect from it, and what reactions we must prepare. Our conception of these effects, whether immediate or remote, is then for us the whole of our conception of the object, so far as that conception has positive significance at all (*Pragmatism,* pp. 46–47).

Let us consider James's version of the pragmatic criterion with reference to some particular concrete object such as a chair. To attain perfect clearness in our idea of what a chair is, we need not try to discover some ineffable essence such as the essential nature of chairness. We need only understand what sensations we may expect from a chair and what reactions we need to be prepared to execute toward it.

What sensations do we expect from a chair? It is a material object and so we expect all the sensations we would expect from material objects, i.e., we expect the chair to give us the sensation of resistance if we try to lift it, we expect it to give us the sensation of color if we shine a light upon it, we expect it to give a sensation of sound if we strike it, a tactile sensation if we touch it, etc. In addition to these sensations which we expect from any material object, there are certain additional sensations which we expect only from chairs. Primarily we expect the sensation of rest and comfort when we sit upon it. One could, of course, sit upon a table or a bed, but he would not expect the degree of comfort and support which he would get from a chair. Or, if he did get it, he might comment that "this would make a good chair," indicating thereby that he got the sensations which he ordinarily expected only from a chair. On the other hand, if one went to a furniture store and the salesman showed him an object which looked like a chair except that the seat was a bed of spikes, he might very well comment, "That's not a chair," indicating thereby that he would not expect from it the sensations which he primarily expected from a chair.

As to the reactions one must prepare toward a chair, there are, again, all those one would customarily prepare toward any material object. One usually makes rather extensive preparations, for example, if walking about in a dark room to keep from bumping into a chair. Or, if we wish to move a chair from one place to another, we prepare ourselves to get a good grip upon it and to be ready to exert our muscles. But also there are certain specific reactions which we prepare primarily for chairs, namely, the reaction of establishing ourselves in a position such that our body is over the seat and then sitting upon it. This is a reaction which we do not prepare toward a hot stove, for example. We do prepare it toward other objects when we are "using them as chairs."

One who has a perfectly clear idea of all the sensations that may be expected and all the reactions we must prepare toward a chair has a perfectly clear idea of what a chair is, and there is nothing more to the idea.

The pragmatism of James can, obviously, be expressed in Peirce's formulation: "If I act in manner x, then I may expect experience y." If I act so as to lift the chair, then I may expect the experience of resistance; if I act so as to look at the chair, then I may expect the experience of a color; if I act so as to sit upon the chair, then I may expect the experience of resting; etc.

The pragmatism of James involves a different emphasis from that of Peirce, however. James is primarily concerned with the "sensations we expect" and the "reactions we must prepare." Peirce, while certainly concerned with these, is primarily concerned with the relations between them. To use Peirce's terminology, James is concerned primarily with the antecedent and the consequent, and only secondarily with the consequence—the relation between the antecedent and consequent. Peirce is concerned primarily with the consequence, and only secondarily with the actions and the sensations. This difference in emphasis is the ground for Peirce's complaint that James's psychological predilections led him to concern himself too much with the sensationalistic side of experience. James concerns himself with firsts and seconds, and tends to ignore thirds. To the extent that James neglects relations, he is guilty of ignoring an important aspect of the analysis of a meaning. It is clear from James's discussions, however, that the neglect is more of the nature of an oversight. He certainly intends that the relations shall be included, as we shall see in the next chapter when we examine his analysis of the meaning of truth, and as we may clearly infer from his statement that "the parts of experience hold together from next to next by relations that are themselves parts of experience" (*Meaning of Truth*, p. xiii).

There are three other points upon which James agrees with Peirce. In the first place, James accepts the type of approach exemplified by pragmatism as an alternative to the traditional Aristotelian method of definition. Secondly, he sees the process of attaining to the full meaning of an object as a process involving the whole community of human investigators because of the many aspects of each object. He stated these two points as early as 1890, when he wrote in his *Psychology:*

When we conceive . . . of vermillion merely as a mercury-compound . . . we neglect all the other attributes which it may have, and attend exclusively to this one. We mutilate the fulness of [its] reality. . . . When we reach more complex facts, the number of ways in which we may regard them is literally endless. Vermillion is not only a mercury-compound, it is vividly red, heavy, and expensive, it comes from China, and so on, *in infinitum.* All objects are well-springs of properties, which are only little by little developed to our knowledge. . . . But each relation forms one of its attributes, one angle by which some one may conceive it, and while so conceiving it may ignore the rest of it. A man is such a complex fact. But out of the complexity all that an army commissary picks out as important for his purposes is his property of eating so many pounds a day; the general, of marching so many miles; the chairmaker, of having such a shape; . . . . Each of these persons singles out the particular side of the entire man which has a bearing on *his* concerns, and not till this side is distinctly and separately conceived can the proper practical conclusions *for that reasoner* be drawn (*Principles*, II, 332–33).

Men are so ingrainedly partial that, for commonsense and scholasticism (which is only commonsense grown articulate), the notion that there is no one quality genuinely, absolutely, and exclusively essential to anything is almost unthinkable. "A thing's essence makes it *what* it is. Without an exclusive essence it would be nothing in particular, would be quite nameless, we could not say it was this rather than that. What you write on, for example, —why talk of its being combustible, rectangular, and the like, when you know that these are mere accidents, and that what it really is, and was made to be, is just *paper* and nothing else?" The reader is pretty sure to make some such comment as this. But he is himself merely insisting on an aspect of the thing which suits his own petty purpose, that of *naming* the thing; or else on an aspect which suits the manufacturer's purpose, that of *producing an article for which there is a vulgar demand.* Meanwhile the reality overflows these purposes at every pore. Our usual purpose with it, our commonest title for it, and the properties which this title suggests have in reality nothing sacramental. They characterize *us* more than they characterize the thing. But we are so stuck in our prejudices, so petrified intellectually, that to our vulgarest names, with their suggestions, we ascribe an eternal and exclusive worth. The thing must be, essentially, what the vulgarest name connotes; . . . . Those are no truer ways of conceiving them than any others; they are only more important ways, more frequently serviceable ways (*Principles,* II, 334–36).

The third way in which James would agree with Peirce— and it is what one would expect after seeing what James thinks of essences—is in his view that concepts are realities that are abstracted from sensible reality. First we have sensations, then we abstract the conceptions from the sensations: "Sensations are *first* things in the way of consciousness (*Principles,* II, 6)"; "Every one of our conceptions is of something which our attention originally tore out of the continuum of felt experience, and provisionally isolated so as to make of it an individual topic of discourse" (*Principles,* I, 465).

Concepts thus being abstracted out of reality are real. Their reality is the reality of sensible things. In speaking of the concept of "aboveness" James says, "It is not an aboveness *ante rem,* it is a *post rem* extract from the aboveness *in rebus*" (*Meaning of Truth,* p. 151).

The great error of the intellectualists, for James as for Peirce, comes in treating the concept as though it had a reality independent of that from which it is extracted. "But no mere floating conception, no mere disconnected rarity, ever displaces vivid things or permanent things from our belief. A conception, to prevail, must *terminate* in the world of orderly sensible experience" (*Principles,* II, 301).

Thus pragmatism, for James as well as for Peirce, culminates in that principle which dominates twentieth-century philosophy. The abstract conception is only meaningful so far as it may be reduced to the concrete experience.

In the next chapter we examine James's pragmatism in more detail by showing how he applied it to the term "truth."

7

The Pragmatic Theory of Truth

For James "truth" is an abstraction. Therefore, to find what it means we have first to deal with the concrete process from which it is abstracted. This process is the process of knowing or cognizing an object. James's theory of cognition is his interpretation of this process.

Basic to James's theory of cognition—or theory of knowledge as we would call it today—is a distinction he makes between an ambulatory and a saltatory relation.[1] The notion behind the term "ambulatory" here is that of a moving along a continuous route by a successive series of steps—as a man walking from one point to another. "Saltatory" means to jump or leap across—as in taking a fort by assault. The question for James is whether the cognitive relation is an ambulatory or a saltatory relation. As he sees it, the traditional view has been that knowing is a saltatory relation. The knower's mind leaps across to the object—or an essence from the object leaps into the mind—and the knowing process is consummated at a flash and with no intermediaries.

For James cognition is an ambulatory process. At one end is the knowing mind, at the other end the object known. Be-

[1] James acquired this terminology from Dickinson S. Miller, who held a similar view.

tween them is a series of intermediary experiences which lead from the mind to the object and thus show that the mind knows *that* object.

Cognition, whenever we take it concretely, means determinate "ambulation," through intermediaries, from a *terminus a quo* to, or toward a *terminus ad quem*. As the intermediaries are other than the termini, and connected with them by the usual associative bonds (be these "external" or be they logical, i.e., classificatory, in character), there would appear to be nothing especially unique about the processes of knowing. They fall wholly within experience; and we need use, in describing them, no other categories than those which we employ in describing other natural processes (*Meaning of Truth*, p. 142).

To know an object is to have an idea which leads you to perform a series of actions, or think a series of thoughts, or to experience a series built of both actions and thoughts—and the terminus of this series must be the object of which you have an idea. This is the process of "knowing" and when you experience the process you know the object. If each term of the original idea corresponds serially with some idea or thought of the process that leads to the object, that object "was what I *meant*, for into it my idea has passed by conjunctive experiences of sameness and fulfilled intention. Nowhere is there a jar, but every later moment continues and corroborates an earlier one" (*Radical Empiricism*, p. 56).

This is the nature of the ambulatory process. The saltatory stage is arrived at by abstraction. We make a skeletal arrangement by thinking of knower and known and knowing. The knower knows what is known by knowing. But, now we are puzzled as to how this wonderful "knowing" relation can come to be. Having removed all the planks that bridged the gap from knower to object, we are left with the epistemological gulf and then "the whole hocus-pocus of erkentnisstheorie begins, and goes on unrestrained by further concrete consideration" (*Meaning of Truth*, p. 143).

For James, accordingly, knowledge is an ambulatory process. Being a process it has a temporal dimension. The elements of this process are thoughts and actions. To *know* the object is to complete the actual process. To think that you could complete the process is not to know. Even to be potentially able to complete it is only to be a "virtual" knower. To actually know, for James, we must actually complete the process, because for him knowing is the result of process. "Knowledge of sensible realities then comes to life inside the tissue of experience. It is *made;* and made by relations that unroll themselves in time" (*Radical Empiricism*, p. 57).

In order to make this process work James needs a theory of mind at one end and a theory of objects at the other end. His theory of mind is set forth in the well-known essay "Does 'Consciousness' Exist?" [2] in which he asserts that mind is not a stuff distinct from material stuff, but is a function. This is a view so familiar nowadays as to appear trite, but in James's day it was a novelty.

We shall return to James's view here in a moment after viewing his difficulty with matter, for matter posed a problem for him analogous to mind, and he solved them both in the same way.

In so far as the process of knowing is in contact with the object, James, had he stayed within the tradition of his time, would have held that the object known is qualitatively the same as the knowing mind and would thus have been an idealist. Or if he rejected that solution he could have asserted that the mind knew only the object's appearances and then have classed the object as an unknowable *ding-an-sich*. In seeking to tread the narrow line between Berkeley and Kant,

[2] *Radical Empiricism*, p. 1*ff.*

James wandered all over the epistemological field. Sometimes he sounds like an idealist, sometimes like a Kantian, sometimes like a naive realist, and finally ends up with his own version of a neutral monism.

As early as 1873, he espoused a phenomenalism that had overtones of John Stuart Mill's definition of substance and which sounded similar to Peirce's view. James says, "My idea of substance is simply that it means that the present phenomenon is not all—that its existence involves other existences —that in addition to its actuality it has a potentiality when it *is* not" (*William James*, I, 498).

He swings from the phenomenalist view toward the Kantian by saying: "But, if, as most reflective people opine, sensible realities are not 'real' realities, but only their appearances, our idea brings us at least so far, puts us in touch with realities' most authentic appearances and substitutes" (*Meaning of Truth*, p. 140).

From language of this sort it is no great jump for James to sound like an idealist. He says that by reality he "means nothing more than the other conceptual or perceptual experiences with which a given experience may find itself mixed up" (*Meaning of Truth*, p. 100).

With James talking in this way it is no wonder that many of his contemporaries took him as some kind of an idealist. To show that he was not he had to repeat often that he was in the tradition of realism. In a footnote to the last quote given above, he says: "This is meant merely to exclude reality of an 'unknowable' sort, of which no account in either perceptual or conceptual terms can be given. It includes of course any amount of empirical reality independent of the knower. Pragmatism is thus 'epistemologically' realistic in its account."

In letters to C. A. Strong, James emphasized, "The object is assumed all along by me, the describing epistemologist, to be 'outside' of the thought" (*William James*, II, 545). "I have always intended (though I may have made verbal slips) to be realistic, and to be called an idealist . . . makes me feel queer" (*William James,* II, 550).

James defines reality very much as Peirce did. He speaks of "This notion of a reality independent of either of us" (*Meaning of Truth,* p. 217) and says "I conceive realities as existent, as having existed, or about to exist, in absolute independence of my thought of them" (*William James,* II, 541). Around this definition James evolves a metaphysics similar to that of Peirce, although the terminology is different. James suggests a kind of neutral stuff which is neither mental nor physical but which may be either depending upon the relations it is found in. "Experience, I believe, has no such inner duplicity; and the separation of it into consciousness and content comes, not by way of subtraction, but by way of addition" (*Radical Empiricism,* p. 9).

An event, as such, is not part of my consciousness nor an aspect of the object. It is either one, depending upon whether I am considering it in relation to me or in relation to the object. As an analogy, one may consider the intersection between two streets—street A and street B. The question is asked, "Is the intersection part of A Street or part of B Street?" The answer might be, "That depends upon whether you are standing on A Street or on B Street"—i.e., which street the intersection belongs to depends upon the relations in which you take it. So the basic stuff may be either physical (material) or mental, depending upon the relations in which you take it. Thus a room is a physical thing considered from the point of view of the life-history of the metal or wood that makes it up. Considered from the point of view of my relations to it, as part of my life-history, it is an experience of mine and so is mental. The basic stuff is only one kind of thing—not two as in the mind-matter metaphysics—and hence the view is a monism. But the basic stuff is neutral with respect to the mind-matter distinction—it is in itself neither, although it may be taken as either—and so the view is called a neutral monism.

To this basic stuff James gives the name "pure experience."

"Pure experience" is the name which I gave to the immediate flux of life which furnishes the material to our later reflection with its conceptual categories. Only new-born babes, or men in semi-coma from sleep, drugs, illnesses, or blows, may be assumed to have an experience pure in the literal sense of a *that* which is not yet any definite *what*, tho' ready to be all sorts of whats (*Radical Empiricism*, p. 93).

With this view, James comes to a doctrine of immediate perception which is so immediate that the knower and the known coalesce into one. In writing to James about the doctrine, Peirce says, "I also agree with every word you say. . . . I have myself preached immediate perception, as you know; and you can't find a place where I distinguish the objective and subjective sides of things" (*William James*, II, 433–34). In reply, James says, "My starting point is, of course, the doctrine of immediate perception" (*William James*, II, 435).

For both Peirce and James, accordingly, the percept is the reality. A reality is no unknowable *ding-an-sich*. It is that which is experienced, and it is as it is experienced, but its reality is evidenced by its nature being independent of how it is experienced.

THE PROBLEM OF TRUTH

For James the problem of truth is a special case of the problem of knowledge. To know truly is one kind of knowing. To understand his solution it is necessary to look for a moment at the problem of truth. The question is, of course, what is truth? What do we mean when we say of something that it is true?

In James's day there were two theories of truth that had

their followers. James's theory takes account of both of them. The first is called the Coherence Theory of Truth. The key concept here is "cohere" which is to be contrasted with "adhere." The distinction refers to the property of sticking-together and may be seen best in an example. Adhesive tape, for example, adheres; that is, it sticks to things other than itself. Liquid mercury, on the other hand, is not adhesive but is cohesive; that is, a drop of mercury will not stick to other things but will stick to—or cohere with—other drops of mercury. So, according to the coherence theory, a proposition that is true will stick to the body of other known truths without difficulty; but a false proposition will not so cohere, it will conflict with them and not join them. In general, the theory is that all true propositions will cohere or stick together, where the false ones will not. James is conscious of this theory in his insistence that in our search for truth we want propositions that will disturb our old truths as little as possible. But, again, for the pragmatist the question always is, what do you mean by "cohere"? How can you tell when a proposition coheres with your other truths?

The other common theory of truth, and the one from which James's theory stems more directly, follows the Aristotelian tradition and is usually associated with the name of John Locke. This theory is called the copy theory, or Correspondence Theory of Truth. According to this theory, an idea is held to be true when it copies, or corresponds with, or agrees with its object.

But to accept this statement is not to complete a theory of truth, but to begin one. While we may understand what we mean by copying or corresponding with in a simple case, what do we mean in more complex cases? How do we know whether our ideas of such complex things as energy and justice are true copies of their objects? Or, to use one of James's examples, we may know what it means for our idea of the face of a clock to be a true copy, but it is not so simple to know what we mean when we say that our idea of the way a clock runs is a true copy of the reality.

Basic to James's theory of truth is a distinction which he makes between "truth" and "reality." If truth is a relation between the idea and the reality, truth cannot be identified with reality. "Realities are not true, they are; and beliefs are true of them" (*Meaning of Truth*, p. 196). "It seems an abuse of language, to say the least, to transfer the word 'truth' from the idea to the object's existence." (*Meaning of Truth*, p. 314). "Objective realities are not *true*, . . . they are taken as simply *being*, while the ideas are true *of* them" (*Meaning of Truth*, p. 155). In a more contemporary terminology, ideas are true, facts are real.

Dewey agrees with James in this usage. At one point in his advocacy of the pragmatic theory of truth, James was inclined to give up this distinction because of the opposition it met with. Dewey wrote him at some length, urging him to maintain the distinction, and concluded his letter: "You will pardon this suggestion, I hope, but it seems to me that to concede, for the sake of a better understanding, to the critic, that a happening is the same as a truth, is to admit the very point in which his own confusion resides, and by encouraging him in that confusion to prevent exactly the better understanding which you have aimed at" (*William James*, II, 530).

On the basis of James's distinction it would be incorrect to say of a fact that it was true. What would be correct would be to say that the idea of the fact was true. The expression that something is "a true fact" would be either nonsense or an elliptical expression for "the idea of that fact is true." This usage is implicit in the present-day view that propositions are what are true or false. A proposition is the meaning of a sentence. A meaning is an idea. Hence, an idea is what is true or false.

If a proposition is true of a fact or false of a fact, the

difference in truth or falsity makes no change in the fact. The fact remains the same when in the relation of truth that it does when in the relation of falsity. Since truth or falsity makes no change in the fact, but only in the idea, truth or falsity must be a function of the idea, not of the fact. "Remember also that Caesar's having existed in fact may make a present statement false or irrelevant as well as it may make it true, and that in neither case does it itself have to alter. It being given, whether truth, untruth, or irrelevancy shall be also given depends on something coming from the statement itself" (*Meaning of Truth,* p. 224).

On the basis of this distinction, "Truth . . . is a property of certain of our ideas. . . ." (*Meaning of Truth,* p. 303). We have now to investigate the question of what property of the idea it is that makes for truth. We have already seen that it is the property of agreeing. An idea is true when it agrees with (copies or corresponds with) some reality. We have here three key concepts for which we need to formulate pragmatic definitions if we wish to find the meaning of truth. These concepts are "idea," "agreeing," and "reality."

We have already seen the pragmatic meaning of the first and last of these. We have seen that for a pragmatist an idea is a potential way of acting, or a habit. A reality is an object whose nature is independent of how I think about it. Both of these are known only in so far as they are parts of my experience. The idea is what we call a subjective part of my experience—that is, something I may change at will. The reality is an objective part of my experience—something the nature of which I cannot change by merely thinking differently about it. So we find that the truth relation begins and ends in experience. It begins with one part of my experience and terminates in another part. The crux of the issue is how we are to determine when the first part "agrees" with the second part.

We discover this, according to James, by acting in accord

with the idea. The idea is a plan, or a guide, for action. We follow this plan and see if it leads us to the objective part of our experience. It is at this point that we return to James's theory of knowledge. It will be recalled that for him "knowing" was an ambulatory process that led us through a series of experiences to the object. If this series of experiences leads us up to the object, then we know it truly; that is, our idea is true of it. "The links of experience sequent upon an idea, which mediate between it and a reality, form and for the pragmatist indeed *are*, the concrete relation of truth that may obtain between the idea and that reality. They, he says, are all that we mean when we speak of the idea 'pointing' to the reality, 'fitting' it, 'corresponding' with it, or 'agreeing' with it" (*Meaning of Truth*, p. 201–2).

That is, our idea is indeed of the object if the idea leads us up to the object. If the idea as a plan of action toward the object works successfully as a plan, it leads us into a satisfactory relation with the object so that we are in contact with it. Accordingly James sometimes refers to the truth relation by saying that an idea is true if it "works," or, since the idea is one part of our experience and the object another part, he sometimes says that the idea is true if it successfully leads us from one part of our experience to another part of our experience to which we wish to be led, so that "working" and "successful leading" become synonyms for "agreeing." Since attaining our goal here is accompanied by a feeling of satisfaction, satisfaction becomes another key term in describing the truth relation.

Each reality verifies and validates its own idea exclusively; and in each case the verification consists in the satisfactorily-ending consequences, mental or physical, which the idea was able to set up. These "workings" differ in every single instance, they never transcend experience, they consist of particulars, mental or sensible, and they admit of concrete description in every individual case. Pragmatists are unable to see what you can possibly *mean* by calling an idea true, unless you mean that between it as a *terminus a quo* in someone's mind and some particular reality as a *terminus ad quem,* such concrete workings do or may intervene. Their direction constitutes the idea's reference to that reality, their satisfactoriness constitutes its adaption thereto, and the two things together constitute the "truth" of the idea for its possessor. Without such intermediate portions of concretely real experience the pragmatist sees no materials out of which the adaptive relation called truth can be built up (*Meaning of Truth,* pp. 237–38).

Considering the idea before the ambulatory process has been carried out, James does not call the idea true—even though subsequent experience may show that it is true. Before the ambulatory process is completed we do not know whether or not it is true. If subsequent experience shows it true, we may speak of its earlier state as a virtual truth or a potential truth. But for James it is only the actual carrying out of the investigatory process that makes the idea true. So that truth is not a relation that "holds" or "obtains" from all eternity; it is a relation that is made and it is made by the experiential process. Thus an idea comes to be true, or is made true, by the completion of the process. "The truth of an idea is not a stagnant property inherent in it. Truth *happens* to an idea. It becomes true, is *made* true by events. Its verity *is* in fact an event, a process, the process namely of its verifying itself, its *verification.* Its validity is the process of its *validation*" (*Meaning of Truth,* p. 304).

One may make an analogy here to imputing value to an object. The pragmatist would say that an object has no value if no one desires it. It becomes valuable when it is desired. Value is something that happens to an object. So truth is something that happens to an idea; it becomes true when it is verified.

Much of James's time was spent in polemics with those

who could not abide his view because of the terminology he used. When he said that the meaning of an idea was only its "cash-value" in experience, his view was thought to be refuted by the suggestion—particularly from some noted British critics—that pragmatism was built around the concept of the American tradition of only taking account of that which could make money. When he said an idea was only true if it worked he was accused of concerning himself solely with the materialistic aspects of life. The term "pragmatic" with its translation into that which is practical aided and abetted this notion. Finally, when James used the term "satisfactory" as a basic criterion for truth, his critics attacked him in full fury. It was pointed out that it might be satisfactory to a lunatic to believe he was Napoleon but this would hardly suffice to make it true. Or, it might be satisfactory to a man to believe he was worth twice the salary he was getting but this would not make it true that he was.

In reply James tried again to make his point:

The pragmatist calls satisfaction indispensable for truth-building, but I have everywhere called them insufficient unless reality be also incidentally led to. If the reality assumed were cancelled from the pragmatist's universe of discourse, he would straightway give the name of falsehoods to the beliefs remaining, in spite of all their satisfactoriness. For him, as for his critic, there can be no truth if there is nothing to be true about. Ideas are so much flat psychological surface unless some mirrored matter gives them cognitive lustre. This is why as a pragmatist I have so carefully posited "reality" *ab initio*, and why, throughout my whole discussion, I remain an epistemological realist (*Meaning of Truth*, p. 195).

Dewey has also said: "I have never identified any satisfaction with the truth of an idea, save *that* satisfaction which arises when the idea as working hypothesis or tentative method is applied to prior existences in such a way as to fulfil what it intends" (*Experimental Logic*, p. 320).

In reference to the whole set of terminological difficulties, Dewey wrote:

It is easier to start a legend than to prevent its continued circulation. No misconception of the instrumental logic has been more persistent than the belief that it makes knowledge merely a means to a practical end, or to the satisfaction of practical needs—practical being taken to signify some quite definite utilities of a material or bread-and-butter type. Habitual associations aroused by the word "pragmatic" have been stronger than the most explicit and emphatic statements which any pragmatist has been able to make. But I again affirm that the term "pragmatic" means only the rule of referring all thinking, all reflective considerations, to *consequences* for final meaning and test; they may be aesthetic, or moral, or political, or religious in quality—anything you please. All that the theory requires is that they be in some way consequences of thinking; not indeed of it alone, but of it acted upon in connection with other things (*Experimental Logic*, p. 330).

In spite of all these efforts the pragmatists have never quite stopped the misconceptions. A noted American mathematician writes as follows:

But is there not, among the various current meanings of the term "truth," one meaning which enables us to say that Euclidean geometry, regarded as a doctrine about our perceptual space, is true? The answer is: yes, there is such a meaning. It is the "instrumental" meaning insisted upon by Professor John Dewey—the "pragmatic" meaning first signalized by C. S. Peirce, subsequently interpreted, elaborated and advocated by William James and others. It is the meaning in accordance with which an idea or a proposition or a doctrine is true if it "works," in so far as it "works," so long as it "works." The meaning is not without merits that commend it to all men and women for all human beings have, below their distinctively human qualities, certain animal propensities and animal impulses, and, in the animal world, the end always justifies the means—all ways that "work" equally well, are equally "effective," are equally good. It is the pragmatic meaning of truth that makes treason a crime, if it fail, and a virtue, if it succeed. It is a meaning that is especially congenial to practicians and "politicians," whose "philosophy" never rises above the question: How can I "get there"? How can I put this thing "through," "over" or "across"? What is the means that will "work"? It is a meaning, too, that is especially congenial to an industrial age,—an experimental age,—an age of laboratories,—an adventurous age when men act more than they think. In the head-long rush and hurly-burly of such an age, men and women are not aware of the fact that the world of human affairs would quickly dash upon utter destruction but for the guiding and saving influence of a nobler truth-conception which they do not consciously own,—the conception, I mean, of truth as having its highest meaning in the unchanging relations and eternal laws of Logical Thought.[3]

The year after the publication of *Pragmatism*, James wrote in a letter to R. B. Perry:

The pragmatism that lives inside of me is so different from that of which I succeed in wakening the idea inside of other people, that theirs makes me feel like cursing God and dying. When *I say* that, *other things being equal*, the view of things that seems morally satisfactory will legitimately be treated by men as truer than the view that seems less so, *they quote me as saying* that anything morally satisfactory can be treated as true, no matter how unsatisfactory it may be from the point of view of its consistency with what we already know or believe to be true about physical or natural facts. Which is rot!! (*William James*, II, 468).

The issue at the heart of the whole group of objections was made concisely in a question from Shadworth Hodgson to

[3] C. J. Keyser, *Mathematical Philosophy* (New York: E. P. Dutton, 1922), pp. 361–62. The above quoted remark was written two years *after* Dewey had said in *Reconstruction in Philosophy* (p. 157), "When truth is defined as utility, it is often thought to mean utility for some purely personal end, some profit upon which a particular individual has set his heart. So repulsive is a conception of truth which makes it a mere tool of private ambition and aggrandizement, that the wonder is that critics have attributed such a notion to sane men."

James: "How can you dream of elevating the needs, the desires, the purposes of Man into a 'measure' of the Universe?" (*William James*, II, 467). This is the oldest objection to a humanistic philosophy. Of course, the pragmatists do not do this. Reality is the measure of the universe, but reality for man can be neither more nor less than what it is known-as to man. Any philosophy which accepts *this* premise and then works out its details from there must end up closely akin to pragmatism.

In the main, both Peirce and Dewey accept the type of theory of truth that James elaborated. In fact, James seems to credit Dewey with the theory, although it should be clear that it would follow from James's theory of knowledge in any event. That Dewey is in complete agreement with James may be seen in *Essays in Experimental Logic*, in Chapter VIII, "The Control of Ideas by Facts," particularly section II.

The three philosophers are also in agreement as to the theory of error which would follow from their theory of truth. It will be recalled that for Peirce the percept is neither true nor false; it is the inferences drawn by the mind which introduce error. James expresses this view succinctly as follows:

Note that in every illusion what is false is what is inferred, not what is immediately given. The "this," if it were only felt by itself alone, would be all right, it only becomes misleading by what it suggests. If it is a sensation of sight, it may suggest a tactile object, for example, which later tactile experiences prove to be not there. *The so-called "fallacy of the senses," of which the ancient sceptics made so much account, is not the fallacy of the senses proper, but rather of the intellect, which interprets wrongly what the senses give* (*Principles*, II, 86).

Dewey accepts the same position (*Influence of Darwin*, pp. 234–35). In fact, since all three subscribe to the doctrine of immediate perception they must of necessity hold to this theory of error.

A GENERAL PRAGMATIC ANALYSIS OF TRUTH

James, in his discussion of truth, is concerned primarily with the nature of truth as the term refers to particular objects or events. A full treatment of truth would have to deal with more general statements as well. The application of the pragmatic approach to the problem of the truth of general statements such as scientific laws is done by Peirce. Dewey has followed Peirce closely in this respect. James, while agreeing with the proposals, never made any detailed analysis of what was involved in the more general problem. In order to complete the pragmatic account of truth we may examine this more general problem as Peirce dealt with it.

It may be seen from the analysis of the pragmatic theory of truth given in the previous section that it is one form of what is known today as a verification theory of truth. A complete development of the pragmatic theory may be obtained by showing how it would deal with some of the objections offered against any form of the verification theory.

Theories which equate truth with verification have difficulty establishing criteria for determining the truth of universal propositions, of counterfactual propositions, and of historical propositions. A proposition which refers to a particular instance may be easily verified. The proposition "This stone, if released, will fall" may be verified by releasing the stone. But how are we to verify a universal proposition such as "All stones when released will fall"? What single event or series of events will suffice to establish the truth of this proposition? No matter how many particular stones may fall, the universal proposition still refers to a large number of events concerning which we have no information. Because of this latter fact we do not, on a verification theory, have proper evidence for asserting the truth of universal propositions.

In discussing this problem, Carnap says:

If verification is understood as a complete and definitive establishment of truth then a universal sentence, e.g., a so-called law of physics or biology can never be verified, a fact which has often been remarked. Even if each single instance of the law were supposed to be verifiable, the number of instances to which the law refers—e.g., the space-time points—is infinite and therefore can never be exhausted by our observations which are always finite in number.[4]

Since all scientific laws are of the form of universal propositions, the problem of adequate criteria for establishing the truth of such propositions is an important one.

A second type of proposition that presents difficulties for a verification theory is counterfactual propositions. On a verification theory of truth the proposition "If I scratch this diamond, then it will be found to be hard" may be verified by actually scratching the diamond. But suppose we have the proposition "If I had scratched this diamond, then it would have been found to be hard, but I did not scratch it." In what way can such a proposition be verified? The proposition has no consequences, either direct or indirect, in experience and so cannot possibly be verified by experience. In short, a counterfactual proposition is by definition a proposition for which neither the antecedent nor the consequent is observed. Obviously what by definition is not observed, by definition cannot be verified by observation.

Counterfactual propositions are, again, an important class of everyday propositions. All regret and blame are based upon them. A man regrets having acted in a certain manner. He regrets it because he believes that if he had acted in some other way, a way in which as a matter of fact he did not act, then some other situation which he finds more desirable would have occurred, i.e., he believes the truth of some counter-

[4] R. Carnap, "Testability and Meaning," *Philosophy of Science*, III (1936), 425.

factual proposition. Similarly, in a court of law a man is blamed for a result produced by his actions because the court believes the counterfactual proposition that if he had acted in a way in which he did not act, some different result would have ensued. In fact, all ethical praise and blame is based on counterfactual propositions. We blame a man for an action because we believe there are other actions he might have done, although he did not, which would have had more desirable results; or we praise him because there are other actions he might have done, although he did not, which would have had less desirable results.

Finally, a verification theory has considerable difficulty dealing with historical propositions. A proposition about the past, although not counterfactual, is nevertheless not susceptible to direct verification. The proposition that "Aristotle was unable to pronounce the letter R" is either true or false, but there is no way of verifying it except inconclusively by indirect evidence which is itself open to the difficulty of being historical in nature. We are assured by several commentators on Aristotle that he was indeed unable to pronounce the letter R. But these comments are themselves historical propositions and we are forced to ask the question, did these commentators actually write the sentences credited to them? We can only establish that they did by other evidence which is itself historical in nature, and we are thus caught in a circular argument. Since we cannot go back into the past, we cannot verify by experience any proposition about the past.

When the complaints are gathered together and read off in this summary fashion they present a serious indictment of a verification theory of truth. To hold to a theory that cannot establish the truth of universal propositions, of counterfactual propositions, or of historical propositions is to hold to a theory on which the basic propositions in science, in law and ethics, and in history cannot be asserted as true or false.

For a verification theory of truth a proposition is held to be true if it agrees with experience. Peirce held to a theory of truth on which this is not the case. Peirce holds that a proposition is true if it does not disagree with experience. He bases his usage on what is meant by a mathematical truth. "The truth of the pure mathematical proposition is constituted by the impossibility of ever finding a case in which it fails" (5.567).

The same definition is held to be meant when we talk of the truth of any proposition: "Every proposition is either *true* or *false*. It is false if any proposition could be legitimately deduced from it, without aid from false propositions, which would conflict with a direct perceptual judgment could such be had. A proposition is true, if it is not false" [5] (2.327; see also 5.569).

The view here is that: 1) a proposition is true if it is not false; 2) a false proposition is one which conflicts with some experience; and 3) a true proposition is, therefore, a proposition that does not conflict with any experience. This definition gives truth a vacuous nature. Truth is not something positive but something negative; it is not the agreement with experience but the absence of disagreement. This is contrary to the customary interpretation which tends to make falsity vacuous: Ordinarily a proposition is true if it agrees with experience, false if this agreement does not occur. In another place Peirce tells us that truth is the opinion which will be ultimately agreed to by all who investigate (5.407).[6] Interpreting this remark in terms of his definition of truth as the absence of disagreement,

[5] Compare James, "We never disbelieve anything except for the reason that we believe something else which contradicts the first thing" (*Principles*, II, 284). Dewey has written, "The mind learns through the contradictions existing between its ideas, that not all can be projected as facts. . . . The fact is the idea which nothing contradicts" ("The Logic of Verification," *Open Court*, IV [1890], p. 2227).

[6] Dewey cites this as "the best definition of truth from the logical standpoint which is known to me" (*Logic,* p. 345n.).

we obtain a full statement of Peirce's position: *To assert that a proposition will be found to be true is to say that that proposition will never be contradicted in the experience of any investigator.*[7] On this view, when we assert the truth of a universal proposition we are not denoting a class of infinite possible situations, but a finite number of instances, namely, all those experiences of a certain sort that will be had by human beings.

This view obviates two of the objections customarily made about universal propositions. We have suggested above that a law of science can never be definitively established as true because the number of instances to which the law refers is infinite. On Peirce's view this is not the case. The number of instances to which the law refers is finite. It refers only to the actual experiences of a certain sort that will be had by members of the human race.

A similar objection to asserting the truth of natural laws was offered by Moritz Schlick, who held that natural laws could only be prescriptions or rules of procedure for the investigator because a law "logically considered, does not have the character of an assertion, for a genuine assertion must admit of being definitively verified." [8]

---

[7] Compare James, "If universal acceptance be, as it surely is, the only mark of truth which we possess, then any system certain not to get it, may be deemed false without further ceremony, false at any rate for us, which is as far as we can inquire" (*William James*, I, 495).

Dewey agrees as follows: "Every proposition concerning truths is really in the last analysis hypothetical and provisional, although a large number of these propositions have been so frequently verified without fail that we are justified in using them as if they were absolutely true. But logically absolute truth is an ideal which cannot be realized, at least not until all the facts have been registered, or as James says 'bagged,' and until it is no longer possible to make other observations and other experiences" (*Philosophy and Civilization*, p. 24).

[8] M. Schlick, "Die Kausalität in der gegenwärtigen Physik," Naturwissenschaften, XIX (1931), p. 156. Quoted in Carnap, "Testability and Meaning," p. 19.

On Peirce's formulation a natural law does admit of being definitively verified. The law says that the experience of no investigator will ever be contrary to this law. When all investigation has ceased the law will be either definitively verified or definitively disverified; that is, either no experience will run against the law or some experience will. This view thus allows a natural law to be a genuine assertion.

If we say that a law of science is true if it is such that it will be accepted as true at that future time when all investigation has ceased, the question immediately occurs: How can we tell now what will be believed in the future? In dealing with this problem we may make two points: 1) By a properly constructed experiment we can eliminate all possible laws about a certain sort of event except for one formulation; 2) We can accumulate evidence substantiating this formulation.

To consider a simple illustration, suppose that we have a scientist investigating how stones behave when released. He releases a stone and it falls. What does this single experiment do? It disproves all general propositions about the direction of movement of stones when released except the one proposition "All stones fall when released." A stone may theoretically travel in an infinite number of directions from a given point. Thus one could formulate an infinite series of universal propositions, one for each direction, asserting that all stones when released will travel in that direction. This one experiment disproves all but one of these universal propositions. It disproves propositions such as "All stones rise when released"; "All stones remain stationary when released," etc. What this experiment says is: "No other universal proposition about the direction in which stones move is true," or "If any universal proposition at all about the direction in which stones move is true it must be this one." With this knowledge—that this is the only possible proposition that can be universally true—what does the scientist do? He deliberately strives to disprove it. He releases stones under all the different circumstances that he can contrive. Each time that the experiment succeeds, his belief in the truth of the law increases; eventually he takes the position that the law is universally true, and by this he means that no kind of experiment that he has been able to construct has shown it to be false and therefore he does not believe that any experience will ever show it to be false and therefore it is universally true.[9]

But if this is the only possible law that can be true, can we gather any evidence substantiating it? It will be recalled that on Peirce's view the law refers to those actual experiences of released stones that will be had by human beings. Even though we do not know the precise number of such experiences there may be that will be had, we nevertheless believe that the number is finite. This number, let us call it Alpha, represents the number of possible cases in which this law may be found false. The observed instances where the law is not contradicted represent favorable instances—let us call the number of such instances Beta. When the first experiment is performed and the law is not contradicted we have a probability of one over Alpha that it will never be contradicted. When a second experiment is successfully performed we have a probability of two over Alpha. With each succeeding experiment the number Beta becomes larger and the ratio between Beta and Alpha approaches nearer to one as a limit. When all experiences have been had, if there are no contradictions,

[9] It might be argued that some experience might some day contradict this law, nevertheless. And this is possible. It is because of this that truth, for Peirce, consists in what will be known when the community of human investigators has completed its investigation. At such a time those propositions which have never been contradicted will be true. It may be that some of the propositions that we know now will be among those. If so, we know the absolute truth now. But we cannot know that it is the absolute truth until the investigation has been completed. This is all in agreement with scientific procedure.

then Beta will equal Alpha and the truth of the law will be that of one over one, or certainty. Thus as long as we believe that the number of experiences of the human race will be finite, even though we do not know what that number is, each succeeding experiment justifies an increased belief in the law.[10]

The most persistent objection to Peirce's theory is that on the basis of it a proposition that is never investigated must be held to be true. The argument is that on Peirce's view a proposition is true if it is not false, and a false proposition is one which conflicts with some experience, so that a true proposition is one that does not conflict with any experience. From these premises the conclusion is drawn that a proposition that is never investigated is true since it does not conflict with any experience.

In speaking of Peirce's definition Bertrand Russell says, "If the definition is interpreted strictly, every proposition which is investigated by no one is 'true,' but I think Peirce means to include only such propositions as some one investigates." [11]

I think Russell is right as to what Peirce means but wrong as to what the definition strictly implies. In his definition Peirce defines truth as the opinion which will be ultimately agreed to "by all who investigate" (5.407). It would seem that the clear implication is that the opinion of those who do not investigate is not to be counted. In another definition—to which Russell also refers—Peirce defines truth as "the ideal limit toward which endless investigation would tend to bring scientific belief" (5.565). It is difficult to see how one can conclude that these definitions strictly imply that propositions investigated by no one are true. Apparently Peirce could have avoided such misinterpretation only by saying that a proposi-

[10] It will be noted that this procedure does not presuppose the uniformity of nature except to the extent that it assumes that our records of experiments will not be changed by the passage of time.

[11] In *The Philosophy of John Dewey*, P. A. Schilpp, ed. (New York: Tudor, 1951), pp. 144–45.

tion is true if it is never contradicted in the experience of any investigator who investigates—the redundancy being necessary to eliminate "investigators" who do not investigate.

The point is, of course, that on no theory of truth can one talk meaningfully about the truth or falsity of a proposition if there is no evidence at all relative to it.

There are two other objections to Peirce's theory of truth which need to be examined. The first is the view that the community of human investigators may not succeed in discovering the truth about something. No one may happen to have an experience that contradicts a law, but if experience were to take place at space-time points where no one happens to be, or to be continued after everyone ceases to exist, perhaps the law would be contradicted. To talk about an experience that would be had when, by definition, no one can have it, is to talk about a logical impossibility, and therefore to talk nonsense.[12] James is explicit on this point: "If objects be represented so devoid of any context as to make no connection whatever (logical or physical) with any item in the world's future, their existence is not only unverifiable, but really meaningless" (*William James*, II, 481).

A second objection offered against this theory is that it gives no absolute universal truths until the last investigation has been completed, and by then it is of little use to know what is absolutely true. About all one can do at this point is to offer such an objector consolations. This may be unfortunate, but is it not, nevertheless, the case? The scientist is looking for a law that will never be contradicted in any human experience. This is, however, Peirce's "ideal limit." The scientist can never know whether he has attained such a law

[12] Peirce says: "Knowledge which should have no possible bearing upon any future experience—bring no expectation whatever—would be information concerning a dream. . . . It were better to hand the reports over to the poets to make something pretty of, and thus turn them to some human use" (5.542).

until all experience has been had and no contradiction has occurred. In what field of human investigation today would any trained investigator be so rash as to assert that he has a universal truth that no further experience will ever contradict? Anyone cognizant of what has been done in the last fifty years to Newtonian physics by relativity physics, to the biology of the fixed species by evolution, to mathematics by non-Euclidean geometries, or to psychology by the theories of Freud and his followers, would hardly care to assert that the present theories are likely to be the last word on these subjects. The last word will be had by the last man. If we do not find this emotionally satisfying, there is, after all, no reason to suppose that the universe must be so constructed as to merit our approbation.[13]

If the above procedure suffices to establish the truth of universal propositions, then it may also suffice to establish the truth or falsity of counterfactual propositions, for the difficulty of establishing the truth or falsity of counterfactual propositions is due simply to our not having evidence for the truth or falsity of some universal proposition of which the counterfactual would have been a particular instance.

A counterfactual proposition must not be confused with a pseudo-proposition. A counterfactual does not refer to experiences that no one could have, but only to experiences that no one does have. Assuming that I am now in Room A, no one

---

[13] James holds to the same view of absolute truth. "Truth absolute . . . means an ideal set of formulations towards which all opinions may in the long run of experience be expected to converge" (*Meaning of Truth*, p. 266).

"The 'absolutely' true, meaning what no farther experience will ever alter, is that ideal vanishing-point towards which we imagine that all our temporary truths will some day converge" (*Pragmatism*, p. 222).

Dewey says, "In scientific inquiry, every conclusion reached, whether of fact or conception, is held subject to determination by its fate in further inquiries. Stability or 'identity,' of meanings is a limiting ideal, as a condition to be progressively satisfied" (*Logic*, p. 345).

would wish to deny that, barring physical restraint, I could be in Room B. To say "If I were now in Room B, I would see a red chair" is not to talk about what is now the case in Room B when no one is there, but about what would be the case if I were there. A counterfactual is an hypothetical that involves neither a logical nor a physical impossibility. It only refers to a contingent fact: I am not in Room B but I could be there, and if I were there then I would see a red chair.

When one asserts such an hypothetical, what he is doing primarily is saying that all x's are y's, therefore if this were an x it would also be a y. Thus the truth of an hypothetical depends simply upon the truth of some universal from which it could be logically deduced. For this reason a criterion of truth which suffices to establish the truth or falsity of universal propositions contributes to establishing the truth or falsity of hypothetical counterfactuals.

Peirce uses the same theory of truth as a basis for accepting historical propositions. "The truth of the proposition that Caesar crossed the Rubicon consists in the fact that the further we push the archaeological and other studies, the more strongly will that conclusion force itself on our minds forever—or would do so, if study were to go on forever" (5.565).[14] The proposition that Caesar crossed the Rubicon is an hypothesis

---

[14] Dewey has put the same thing thus: "That evidential data for all historical propositions must exist at the time the propositions are made and be contemporaneously observable is an evident fact. The data are such things as records and documents; legends and stories orally transmitted; graves and inscriptions; urns, coins, medals, seals; implements and ornaments; charters, diplomas, manuscripts; ruins, buildings and works of art; existing physiographical formations, and so on indefinitely. Where the past has left no trace or vestige of any sort that endures into the present its history is irrecoverable. Propositions about the things which can be contemporaneously observed are the ultimate data from which to infer the happenings of the past" (*Logic,* p. 234).

In an illuminating comment, Santayana has referred slightingly to this view of the truth of historical propositions as the pragmatic reduction of yesterday to tomorrow.

which we adopt to explain certain facts. If the hypothesis were false we would expect further investigation to contradict it. We continue to investigate and fail to find any contradictory evidence. Each failure is a further confirmation of the truth of the proposition, i.e., each failure demonstrates that it is false that "this proposition is false." We do not verify the truth of the proposition, but we fail to verify its falsity. "Truth is the concordance of an abstract statement with the ideal limit toward which endless investigation would tend to bring scientific belief" (5.565).

Certainly Peirce does not hesitate to accept verification of a singly quantified proposition (i.e., a proposition referring to a single event) as a basis for admitting its truth. It seems to me possible to interpret verification in terms of his position and thus reduce the former to a version of the latter. One might say, for example, that when we assert that a singly quantified proposition, A, is verified by an experience, B, we mean that we know with certainty that no experience will ever contradict A because the only experience that could have done so was B, and B did not do so, therefore A is true.

From the experiences of human beings it is no surprise that verification has been taken as the meaning of truth. The vast majority of our inquiries have to do with single facts which may be verified completely. Also, such verifications are immediate, they come now, they do not depend upon any long run experience. It is therefore natural that we should take the meaning of truth which we encounter most often and most immediately, and seek to project it into all cases of truth seeking. Unfortunately it is not adequate to deal with them. We are thus forced to formulate a wider concept of truth which includes verification as a special case. If verification can be reduced to a form of Peirce's position, it would appear that his view is the basic or most general meaning of truth. And this seems to me to be the case.

In conclusion, it may be helpful to point out that the pragmatic, or empirical, theory of truth is a compromise between two extremes. At one end is the position of the absolutist. According to this view there is absolute truth now; we can know it; we can know that we know it. At the other extreme is the sceptic. According to his view there is no absolute truth; if there were, we couldn't know it; if we did know it, we couldn't know that we know it. According to the pragmatic view, there is absolute truth only in the future; we can know it; we can only know that we know it then. The pragmatist rejects the absolutist view on the grounds that it is dogmatic. It is asserted, but no reasons are given for believing it. The sceptical position is rejected because it is irrational. It blocks the way to inquiry; one who accepted it would not be motivated to try to find any truth that might exist. The empirical view is only a hope, but it is the kind of hope that so far in the history of mankind has proven fruitful in providing that control and understanding of the natural world which are the basic motives in our search for truth.

Part III

THE INSTRUMENTALISM OF JOHN DEWEY

8

Theory of Inquiry

John Dewey was born in 1859 in Burlington, Vermont, of pioneer American stock. His father was a grocer in Burlington, and because the University of Vermont was in Burlington, John Dewey attended it, graduating in 1879. The university was small at that time, with a faculty of eight. Philosophy was taught by Professor H. A. P. Torrey and was based largely on the work of the Scottish Commonsense Realists. The controversy over the theory of evolution was in its early stages, and Dewey studied and read a good bit about it. He was an excellent student, although inclined to be bookish.

Upon graduation he went into school teaching. He taught two years in a Pennsylvania high school, and returned to Charlotte, Vermont, for a third year. During this time he began to think seriously of philosophy as a career. W. T. Harris, who was superintendent of schools in St. Louis, edited a publication called *The Journal of Speculative Philosophy*. In the throes of indecision Dewey sent Harris an essay on "The Metaphysical Assumptions of Materialism," and inquired hesitatingly of the editor whether the author should go into philosophy as a profession. Harris replied that the essay showed a philosophical mind of high rank, and published the essay in the April, 1882, issue of his journal.

Thus encouraged, Dewey entered Johns Hopkins University in the fall of 1882. Johns Hopkins had been open only a few years, and the graduate program was carried on with great intellectual zest. Dewey had two courses in logic from Peirce who was teaching at Hopkins at that time, although most of the philosophy was taught by George S. Morris and G. Stanley Hall. Morris was an Hegelian of a sort and exerted considerable influence on Dewey's formative years. Morris and Dewey became firm friends, and when Dewey received his Ph.D. from Johns Hopkins in 1884, Morris, who had in the meantime gone to Ann Arbor, was able to offer Dewey an instructorship in philosophy at the University of Michigan. Dewey was an instructor and assistant professor of philosophy at Michigan from 1884 to 1888. He then went to the University of Minnesota for a year as a full professor. During that year George S. Morris died, and Dewey was invited to return to Michigan as head of the department. He remained at Michigan in this capacity from 1889 to 1894.

While he was at Michigan, Dewey met and, in 1886, married Alice Chipman of Fenton, Michigan. Miss Chipman had been teaching school for several years to earn money to complete her education. She was the same age as Dewey and had returned to Ann Arbor as one of the first "coeds" of that institution. She seems to have been a woman of exceptional intelligence and was a co-worker of Dewey's in much of his experimental work in education. The Deweys had six children and adopted three more.

In 1894 Dewey accepted an offer from the University of Chicago to head the Department of Philosophy and Psychology. During his years at Michigan, Dewey had developed a considerable interest in educational theory. A major inducement leading him to accept the offer from Chicago was that Pedagogy would be a part of his department. In 1896, with the help of some interested parents, Dewey founded at Chicago the University Elementary School, generally known as the Laboratory School or the Dewey School. For the next seven and one-half years, he worked at Chicago developing the educational theories which have since become world famous. In 1904 Dewey resigned from Chicago because of differences of opinion with the University administration concerning the Laboratory School.

At the time of his resignation, Dewey had no other position at hand. With the help of his friend J. McKeen Cattell, he obtained a position at Columbia University in 1905. He taught there until his retirement in 1929, continuing after that as professor emeritus. He died in 1952 at the age of ninety-two.

It is almost impossible to summarize Dewey's published work. His first article was printed in 1882, and he was still intellectually alert and publishing regularly at the time of his death. This gives him a writing career of seventy years, or about twice that of the average individual. A recent bibliography of Dewey's writings consists of seventy-five large pages, enough to make a small book in itself.

In education his most widely read books are *School and Society* (1900), which has been translated into thirteen languages, and *Democracy and Education* (1916), which has had ten translations. In general philosophy, his most enduring work, in the opinion of the present writer, is *Human Nature and Conduct* (1922). Other major works include *Experience and Nature* (1929), *Quest for Certainty* (1929), *Art as Experience* (1934), and *Logic: The Theory of Inquiry* (1938).

Our examination of the philosophies of Peirce and James has shown that there is a strong current of what may be called "process" philosophy in the thought of the pragmatists. Peirce's attacks against nominalism and his development of his synechistic view, James's attacks against the atomistic psychologies of Hume and his followers and his insistence on the reality of conjunctive relations will serve to indicate the basic view common to all pragmatists that what A. N. Whitehead has called the "fallacy of bifurcation" *is* a fallacy in philosophy. The attempt to reunite what earlier philosophies have separated is even more persistent in the philosophy of Dewey. Although Dewey refers his emphasis on continuity to both Peirce and James, he carries the position into areas not previously discussed by either of his predecessors.

It is a natural tendency in thought to analyze a complex situation, to break it up into its parts. Parts being simpler to understand than wholes, we tend to study the parts more carefully and, by this emphasis, to give them an honorific position and eventually to hypostatize them. We ignore their relations to the whole and treat as a feature of reality what is only a feature of our limited understanding. Throughout more than two thousand years of the history of thought, we have crystallized these partial aspects of experience until they have come to form such a dominant background of our thinking that we cannot conceive the universe in any other way—except as a result of a rigorous training in one of the arts or sciences, and even then we tend to lapse back into the older view when we get out of the field in which we may be a specialist.

One of the essential traits of a clear thinker in every field—but especially in philosophy—is the ability to get out of the intellectual framework of his predecessors and to see things without looking through the constructs of the past. Each era makes its new discoveries as knowledge progresses. A major function of philosophy is to undertake to see the world over again in the terms set up by increased knowledge. This effort to get out of the stream of history long enough to see the world afresh, to get a new vision of things, is the trait which has persistently characterized the greatest philosophers. Dewey has demonstrated this ability more consistently than any of his contemporaries. Whether or not his view has been a correct one, it is at least a new one. Being new, it calls for an effort on the part of those who wish to understand him. Those who are satisfied with the framework of the past and try to place Dewey's thought in relation to it will not understand him.

From the time of Newton in science and John Locke in psychology, education, political and social philosophy, no new vision of the world about us came until the last hundred years. The revolutions which Darwin instituted in biology, Einstein in physics, Freud in psychology, and Marx in social and political thought, all happened during Dewey's lifetime. Dewey's thought is an effort to see the world in these new ways. Not that Dewey is a Freudian or a Marxist, for example, but he does recognize a fresh *aperçu* when he meets one, and he tries to see what the world looks like in the light of it.

Because Dewey tries to reunite what has been divided in traditional thought and language, and because he does his uniting in the light of these new points of view, his philosophy is easier to misunderstand than that of most philosophers.

THE HISTORY OF IDEAS

The realization that ideas have a history is not something new, but the formal recognition of the area of the history of ideas as a separate discipline in our larger universities has come about only recently. It is probably no mere coincidence that the university with which Dewey has been professionally associated for much of his life has been one of the pioneers in this development. This much is certainly true, that Dewey's writings show a greater concern with the history of our ideas than do those of any other contemporary philosopher.

Why should an examination of the genesis of our ideas be of concern to a philosopher? Dewey's concern has been motivated by his interest in replacing older ideas with a new intel-

lectual framework. Most of us incline to the view that our ideas
are ideas of reality, but if it can be shown that they are,
genetically, simply offshoots of historical situations, we are
more willing to consider the likelihood that they are not the
final view of things and to consider with more leniency new
ideas suggested for our consideration.

The theme around which Dewey builds his treatment of the
history of our ideas is the title for his Gifford Lectures in 1929,
*The Quest for Certainty: A Study of the Relation of Knowl-
edge and Action*. As Dewey sees it, a basic thread in the pattern of human history has been the quest for certainty. Man
finds himself in a precarious world, a world in which there are
elemental forces and natural enemies which harm him and
destroy him. In his primitive ignorance he does not know when
or where the next blow will fall upon him. In this world of
uncertainty his quest is for that which is certain. His initial
reaction to this environment is to personify those natural forces
which threaten him. He sees them as living beings who either
capriciously harm him or to whom he has inadvertently done
evil. His first efforts are toward appeasement of them by ceremonies and rites so that they will treat him well rather than
ill. Thus are born primitive religions. Another type of reaction
to these forces may accompany the first or follow it. This is
the attempt to control the forces through action. Instead of,
or in addition to, fertility rites to promote harvests, man acts to
provide water for his fields in dry seasons; he develops the art
of agriculture.

A second stage in this development in the history of western
man comes with the Greeks. The Greek philosophers saw that
the world of experience cannot give absolute certainty; at
best it can give only probability. The world of experience was
for them a world of flux, a world of change. The world of ideas,
the world of theoretical as contrasted with practical knowledge, became for the Greek thinkers the goal of the wise man,

the aim of the philosopher. Philosophy was marked out as the discipline concerned with the eternal truths of immutable being. Where, in the first stage, religion was separated from the practical arts, in the second stage philosophy becomes separated also.

After 1,500 years of this situation, modern science appeared *television* upon the scene. The practical arts, the arts of action, of doing, of controlling the universe by working upon it, of correcting evils rather than accepting them as inevitable, once again came into dominance.

With the rise of science there came what Dewey calls a "changed attitude toward change" (*Quest for Certainty*, p. 101). Where the Greeks had looked upon change as something to be abhorred, science looks upon the correlation between changes as the only method of control of the universe. The primitive view was to react to experience by rites and ceremonies; the classical view was to classify what was given in experience—thus forming experience into a rigid schema from which change was eliminated; the modern view is to control change by discovering what it is associated with so as to produce change when it is desired and to avert it when it is not wanted.

But the development of science produced a new problem. In a philosophic dialogue titled "Nature's Good," Dewey has one of the characters say: "Modern science has completely transformed our conceptions of Nature. It has stripped the universe bare not only of all the moral values which it wore alike to antique pagan and to our medieval ancestors, but also of any regard, any preference, for such values. They are mere incidents, transitory accidents, in her everlasting redistribution of matter in motion" (*Influence of Darwin*, p. 22).

In the same context in another book, Dewey says: "This effect of modern science has, it is notorious, set the main problems of modern philosophy. How is science to be accepted and yet the realm of values to be conserved? This question forms the philosophic version of the popular conflict of science and religion" (*Quest for Certainty*, p. 40). "Thus is created the standing problem of modern philosophy:—the relation of science to the things we prize and love and which have authority in the direction of conduct" (*Quest for Certainty*, p. 102).

This problem is the basic problem Dewey seeks to solve in his philosophy. It is no less basic in the age of the atom bomb than it was when Dewey was first disturbed by it. To understand Dewey's solution we need to see first how he conceives science and then how he conceives the relation of science to values. The first task will occupy us in the remainder of the present chapter; the next chapter will discuss his theory of value.

ORGANISM AND ENVIRONMENT

Traditional epistemologies distinguish between the knower and the known, the perceiving subject and the perceived object. In this framework, knowing of the object by the subject is something that goes on in the mind of the knower and is therefore subjective and private. This creates the problem of how the private and subjective knowledge can become related to the public and objective thing known. On Dewey's view this position is a carry-over from an outmoded mentalistic psychology. He does not think we start from a knower, a knowing, and a known. Dewey and Bentley, in their book *Knowing and the Known*, eliminate the knower even from the title. In the body of the book we are advised that even the two remaining are but one, "*knowings* are always and everywhere inseparable from *the knowns*," "the two are twin aspects of common fact" (*Knowing and the Known*, p. 53). They take these two "as forming together one event for inquiry—one transaction—since, in any full observation, if one vanishes, the other vanishes also" (*Knowing and the Known*, p. 82).

What we have here is what Dewey calls variously a "situation," a "transaction," or a "field." Knowing is essentially, for him, an interaction of an organism with its environment. It does not take place in the organism alone nor the environment alone. It takes place in a situation of which they are both part. Within this situation or field, there is an interaction or transaction to which each contributes.

In this sense, knowing is analogous to eating or any other natural function. In order that eating take place there must be an eating situation in which there is an eater and an environment that is edible. But eating is not something separate from these two; it is what goes on when they interact—when eating takes place. If we seek to distinguish the eater from the edible, we can do so for purposes of reference as long as we remember that eating is a functional relation and that the eater and the edible are the elements of the function.

Having seen that eating is nothing separate from the eater and the edible, we must see further that either of these is not what he is without the other. An eater is not an eater without something to eat; an edible object cannot be meaningfully said to be edible unless someone has eaten it. It is eating which makes the eater an eater and the edible object edible. They are twin aspects of a common fact—eating.

The knowing situation is identical. When an organism enters into a knowing function with its environment, there is no knower without something that is known; there is nothing that is known without a knower. But the knower is not a knower without a known, and the known is not a known without a knower. They are twin aspects of the common fact—knowing.

In the historical systems of epistemology

It was assumed that whatever else knowledge is or is not, it is dependent upon the independent existence of a *knower* and of something *to be known;* occurring, that is, between mind and the world; between self and not-self; or, in words made familiar by use, between subject and object. The assumption consisted in holding that the subjectmatters designated by these antithetical terms are separate and independent; hence the problem of problems was to determine some method of harmonizing the status of one with the status of the other with respect to the possibility and nature of knowledge (*Knowing and the Known,* p. 322).

Dewey says that he sought to pursue inquiry into this situation by examining the knowledge process not as an epistemologist but simply as a scientist would in observing a new biological process that might come to his attention. In so doing, it seemed to him that the separation as an ontological fact disappeared. The separateness of subject and object appeared as a carryover from a prior ontology. What remained was a difference in use.

Consideration of the simpler physiological activities which significantly enough already bore the name "functions" served to indicate that a life-activity is not anything going on *between* one thing, the organism, and another thing, the environment, but that, *as* life-activity it is a simple event over and across that distinction (not to say separation). Anything that can be entitled to either of these names has first to be located and identified as it is incorporated, engrossed, in life-activity. . . .

The obvious suggestion was that the subject matters to which the names "organism" and "environment," respectively, apply are distinguished when some function, say digestion, is disturbed, unsettled, and it is necessary, *in order to do something about it* which will restore the normal activity (in which organs and foods work together in a single unified process) to *locate* the source of the trouble. Is there something wrong inside? Or is the source of the disturbance located in water or in food that has been taken into the system? When such a distinction is once clearly made there are those who devote themselves especially to inquiry into the structures and processes that can be *referred* distinctively to the organisms, (although they could not take place and be capable of such reference without continuous partnership in a single transaction), while others study the relations of air, climate, foods, water, etc., to the maintenance of health—that is, of unified functionings (*Knowing and the Known,* pp. 323–24).

The analogy between eating and knowing may be carried further to illustrate another major point in Dewey's view. Eating is not a passive but an active situation. That it involves activity is demonstrated by the fact that it makes a difference to both the organism and the environment. The organism actively interacts with the environment. When the eating process is completed the organism is changed and the environment is changed. Similarly with knowing—knowing makes a difference not only to the knower but to the object known.

The view that knowing makes a difference to the object known is, for the traditional epistemologist, the primary paradox in Dewey's position. If knowing is an activity, it would be expected that it would act on what is known and thus change it. However, the road to understanding how this is the case is a somewhat devious one. Dewey begins his attack by rejecting the traditional theory of knowledge according to which the mind is a passive spectator in the knowing process. He calls this the spectator theory of knowledge and traces it back to the Greek view that knowledge is of something fixed and timeless to which human knowing makes no difference.

There is involved in these doctrines a whole system of philosophical conclusions. The first and foremost is that there is complete correspondence between knowledge in its true meaning and what is real. What is known, what is true for cognition, is what is real in being. The objects of knowledge form the standards of measure of the reality of all other objects of experience. . . . Secondly, the theory of knowledge has its basic metaphysics fixed by the same doctrine. For knowledge to be certain must relate to that which has antecedent existence or essential being. . . .

The common essence of all these theories, in short, is that what is known is antecedent to the mental act of observation and inquiry, and is totally unaffected by these acts; otherwise it would not be fixed and unchangeable. . . .

The theory of knowing is modeled after what was supposed to take place in the act of vision. The object refracts light to the eye and is seen; it makes a difference to the eye and to the person having an optical apparatus, but none to the thing seen. The real object is the object so fixed in its regal aloofness that it is a king to any beholding mind that may gaze upon it. A spectator theory of knowledge is the inevitable outcome (*Quest for Certainty*, pp. 21–23).

To understand the view Dewey opposes to this, it is first necessary to notice a distinction which he makes between "experience" and "knowledge." He uses the term experience to denote what is given in immediate sensation and the term knowledge to denote the end-product of the active process of thinking. The distinction here is analogous to that which Peirce makes between a secondness and a thirdness. The secondness is the given, the thirdness the result of thought about the given. In fact, in his earlier writings Dewey seems to agree with Peirce in calling brute experience "existence" and knowledge "reality" (*Influence of Darwin*, p. 235n.).

For Dewey, experience is not of something that is subjective but of something that is objective. We do not experience our sense-data as the idealist would have it; we experience the object. In short, he accepts the postulate of immediate experience. "Immediate empiricism postulates that things—anything, everything, in the ordinary or nontechnical use of the term 'thing'—are what they are experienced as" (*Influence of Darwin*, p. 227). But immediate experience is not to be confused with immediate knowledge. The spectator theory of knowledge holds to a doctrine of immediate knowledge. It holds that the object is known immediately; for Dewey the object is experienced immediately but known mediately through acting upon it, so that knowing is a temporal process and therefore comes at a later time.

Dewey traces his usage of experience back through Peirce and James to the British empiricists.

Experience thus comes to mean, to use the words of Peirce, "that which is forced upon a man's recognition will-he, nill-he, and shapes his thoughts to something quite different from what they naturally would have taken" (C. S. Peirce, *Monist*, Vol. XVI, p. 150). The same definition is found in James in his chapter on Necessary Truths: "Experience means experience of something foreign supposed to impress us whether spontaneously or in consequence of our own exertions and acts" (*Psychology*, Vol. II, p. 618). As Peirce points out, this notion of experience as the foreign element that forces the hand of thought and controls its efficacy, goes back to Locke. Experience is "observation employed either about external sensible objects or about the internal operations of our minds" [1]—as furnishing in short all the valid data and tests of thinking and knowledge. This meaning, thinks Peirce, should be accepted "as a landmark which it would be a crime to disturb or displace" (*Influence of Darwin*, 202–3).

But to experience something is not to know it. A thing as it is sensed, or experienced, has no significance. The word significance is an important word in Dewey. He takes it in its literal sense as meaning a sign of. Things have significance for thought, that is, they are signs of something else. What they are signs of is not given in experience but discovered by the activity of investigation. "There is moreover no particular limit to the possibilities of growth in the fusion of a thing as it is to sense and as it is to thought, or as a sign of other things" (*How We Think*, p. 18).

Let us take a concrete example. Suppose that I place on a table in front of you a small green object about the size of a

[1] "Essay concerning Human Understanding," Book II, Chapter II, Section 2. Locke doubtless derived this notion from Bacon (Dewey's footnote —ECM).

cantaloupe and tell you that it is an "alpowa." Would you, because you saw the object, know thereby what an alpowa was? Would the object have any significance for you? Clearly, not until you had thought about it. But would thinking be simply a matter of sitting down and gazing in soulful meditation at the object? Could you thus get to know what it was? What you would have to do would be to accept the object as a part of your environment and actively think about it. You would lift it, smell it, cut it open, inquire as to where it came from, how much it cost; you might conduct an experiment to find out whether it was edible or poisonous; if edible, you might take it into the laboratory and analyze it to find out what nutrients good for the human body were present in it; if it possessed a quantity of some rare nutrient you might investigate as to what the climatic conditions were under which alpowas grew so that these conditions might be artificially prepared to further the production of alpowas; etc., etc. When you had completed a series of investigations of this sort you would come to have some knowledge of what an alpowa was; an alpowa would have significance for you and for your thought as a result of your thinking about it. It should also be clear that your thinking affected the object thought about, not merely in the brute sense in which you physically handle it, but in the sense that your investigations make the thing as known different from the thing as experienced. As experienced it was not edible, as known it was edible; as experienced it was not a fruit, as known it was. The known object, then, is a construct out of the knowing process. The object that is known is affected by the knowing process; it is not too much to say it is made by the knowing of it.

This is not to say that the experienced object is not an antecedent reality. It is only the known object that is not antecedent. "There is nothing in the text that denies the existence of things temporally prior to human experiencing of them.

Indeed, I should think it fairly obvious that we experience most things *as* temporally prior to our experiencing of them" (*Influence of Darwin,* p. 240). Although the perceived object is antecedent to perception, the known object is consequent to knowing. Another way of putting the same thing is to use the pragmatic terminology that knowledge is prospective, not retrospective—it is not a function of the past but of the future.

Dewey got reinforcement for his position from the development of the concept of an operational definition in physics. In commenting on a passage in Eddington's *The Nature of the Physical World,* Dewey says:

It is implied in the quotation that concepts are recognized by means of the experimental operations by which they are determined; that is, operations define and test the validity of the meanings by which we state natural happenings. This implication is made explicit a few sentences further along when in speaking of Einstein Mr. Eddington says his theory "insists that each physical quantity should be defined as the result of certain operations of measurement and calculation." The principle is anticipated in Peirce's essay on *How to Make Our Ideas Clear* published as far back as 1881. . . . Peirce states that the sole meaning of the idea of an object consists of the consequences which result when the object is acted upon in a particular way. The principle is one element in the pragmatism of James. The idea is also akin to the "instrumental" theory of conceptions, according to which they are intellectual instruments for directing our activities in relation to existence. . . . On account of ambiguities in the notion of pragmatism—although its *logical* import is identical—I shall follow Bridgman in speaking of "operational thinking" (*Quest for Certainty,* p. 111, n.2).[2]

It should be clear that such thinking, since it actually acts upon what is known, affects it, changes it. The change is not something that goes on just in the knower; knowing changes

[2] See also, *Experimental Logic,* p. 8, n.1.

what is known. " 'Thought' is not a property of something termed intellect or reason apart from nature. It is a mode of directed overt action. Ideas are anticipatory plans and designs which take effect in concrete reconstruction of antecedent conditions of existence" (*Quest for Certainty,* p. 166).

Part of the confusion in understanding Dewey is terminological. When he denies that antecedent conditions are the object of knowledge he is interpreted to be denying that antecedent conditions are the subject of inquiry. The object of knowledge—in the sense of objective—is a solution of some difficulty. The subject of inquiry—in the sense of subject matter—is a situation which poses the difficulty. Inquiry solves the problem by changing the antecedent difficulty into the consequent solution. And since the object of knowledge is the solution, the object of knowledge is *made* by thinking about it. "Made by thinking" in this context means Dewey's view "of *acts* performed, acts in the literal sense of the word, deeds done" (*Quest for Certainty,* p. 112).

A final point in Dewey's theory of knowledge may be indicated by calling attention to the fact that the known object is not entirely new. It is a construct but also a re-construct. It is a new arrangement of old materials and so refers back to them. This circular nature of knowledge forces Dewey to a rejection of the simple stimulus-response reflex arc as the basic unit in describing human behavior. The stimulus-response formula is usually taken to imply a direction of energy from the stimulus to the response. But this is only half the picture; there is a return of energy from the response to the stimulus. It is customarily held that the stimulus causes the response. But what is there about the stimulus that causes the response? The response is caused by the fact that the stimulus lacks significance. It is precisely this non-significant feature of the stimulus which moves us to respond. We respond to discover the significance of the stimulus.

Consider a man walking in the woods. He hears a sound off the trail. He does not know what it is. Is it a harmless deer, a threatening bear, or an innocuous wind in the trees? Because the sound lacks significance, he responds to it in order to discover its significance. He cautiously enters the woods and sees a mule deer peacefully grazing. He now refers back to the sound, the significance "deer-grazing." He thus completes the circuit of which the reflex-arc is only half. "What we have is a circuit, not an arc or broken segment of a circle. This circuit is more truly termed organic than reflex, because the motor response determines the stimulus, just as truly as sensory stimulus determines movement. Indeed, the movement is only for the sake of determining the stimulus, of fixing what kind of stimulus it is, of interpreting it" (*Philosophy and Civilization*, p. 240).

Having established the significance of the stimulus, the individual then builds up out of these significant stimuli, organic circuits or habits (*Logic*, p. 31). That habits are functions not merely of stimuli *qua* stimuli, but of stimuli as significant is indicated by the fact that different people will respond to the same stimulus in different ways. Two men working on different shifts in the same factory will respond differently to the same whistle. For one it will be a quitting whistle, for the other a starting whistle. They have formed different habits with reference to the whistle because it has a different significance for each of them.

The sum total of all habitual ways of entering into relations with the environment constitute the self, the individual (*Human Nature*, p. 25, p. 39). The self is the habit of habits.

Everything that a man who has the habit of locomotion does and thinks, he does and thinks differently on that account. This fact is recognized in current psychology, but is falsified into an association of sensations. Were it not for the continued operation of all habits in every act, no such thing as character could exist.

Character is the interpenetration of habits. If each habit existed in an insulated compartment and operated without affecting or being affected by others, character would not exist. That is, conduct would lack unity being only a juxtaposition of disconnected reactions to separated situations. But since environments overlap, since situations are continuous and those remote from one another contain like elements, a continuous modification of habits by one another is constantly going on. A man may give himself away in a look or a gesture. Character can be read through the medium of individual acts (*Human Nature*, p. 38).

Because character, or personality, or the self is constituted of habits, it is not some private, subjective metaphysical entity, it is something public and observable. It may be observed by observing a man's habits.

This completes our discussion of Dewey's view of the nature of the organism in the organism-environment situation. Before examining what he has to say about the environment, we must look at the process of inquiry, for it is through inquiry that the organism and the environment come to interact.

THE PROCESS OF INQUIRY

One of the basic themes in Dewey's philosophy has been his treatment of logic. *Studies in Logical Theory* in 1903 formed the alliance between Dewey and James that led to the pragmatic movement. The material in this early book was included with other material in *Essays in Experimental Logic* in 1916; the whole development culminated in Dewey's full-blown statement of his logical position in 1938 in *Logic, the Theory of Inquiry*. The title of the last named book indicates Dewey's conviction that logic is essentially a study of the methods by which inquiry or investigation is carried out.

It is often held that while logic and psychology are both concerned with human thinking, the difference between them lies in the fact that psychology is concerned with how men do think and logic with how men ought to think. Dewey finds this to be a puerile distinction. Unless one believes that there is some *a priori* method of discovering rules of logic, the only way to discover how men ought to think is by a study of how they do think, and thus, by separating the successful methods from the unsuccessful, to develop gradually a set of logical norms. These norms will necessarily change from time to time as new methods of pursuing inquiry are discovered.

The way in which men *do* "think" denotes as it is *here* interpreted, simply the ways in which men at a given time carry on their inquiries. So far as it is used to register a difference from the ways in which they *ought* to think, it denotes a difference like that between good and bad farming or good and bad medical practice. Men think in ways they should not when they follow methods of inquiry that experience of past inquiries shows are not competent to reach the intended end of the inquiries in question (*Logic,* p. 104).

On this approach the subject matter of logic is actual methods of inquiry. Men have selected many kinds of things to study. Some collect insects and study them, some collect rocks and study them; in the same spirit Dewey thinks logicians ought to collect methods of pursuing inquiry and study them (*Knowing and the Known,* p. 50). The business of logic is "to analyze and report how and to what effect inquiries actually proceed, genetically and functionally in their experiential context" (*Rejoinder,* p. 533).

In so far as logic is the study of methods of inquiry, some light may be thrown on the nature of logic by an examination of Dewey's definition of inquiry: "Inquiry is the controlled or directed transformation of an indeterminate situation into one that is so determinate in its constituent distinctions and relations as to convert the elements of the original situation into a unified whole" (*Logic,* p. 104). In this notion that inquiry is the process whereby an indeterminate situation is converted into a determinate one, it is possible to recognize Peirce's view that inquiry is the process whereby a doubtful situation is transformed into one where doubt is removed, i.e., where belief is attained.

Other points which Dewey has obtained from Peirce are "the principle of the continuum of inquiry, a principle whose importance, as far as I am aware, only Peirce had previously noted" (*Logic*, p. iii). We have already seen this principle in Peirce and in James; Dewey expresses it as follows: "The attainment of settled beliefs is a progressive matter; there is no belief so settled as not to be exposed to further inquiry. It is the convergent and cumulative effect of continued inquiry that defines knowledge in its general meaning" (*Logic*, p. 8). Finally, Dewey credits Peirce with the general position that logical principles are those habitual ways of investigating that are successful. Dewey refers to Peirce's theory of the formulation of guiding principles for settling doubt, and says Peirce was the first logician to give these principles a concrete context by associating them with the biological facts of habit formation (*Logic*, pp. 12–14; see also, *Problems of Men*, p. 228, n.7, written in 1903).

It should not be thought from the above that for Dewey logical principles are formulated solely by an examination of methods of inquiry. That is true, but it is also the case that logical principles originate in inquiry (*Logic*, p. 4). Every investigation is not only an investigation into the subject matter being investigated; it is also an investigation as to the worth of the method of investigation. Will this method successfully resolve this problem? If the method is not successful, new methods are devised until one is found that is successful. Thus the development of logical principles is a dynamic activity that goes on within the process of inquiry.

The organism is in constant contact with its environment.

When friction occurs between the two, the process of inquiry is instituted to ascertain the significance of the friction and to resolve the difficulty that produces it. For the most part, the organism proceeds primarily by virtue of its established habits. But when a situation develops that habit cannot deal with, thinking is called upon to solve the situation and form a new habit.

To connote what Dewey means by thinking or reflection, it were better to use the terms inquiry or investigation, for they suggest the element of activity more emphatically. When the individual is faced by a problematic situation, there are two ways in which he may react. He may use direct or indirect activity to solve his problem. Direct activity is blind, unreasoned, brute force directed against the locus of the problem. It is what we call panic in an individual's response. Such activity is rarely successful. Indirect activity is of a different nature. It is activity on things only indirectly connected with the problem in order to find a means of controlling the difficulty. Thus a medical investigator seeking a cure for a disease will not take a hammer and seek to kill the germs by hitting them. He will act indirectly. He goes off into his laboratory and spends long periods of time trying to develop antibodies or antitoxins. This latter activity is only indirectly related to the problem he is investigating.

A story appeared in the newspapers recently of a man whose automobile engine would not start. He went into his house and got a gun and came out and shot the engine. This is direct action with a vengeance. Indirect action would have led him to check his gasoline, his battery, his spark plugs, etc. Such indirect action need not necessarily be overt. It may be the calling before the imagination of various plans for action, some of which will be rejected before any overt activity is undertaken. But even here the ideas are not mere "mental" phenomena; they are projected activities which are rejected on the basis of previous experiences. Thus thinking is not mere passive reflection of the situation, in the sense in which a mirror reflects; thinking has the active function of reconstructing the situation in imagination so as to suggest activity which will make a new situation in which the problem is solved. "For the holding an end in view and the selecting and organizing out of the natural flux, on the basis of this end, conditions that are means, *is* intelligence" (*Influence of Darwin,* p. 43).

One of Dewey's earliest statements of this position (1910) remains one of his most lucid statements:

Let us then by way of experiment, follow this suggestion. Let us assume that among real objects in their values and significances, real oppositions and incompatibilities exist; that these conflicts are both troublesome in themselves, and the source of all manner of further difficulties—so much so that they may be suspected of being the source of all man's woe, of all encroachment upon and destruction of value, of good. Suppose that thinking is, not accidentally, but essentially, a way, and the only way that proves adequate, of dealing with these predicaments—that being "in a hole," in difficulty, is the fundamental "predicament" of intelligence. Suppose when effort is made in a brute way to remove these oppositions and to secure an arrangement of things which means satisfaction, fulfillment, happiness, that the method of brute attack, of trying directly to force warrings into peace fails; suppose then an effort to effect the transformation by an indirect method—by inquiry into the disordered state of affairs and by framing views, conceptions, of what the situation would be like were it reduced to harmonious order. Finally, suppose that upon this basis a plan of action is worked out, and that this plan, when carried into overt effect, succeeds infinitely better than the brute method of attack in bringing about the desired consummation. Suppose again this indirection of activity is precisely what we mean by thinking. Would it not hold that harmony is the end and the test of thinking? that observations are pertinent and ideas correct just so far as, overtly acted upon, they succeed in removing the undesirable, the inconsistent (*Influence of Darwin,* pp. 132–33).

We have in this quotation all of the fundamental traits of Dewey's position as he has developed them in his later books. Dewey has often said that his view was suggested to him by passages in James's *Psychology.* The extent to which this is the case may be seen from the following paragraph from James's book:

If the end by its simple presence does not instantaneously suggest the means, the search for the latter becomes an intellectual *problem.* The solution of problems is the most characteristic and peculiar sort of voluntary thinking. Where the end thought of is some outward deed or gain, the solution is largely composed of the actual motor processes, walking, speaking, writing, etc., which lead up to it. Where the end is in the first instance only ideal, as in laying out a plan of operations, the steps are purely imaginary. In both of these cases the discovery of the means may form a new sort of end, of an entirely peculiar nature, an end, namely, which we intensely desire before we have attained it, but of the nature of which, even whilst most strongly craving it, we have no distinct imagination whatever. Such an end is a problem (*Principles,* I, 584).

INSTRUMENTALISM

Instrumentalism is Dewey's version of pragmatism. We have just seen that for Dewey a thought is essentially an instrument. It is an instrument for resolving a difficulty. To discover what the instrument will do, you put it into action. Instrumentalism is not a purely practical position any more than pragmatism is. One may have to formulate an instrument for dealing with a theoretical situation as well as a practical one. But so far as the instrument is adequate to the situation, it has practical character. But "There is no warrant in the doctrine for carrying over *this* practical quality into the consequences in which action culminates, and by which it is tested and corrected. A knowing as an act is instrumental to the resultant controlled and more significant situation; this does not imply anything about the intrinsic or the instrumental character of the consequent situation. That is as it may be in a given case" (*Experimental Logic*, p. 332).

The basis of instrumentalism is the conception of the unity of theory and practice. Philosophy prior to pragmatism concerned itself with a theory of reality which, so far as everyday affairs were concerned, had few practical implications. A recognition of this is suggested in the layman's view of the philosopher as a man who lives in the clouds. This position, that the study of reality has little implication for practice, is what Dewey is concerned to reject. In fact, he defines pragmatism as "the doctrine that reality possesses practical character and that this character is most efficaciously expressed in the function of intelligence" (*Philosophy and Civilization,* pp. 39–40).

The most complete statement of Dewey's pragmatism in the tradition of Peirce and James is to be found in his *Essays in Experimental Logic* in the chapter titled "The Control of Ideas by Facts." The title is indicative and informative. For the pragmatist, ideas are controlled by facts. The idea starts from facts and returns to facts, and it is the differences that it makes to the world of fact that indicate its meaning. "We estimate the import or significance of any present desire or impulse by forecasting what it will come or amount to if carried out; literally its consequences define its *consequence,* its meaning or import" (*Ethics*, p. 302).

Dewey had the pragmatic approach even before pragmatism became a philosophical movement. In 1894 he wrote, "A man's real (as distinct from his nominal or symbolical) theory of conduct can be told only from his act" (*Study of Ethics*, p. 1). A more mature statement is as follows:

Acts . . . have different consequences. It is impossible to regard these differences of objective result as indifferent to the quality of the acts. They are immediately sensed if not clearly perceived; and they are the only *components of the meaning* of the act. When feelings dwelling antecedently in the soul, were supposed to be the causes of acts, it was natural to suppose that each psychic element had its own inherent quality which might be directly read off by introspection. But when we surrender this notion, it becomes evident that the only way of telling what an organic act is like is by the sensed or perceptible changes which it occasions (*Human Nature*, p. 151).

Dewey combines his instrumentalism with the doctrine of immediate experience to formulate a new theory about the nature of the objects in the world about us. Since the time of Galileo, science has been concerned in the main with what are called the primary properties of objects—size, shape, position, motion, and mass. These properties are contrasted with the secondary properties of color, sound, odor, taste, and heat. The view here is that the scientist is not concerned with color *qua* color, but rather with a wave length of a certain frequency. He is not concerned with heat as something hot, but with the average molecular velocity of a collection of molecules. Another way of putting it is that the scientist is concerned with those properties of an object that can be reduced to measurement. A given shade of red is of concern to the painter or the interior decorator in a way in which it is not of concern to the scientist. His interest is in those features that can be measured quantitatively.

Because of this, it is sometimes said that science is concerned with the quantitative features of objects, while in practical affairs we are concerned with the qualitative features. The painter, the interior decorator, the dress designer, the furniture upholsterer are concerned with the color, not the wave length. So we seem to develop a schism between the scientific view of the world and the view of practical affairs. For the scientist a table top is a surface that is made up of particles between which there are large holes. The particles are moving about very rapidly and give the surface an ir-regular contour. For the practical man using the table, the table has no holes in it. It is a solid surface of regular contour and made up of parts which do not move but are fixed in place year after year.

John Locke attributed the primary properties to the object and the secondary properties to the mind of the perceiver. Color was what occurred in the perceiving mind when a light ray of a given frequency stimulated the optical apparatus, so that color was not a property of the object—the only prop-erty the object had was that it reflected light rays of a certain frequency; color was something found only in the mind of the perceiver. So with all the secondary properties; the view thus was that the real world, the scientific world, was a color-less, soundless world without any qualities—a world of atoms in motion. Whereas the world of practical affairs was a world of qualities, a world of colors, sounds, odors, heat, etc.

Even more disturbing was the fact that this scientific world left out all value features—ethical good and bad, aesthetic beauty and ugliness, all the emotional properties of poignancy and pathos were not to be found in the scientific world of the meaningless scurrying of atoms. Borrowing a term from Santayana, Dewey calls the value properties of objects, ter-tiary properties. Using this terminology, the position held was that the world of science—of quantitative primary properties —was the real world; the world of practical affairs—of quali-tative secondary and tertiary properties—existed only in the human mind and had no objective reality.

This bifurcation of the universe is rejected by Dewey. Fol-lowing consistently his doctrine of immediate experience, Dewey holds that objects really are what they appear to be. They appear to be colored, therefore they are colored; they appear to be good or to be beautiful, then they are good or beautiful. "Fear, whether an instinct or an acquisition, is a function of the environment. Man fears because he exists in a fearful, an awful world. The *world* is precarious and perilous" (*Experience and Nature,* p. 42). Dewey argues that if the fear belonged only to us, if it were not a property of reality, it could be corrected by simply changing our minds. But to think that you can change a fearful situation into a happy one by simply thinking that it is happy is the essence of insanity. It is to divorce yourself from reality and to retire to a private world of your own devising. To refer the qualitative aspects of experience to the real world and to act upon it to change a precarious existential situation into a satisfactory one is to recognize that the primary properties described by science are only a partial description of reality; a full description would include secondary and tertiary properties as equally real with primary properties.

To understand this view more clearly we need to examine it in greater detail. First of all, it is necessary to see what a scientific object is for Dewey; it is not so much a matter of primary qualities, as a matter of the relations between such properties.

The propositions significant in physical science are oblivious of qualitative considerations as such; they deal with "primary qualities" in distinction from secondary and tertiary; in actual treatment, moreover, these primary qualities are not qualities, but relations. Consider the difference between movement as qualitative alteration, and motion as $F = ma$; between stress as involving effort and tension, and as force per unit surface; between the red of the blood issuing from a wound, and red as signifying 400 trillion vibrations per time unit (*Philosophy and Civilization,* p. 93).

Thus the objects of science are not primary qualities as such but the relations that exist between one set of primary qualities and another set of such qualities. This does not mean that scientific objects are not real. Dewey agrees with Peirce and James that relations are realities: "*connections* exist. . . . Long ago I learned from William James that there are immediate experiences of the connections linguistically expressed by conjunctions and prepositions. My doctrinal position is but a generalization of what is involved in this fact" (*Rejoinder*, p. 532 and n.).

The above points taken from the doctrine of immediate experience are combined with instrumentalism to make scientific objects instruments.

Scientific objects as statements of these interrelations are instrumentalities of control. (*Quest for Certainty*, p. 128).

Extent of control is dependent, as was suggested a moment ago, upon capacity to find a connected series of correlated change, such that each linked pair leads on to another in the direction of a terminal one which can be brought about by our own action. It is this latter condition which is especially fulfilled by the objects of scientific thought. Physical science disregards the qualitative heterogeneity of experienced objects so as to make them all members of one comprehensive homogenous scheme, and hence capable of translation or conversion one into another. This homogeneity of subject-matter over a broad range of things which are as disparate from each other in direct experience as sound and color, heat and light, friction and electricity, is the source of the wide and free control of events found in modern technology. Common sense knowledge can connect things as sign and things indicated here and there by isolated couples. But it cannot possibly join them all up together so that we can pass from any one to any other. In ideal at least, we can travel from any meaning—or relation—found anywhere in nature to the meaning to be expected anywhere else (*Quest for Certainty*, p. 133).

Science, by ignoring secondary and tertiary properties, provides itself with a world which is simpler than the real world—because only a part of it. Dealing with this simpler world has great advantages. It makes inquiry and experimentation less complex and provides a world which can be expressed completely in quantitative units and hence may be dealt with by using mathematics as a tool. In this simpler world the scientist does not concern himself with the quantities as such, but with the functional relations between quantities. He formulates these relations in terms of laws. His ideal is to formulate a set of laws such that the world of primary properties provides a continuum, i.e., given any particular existential set of primary properties he can move by his knowledge of the relations between primary properties to any other desired set of such properties.

Consider an individual who wishes to move from a given set of secondary or tertiary properties, say set A, to some other set, B. He needs only to reduce sets A and B to their corresponding primary properties and the scientist can, ideally, describe for him the route he must travel to get from one to another. Thus science becomes a refined tool, an instrument, for enabling us to change a given situation into a desired situation. Science, then, is not the whole of reality but an abstraction from it—an abstraction whose value lies in its utility and in the fact that it can be connected with the other parts of reality. Science is not separated from aesthetic and ethical properties in any ultimate sense but is intimately associated with them on the level of practical reality.

A final point that needs some further comment here is how a philosophy that makes secondary and tertiary properties real can account for illusion and for individual differences in perception. Illusion is accounted for by the fact that the mind infers that what is given in immediate experience is what will be verified in future knowledge. What is given in immediate experience is a sign of something, but what it is a sign of only further investigation can tell. The mind may infer that it is the sign of one thing, when it is really the sign of something else. " 'The stick seems bent in water' does not mean that the appearing object *seems* bent. It means that what appears *is* something bent, though not necessarily the stick; perhaps it is light" (*Philosophy and Civilization,* p. 71). Individual differences in perception may be accounted for either by physiological differences between individuals, by sociological differences (seeing objects from a different cultural perspective), or by different mental abilities (different minds making different inferences from the same observed data). All such differences are resolved for Dewey, as for Peirce and James, by the continuum of inquiry and the community of investigators.

9

Ethical Theory

According to Dewey, ethics is the science of conduct. Conduct is a form of action. But conduct is not any and every action but only action undertaken with an end in view. There is a goal the individual desires to attain. He conducts himself in a certain way in order to attain this goal. Thus we may make judgments about his actions in terms of the value of the ends he is trying to reach and in terms of the value of his actions as means of reaching his ends.

Conduct implies more than something taking place; it implies purpose, motive, intention; that the agent knows what he is about, that he has something which he is aiming at. All action accomplishes something or brings about results, but conduct has the result *in view*. It occurs for the sake of producing this result. Conduct does not simply, like action in general, have a cause, but also a reason, and the reason is present to the mind of the agent. There can be conduct only when there is a being who can propose to himself, as an end to be reached by himself, something which he regards as worthwhile. Such a being is a moral agent, and his action, when conscious, is conduct (*Outlines,* p. 3).

The essential element of ethical behavior is that it have the end in view. "Conduct is not that which simply reaches certain consequences—a bullet shot from a rifle does that; there is conduct only when the consequences are foreseen; made the reason of action" (*Outlines,* p. 97). So that ethics is not simply the study of human activity, but the study of directed activity, i.e., activity directed by an end in view, or activity directed by an idea of value. The questions for ethics are, "What ends ought we to strive for?" and "What conduct ought we to engage in in order to attain these ends?" Dewey begins developing his answers to these questions by a study of the efforts of his predecessors.

ethics is the study of conduct with a view in mind

HISTORICAL BACKGROUND

Dewey's position evolves out of what he considers to be the one-sidedness of two of the traditional approaches to ethics. On the one hand we have the traditional religious ethic according to which an action is judged to be good primarily in terms of its motive. An action is good if it is done from a good motive, bad if done from an evil motive. This view attains a classical formulation in the ethics of Kant, according to whom the rightness of an action is not to be determined by any of its consequences but solely by the motive from which it is done. An action is good if it is done on the grounds that it is right to do it. If it is done because of the consequences which ensue, it may not be evil, but it has no ethical quality. Dewey finds two points of value in Kant's position:

Kant's positive service was, first, his clear insight into the fact that the good is to be found only in activity; that the will itself, and nothing beyond itself, is the end; and that to adopt any other doctrine, is to adopt an immoral principle, since it is to subordinate the will (character, self and personality) to some outside end. His second great service was in showing the necessity of putting in abeyance the immediate satisfaction of each desire as it happens to arise, and of subordinating it to some law not to be found in the particular desire. He showed that not the particular desire, but only the desire as controlled by the idea of law could be the motive of moral action (*Outlines,* pp. 94–95).

The other traditional approach in ethics is the hedonistic view, that that action is good which produces pleasant consequences. In contrast to Kant, this view, as exemplified, for example, in the utilitarianism of Bentham and Mill, judges the good of an action not in terms of its motives, but rather in terms of the consequences which flow from it. Again Dewey finds some worth in this view in spite of its one-sidedness.

The truth in hedonism is its conviction that the good, the end of man, is not to be found in any outward object, but only in what comes home to man in his own conscious experience. The error is in reducing this experience to mere having, to bare feelings or affections, eliminating the element of doing. It is this doing which satisfies man, and it is this which involves as its content . . . objective and permanent ends. When Mill speaks of the end of desire as a "satisfied life," he carries our assent; but to reduce this satisfied life to feelings of pleasure and absence of pains, is to destroy the life and hence the satisfaction (*Outlines,* p. 30).

Dewey, in his own position, seeks to eliminate the one-sidedness of each of these views by combining them. Where Kant held that only acts done from a good motive are good, and the utilitarians that only acts which have good consequences are good, Dewey's position is that to be good an act must be done from a good motive and have good consequences —where both motive and consequences are definable in terms of human experiences. Or, where Kant advises us to act according to moral law and the utilitarians advise us to aim to satisfy our desires, Dewey tells us to aim to satisfy our desires according to moral law.

The end of action, or the good, is the realized will, the developed or satisfied self. This satisfied self is found neither in the getting of a lot of pleasures through the satisfaction of desires just as they happen to arise, nor in obedience to law simply because it is law.

It is found in *satisfaction of desires according to law.* This law, however, is not something external to the desires, but is their own law. Each desire is only one striving of character for larger action, and the only way in which it can really find satisfaction (that is, pass from inward striving into outward action) is *as* a manifestation of character. A desire, taken as a desire for its own apparent or direct end *only,* is an abstraction. It is a desire for an entire and continuous activity, and its satisfaction requires that it be fitted into this entire and continuous activity; that it be made conformable to the conditions which will bring the whole man into action. . . . The problem then is to find that special form of character, of self, which includes and transforms all special desires. This form of character is at once the Good and the Law of man (*Outlines,* pp. 95–96).

The above quotations are all taken from *Outlines of a Critical Theory of Ethics* published in 1891. They indicate Dewey's approach in terms of the traditional ethical concepts. However, his more mature ethical position, while embodying most of the points in the earlier view, looks at ethics from a different perspective.

This new perspective may be attributed to the influence of Darwin on philosophy. In Dewey's book with this title, the leading essay expounds the nature of this influence. Dewey indicates three major areas of human activity. These are the study of the inorganic world, of the organic world, and of the world of ethical, political, and social values. The ancients treated all of these as consisting of static, unchanging forms. The function of science and philosophy was to grasp the nature of these fixed forms and to classify them. The scientific revolution came about when Galileo, Kepler, and Newton rejected this view as it applied to the inorganic sciences. Instead of looking upon what was given in experience as objects to be classified and filed away, they looked upon what was given as data to be investigated, to be experimented with, to be manipulated. The result of this shift from considering the given as objects in their finalities to data for the beginning of inquiry was to develop arts of control over the inorganic world.

Before these arts of control could be applied to the study and development of human values and goals, it had to be demonstrated that the methods of science were equally applicable to the organic world, that is, that we did not have objective finalities there any more than in the inorganic world. It was this task which Darwin accomplished. He showed that the organic world was a world that must be interpreted in terms of scientific methods and techniques. This opened the door to the application of these methods to the realm of ethics and value.

But prior to Darwin the impact of the new scientific method upon life, mind, and politics, had been arrested, because between these ideal or moral interests and the inorganic world intervened the kingdom of plants and animals. The gates of the garden of life were barred to the new ideas; and only through this garden was there access to mind and politics. The influence of Darwin upon philosophy resides in his having conquered the phenomena of life for the principle of transition, and thereby freed the new logic for application to mind and morals and life (*Influence of Darwin*, p. 8).

From the influence of evolution and biology generally on philosophy, Dewey drew two conclusions. The first was that "moral conceptions and processes grow naturally out of the very conditions of human life" (*Ethics*, p. 343). Which is to say that human experience is the source of our notions of good and evil and right and wrong. This being the case, we need not go outside of human experience for the discovery of standards of good and right—human experience has the capacity to develop its own regulative standards.

But if human experience is the source of our welfare and our woe, the place to develop methods for promoting the goods and eliminating the evils is within such experience. By considering what is given in ethical experience as data—not final goods and bads—we may apply the scientific method to ethics and develop arts of control in that realm. "Through instrumental arts, arts of control based on study of nature, objects which are fulfilling and good, may be multiplied and rendered secure" (*Experience and Nature*, p. 127).

These two elements constitute Dewey's naturalism. Good and evil spring from and are found in nature, including human nature, and the means of promoting more good and less evil is to be found by the study and control of things within nature, not by appeal to something outside of it. It is from this naturalistic point of view that Dewey develops his own ethical position.

DEWEY'S POSITION

Dewey's interpretation of ethical concepts is thoroughly in accord with the pragmatic theory of meaning. "It is not too much to say that the key to a correct theory of morality is recognition of the *essential unity of the self and its acts,* if the latter have any moral significance; while errors in theory arise as soon as the self and acts (and their consequences) are separated from each other, and moral worth is attributed to one more than the other" (*Ethics*, pp. 318–19).

Since ethical activity is a form of activity—not of "inner" feelings—ethics is something that may be studied and observed in a public fashion.

Honesty, chastity, malice, peevishness, courage, triviality, industry, irresponsibility are not private possessions of a person. They are working adaptations of personal capacities with environing forces. All virtues and vices are habits which incorporate objective forces. They are interactions of elements contributed by the make-up of an individual with elements supplied by the out-door world.

They can be studied as objectively as physiological functions, and they can be modified by change of either personal or social elements (*Human Nature*, p. 16).

The basic elements in Dewey's ethics are indicated in the titles to the sub-sections of his *Human Nature and Conduct.* These titles are "The Place of Habit in Conduct," "The Place of Impulse in Conduct," and "The Place of Intelligence in Conduct." For him ethics is basically a matter of the opposition between habit on the one hand and impulse on the other, with intelligence serving as the mediating factor.

He begins his discussion by asserting that "Morals are concerned with the health, efficiency and happiness of a development of human nature" (*Human Nature*, p. 3).

To separate morals from human nature is to invite either a hedonistic bohemianism which glorifies natural impulses as above morals, or a puritanism that glorifies morals as above human nature. Combining human nature with morals also has its pitfalls, however. On the one hand we may coop morals up within human nature and look upon them as distinct from their environment, in which case we say that the only way to change the world is to change the hearts of men. On the other hand, we may blame morals entirely on the social environment and say that human nature is a product of the environment and that nothing can be done until social institutions are changed. Dewey's view consists in considering conduct to be an interaction between the individual and the environment. The environment affects the conduct of the individual; the conduct of the individual affects the environment.

Dewey begins by analyzing the place of habit in conduct. We have already indicated that for him the self is its habits. In the present context, in talking of the power that habits have over us, he says that "When we are honest with ourselves we acknowledge that a habit has this power because it is so intimately a part of ourselves. It has a hold upon us because we are the habit" (*Human Nature*, p. 24).

The habits make the individual. When born, a baby has no individuality. He acquires individuality and literally becomes a person as he develops habits. These habits are formed —i.e., the individual is formed—as a result of contacts with the environment, both natural and social. Thus an individual literally incorporates his environment into his personality. He is partly the individual he is because of his environment being what it is. Again there is the merging in Dewey's thought of traditionally diverse elements. The individual is not something set down in the environment; he is a part of the environment and the environment is part of him. Habits are functions of the individual and his environment. They are ways of using and incorporating the environment into his activities.

In human society the dominant portion of the earliest environment is not natural but social. It is the effect of parents and other adults on the child. He incorporates their behavior into his. The influence of this social environment is important all through life and is vital to the formation of habits.

Some activity proceeds from a man; then it sets up reactions in the surroundings. Others approve, disapprove, protest, encourage, share and resist. Even letting a man alone is a definite response. Envy, admiration, and imitation are complicities. Neutrality is nonexistent. Conduct is always shared; this is the difference between it and a physiological process. It is not an ethical "ought" that conduct *should* be social. It *is* social, whether bad or good (*Human Nature*, pp. 16–17).

Because of the social nature of conduct, society is concerned with the quality of conduct. It strives to control it, to develop it along approved lines. "For practical purposes, morals mean customs, folkways, established collective habits" (*Human Nature*, p. 75).

The habits formed under the influence of social pressure

are often desirable customs. But it is also often the case that, when perpetuated, they are ways of behavior formulated in terms of past conditions which no longer exist. They are what was once good, once solved problems effectively. Whether such habits are still good depends upon whether the problems are still the same today, or whether the conditions have changed so that the habits which once sufficed are no longer adequate to new conditions.

The habits of a social group need to be constantly re-examined and criticized anew in the light of changes in social patterns. Dewey is fond of saying that Socrates initiated ethics with the comment that "The unexamined life is not worth living." If we let our customs go too long without adjusting them to changing conditions, the day comes when we can only catch up with the times by a drastic upheaval, a social revolution. Then there is great moral disturbance, and hue and cry by the adherents of the older morality that the younger generation is immoral.

The opposition is not between intelligence and habit. Habits may be good and desirable. The real opposition is "between routine, unintelligent habit, and intelligent habit or art. Even a savage custom may be reasonable in that it is adapted to social needs and uses" (*Human Nature,* p. 77). Intelligent habit is found in the case of the master violinist whose habits are developed laboriously and carefully, but who in using the habits to give a performance guides his activity by thought about what he is trying to do. Routine, unintelligent habit is found in the case of the moralist who holds that some kind of action, e.g., telling a lie, is wrong at all times, for all persons, under all circumstances. Mechanism is a part of habit, but habit need not be mechanical. When a nation's habits become mechanical, the nation gets old, or rather, "Not the nation but its customs get old. Its institutions petrify into rigidity; there is social arterial sclerosis" (*Human Nature,* p. 102).

Because habits are functions of our selves and our environment, they constitute our means for doing. They furnish us
with our working capacities for changing ourselves or changing
our environment. The neglect of habits as means is a characteristic of traditional ethics. By and large our ethical judgments seem to be based on what Dewey calls a belief in magic
—a belief that results may be obtained without use of means.
Aladdin with his lamp could dispense with means. He merely
rubbed his lamp, said "Let it be so," and by some magical
fiat it was so. In most of our ethical judgments we proceed on
the same basis. If a man does something wrong—such as drinking too much—we often say that he could stop if he only
wanted to, as though he has only to visualize the right end, to
wish for it, and it is attained. To think and talk thus is to
believe in magic.

Actually we can only deal successfully with our conduct
through the medium of our habits. A man becomes a drunkard
because of certain relations which hold between himself and
his environment. He cannot cease being a drunkard by merely
exercising an act of will; he can only change when the conditions are changed. "Conditions have been formed for producing a bad result, and the bad result will occur as long as
those conditions exist. They can no more be dismissed by a
direct effort of will than the conditions which create drought
can be dispelled by whistling for wind" (*Human Nature*,
p. 29).

The way to correct our behavior is not by wishing to be
different—after all, the man who keeps saying to himself, "I
will not drink," is doing his best to make himself drink by
conjuring up a mental image of drinking and thus producing
the stimulus which leads to drinking. The means for changing
his behavior is through his habits. He begins by seeking to
discover why he has the habit he has. What are the conditions
which produce it? What goal is he seeking to attain by acting

in this way? Once he has discovered the meaning of his habit, he then proceeds to try to develop a different habit which will attain the goal his drinking was oriented toward, but which is socially acceptable and not as destructive to his health. His behavior is now directed positively. It is directed toward developing this new habit, not simply negatively toward avoiding an old one. Taking habits seriously as the means of changing behavior is the only way in which conduct will be improved.

The same situation exists on the group level as on the individual level. Social customs are habits common to a social group. These customs, or common habits, exist because members of a group face the same situation, i.e., share a common environment, and, sharing a common human nature, react to the environment in the same fashion. As customs come to be widely adopted and venerable with age, they petrify into rigidity. It is this rigidity of custom and habit which leads us to think of them as essentially conservative in nature. But habit is neither essentially conservative nor progressive. A habit is an ability to do something—a way of behavior. If this ability is oriented toward the past, it is conservative, i.e., if the ability is exercised merely to repeat past acts adapted to past conditions. What makes a habit conservative is enslavement to old ruts; a progressive habit is one that holds energies in readiness for new emergencies. "The genuine heart of reasonableness (and of goodness in conduct) lies in effective mastery of the conditions which *now* enter into action. To be satisfied with repeating, with traversing the ruts which in other conditions led to good, is the surest way of creating carelessness about present and actual good" (*Human Nature,* p. 67).

Habit is discussed at such length by Dewey because ethics is concerned primarily with how we shall conduct ourselves or what habits we shall have. Once ethics has told us how we ought to behave it has completed its function.

Why do this act if I feel like doing something else? Any moral question may reduce itself to this question if we so choose. But in an empirical sense the answer is simple. The authority is that of life. Why employ language, cultivate literature, acquire and develop science, sustain industry and submit to the refinements of art? To ask these questions is equivalent to asking: Why live? And the only answer is that if one is going to live one must live a life of which these things form the substance. The only question having sense is *how* we are going to use and be used by these things, not whether we are going to use them. Reason, moral principles, cannot in any case be shoved behind these affairs, for reason and morality grow out of them. But they have grown into them as well as out of them. They are there as part of them. No one can escape them if he wants to. He cannot escape the problem of *how* to engage in life, since in any case he must engage in it some way or other—or else quit and get out (*Human Nature*, p. 81).

Habits, of course, are acquired. They are, therefore, secondary in time to our native impulses which are part of our original endowment at birth. Dewey uses the generic term "impulse" to describe what are sometimes referred to as instincts or needs or drives. Although impulses are primary in time, the impulse is originally without meaning. It is a blind, unconscious action. The meaning of impulses is acquired through the development of habits.

A child instinctively puts things in his mouth. But this impulse is without meaning. He puts anything in his mouth. He develops habits as he gets older and learns that food put in his mouth is valuable, whereas many other things are not. Some impulses never develop habits. What selects the impulses and determines the habits an individual will have is his environment. Or, since the meaning of the impulse is found in the habit through which it expresses itself, the meaning of the impulse is a function of the environment.

It is obvious, then, that impulses are highly plastic and

flexible in terms of the ways in which they may be expressed. The same impulse may give rise to many different ways of behaving in different environments.

Fear may become abject cowardice, prudent caution, reverence for superiors or respect for equals; an agency for credulous swallowing of absurd superstitions or for wary scepticism. A man may be chiefly afraid of the spirits of his ancestors, of officials, of arousing the disapproval of his associates, of being deceived, of fresh air, or of Bolshevism. The actual outcome depends upon how the impulse of fear is interwoven with other impulses. This depends in turn upon the outlets and inhibitions supplied by the social environment (*Human Nature*, p. 95).

Impulses are usually exerted within the circle of customary habits. When the impulse does not find fulfillment because changed environmental conditions render the habit inoperative, or when a conflict of habits occurs, then the impulse is freed from its bondage to habit. It is released to find a new habit within which it may act and which will allow it to fulfill itself without conflict.

Life is an onward flow of active participation. When activity is frustrated, this onward flow is dammed up, it is pent in, its immediate drive is to burst the bonds that hold it and to move on to its object. Mediated impulse comes about when thought intervenes and seeks a way of activity which removes the obstacle—or, if the obstacle is a competing impulse, combines and unifies the two impulses and focuses their energies upon some different object which can satisfy them both. If no such object can be discovered, the impulse may be dammed up until it explodes violently. In the case of an individual this may mean insanity; in the case of a nation, social revolution.

Thus, for Dewey, "Impulses are the pivots upon which the re-organization of activities turn, they are agencies of deviation, for giving new directions to old habits and changing their quality" (*Human Nature*, p. 93). The situation may be stated as follows: There are certain human impulses; under a specific social environment they take on a certain form; we cannot eradicate the impulse, but we can alter the form it takes by changing the social environment.

We may refer here to certain psychological terminology which Dewey mentions in passing (*Human Nature*, pp. 156–57). The psychologists sometimes portray the situation by saying that every impulse produces a certain quantity of psychic energy. This energy must be discharged in activity sooner or later. If a normal channel is available for attaining its object, the energy is used in that channel and no difficulties ensue. If the impulse is blocked from attaining its goal directly, the frustration may divert the energy into two other channels. The energy may be degraded, that is, it may be worked off in activities society does not approve of, or it may be sublimated, it may be worked off in socially acceptable channels. The stock example is the energy of the sex impulse in unmarried persons. A young man, finding there are no socially accepted channels for sex activity for him, may either work off the energy in activities described as juvenile delinquencies, or he may sublimate it by writing a love poem. The latter activity is socially approved, the former is not.

The function of intelligence is to find ways of altering the social environment so that impulses may either work themselves out directly or may find some sublimate activities in which they may engage.

Blocked impulses pose a problem. The function of thought is to solve problems. The blocked impulse may act immediately upon the object which frustrates it. Such action is blind, irrational action. Or intelligence may prevent the impulse from acting immediately. It may strive for what Dewey calls "the mediation of impulse" (*Human Nature*, p. 197). The mediation of impulse means to keep the impulse from being immediate—to mediate it by other factors—to delay the immediate action and eventually, probably, not to act upon the same object the impulse was toward, but to act indirectly upon some other objects and through their mediation eventually to satisfy the impulse.

We act by habit until habit is blocked. Then thought is called upon to find a way of resolving the frustration. "Thought is born as the twin of impulse in every moment of impeded habit" (*Human Nature*, p. 171). It is in the use of intelligence to free impulse that Dewey finds the function of ethical activity. "The moral correlate of liberated impulse is not immediate activity, but reflection upon the way in which to use impulse to renew disposition and reorganize habit" (*Human Nature*, p. 170).

In pursuing this activity we are undertaking what Dewey has called "the construction of the good." We turn now to an examination of what the good is for Dewey and how we construct it.

If we inquire of Dewey as to what the ethical goal is, we are told that:

The process of growth, of improvement and progress, rather than the static outcome and result, becomes the significant thing. . . . The end is no longer a terminus or limit to be reached. It is the active process of transforming the existent situation. Not perfection as a final goal, but the ever-enduring process of perfecting, maturing, refining is the aim in living. . . . Growth itself is the only moral "end" (*Reconstruction*, p. 177).

To many a reader the doctrine that growth is the only moral end will seem queer indeed. One tends to think of growth as growing toward something, and then tends to evaluate the growth in terms of the value of that toward which it is growing. If we inquire of Dewey as to the end or goal of this growing process, we are told that it has "as its aim at every stage an added capacity for growth" (*Democracy and Education*, p. 63).

At this point one begins to wonder why this continuous harping on growth and what the value of growth as such may be anyway. To understand what Dewey has in mind here it is necessary to recall that he is an ethical naturalist. Which is to say that so far as he is to find values, he must find them in the natural realm, not in the supernatural. Hence he is willing to use the notion of human happiness as the goal of human endeavor. "Moral good, like every good, consists in a satisfaction of the forces of human nature, in welfare, happiness" (*Human Nature*, p. 211). But this does not solve the question, for in what does human happiness consist? A human being is a living being, and in common with all living things his most characteristic trait is that of being alive. Hence he finds his happiness in the exercise of this, his most characteristic function. Not life in the static sense but living in the dynamic sense is the source of human happiness. But again we need to ask what living is in its fullest sense. Dewey's answer is that "Life means growth" (*Democracy and Education*, p. 61). Hence, one who is growing is living life to its fullest. Of course, it is necessary to qualify this statement somewhat. Not all growth is equally valuable. One who grows into a vicious hoodlum is growing. Or one who grows into a mere animal existence is growing. The criterion that distinguishes desirable growth from undesirable is that the former is a type of growth that makes further growth possible, whereas the latter inhibits further growth. In more prosaic terminology, that life is best which consists in living in such a way as to make fuller living possible in the future.

A term which Dewey is fond of using and which epitomizes desirable growth is the term "reconstruction." To see what is involved here it is necessary to digress long enough to see what it is that needs to be reconstructed. Dewey tells us that "living has its own intrinsic quality" (*Democracy and Education*, p. 61). It is this quality of living that needs to be continuously reconstructed. What is this quality? Obviously growth, but growth, like all qualities, cannot be described; it can only be defined by denotation. We can indicate it best by pointing to the period in our lives when, for most of us, growth is most prominent; namely, our childhood. In fact, Dewey thinks that it is because we are living most intensely then, that is, growing most fully, that we tend to idealize childhood. "For with all its extravagancies and uncertainties, its effusions and reticences, it remains a standing proof of a life wherein growth is normal not an anomaly, activity a delight not a task, and where habit-forming is an expansion of power not its shrinkage" (*Human Nature*, p. 99).

This does not imply that we should remain little children all our lives, for every stage of living has its values. But as an instance of the process of growth and of a kind of growth which means the acquisition of habits—such as the arts of communication—which make further growth possible, childhood stands as an eminent example. However, "It is the chief business of life at every point to make living thus contribute to an enrichment of its own perceptible meaning" (*Democracy and Education*, p. 89). That is, it is the business of life to reorganize itself continuously, to reconstruct the quality of experience so as to free our energies for further expansion. In order to develop this concept more fully, it may be worthwhile to restate it in terms of the analysis of habits and impulses set forth in the previous section.

It is generally held that when we think about an ethical problem we are trying to call to mind some object that will satisfy a need. But, if Dewey's analysis of the ethical difficulty is correct, what we are seeking is not an object. We are dealing with a blocked impulse and the impulse is seeking a

way to act, so that ethical thought is concerned with finding
a channel in which the impulse may be released.

We want things that are incompatible with one another; therefore
we have to make a choice of what we *really* want, of the course
of action, that is, which most fully releases activities. . . . The
moment arrives when imagination pictures an objective consequence of action which supplies an adequate stimulus and releases
definitive action. All deliberation is a search for a *way* to act, not
for a final terminus. Its office is to facilitate stimulation (*Human
Nature*, p. 193).

Thus ethics is concerned with finding ways to act; activity
becomes the ethical goal. But the ethical goal is not any
activity at all, but creative activity, or growth. Creative activity is not simply retrospective, it does not simply look to
the past, to the fulfillment of the blocked impulse; it also looks
to the future, it is activity that will provide release for further
impulse as life flows on. The activity not only fulfills the impulse which motivated it, but it has a plus value in that it
sets the stage for the fulfillment of future impulses.

Activity is creative in so far as it moves to its own enrichment as
activity, that is bringing along with itself a release of further
activities. Scientific inquiry, artistic production, social companion-
ship possess this trait to a marked degree; some amount of it is a
normal accompaniment of all successfully coordinated action.
While from the standpoint of what precedes it is a fulfilment, it
is a liberative expansion with respect to what comes after (*Human
Nature*, p. 143).

Thus the activity of a worker operating a machine on an
assembly line is not creative. The task opens up no new vistas
of activity—it is a dead end. Pulling a lever punches out a
piece of metal, pulling the lever again accomplishes the same
end—and punching the metal *is* the end. For the creative
artist, painting a picture is an activity which is its own fulfill-

ment, but it also opens the door to new activities and their fulfillments—most specifically, future visual experiences of the picture and the satisfaction of the impulses that lead one to look at pictures.

It is reported that the publisher of a famous British newspaper was concerned over the number of typographical errors that occurred in his paper. The activity his employees were engaged in was mechanical, they did not see beyond their tasks; they did not envision someone reading the paper with interest and desire for information and being annoyed and baffled by printing errors. Accordingly he announced to his employees that before any papers were printed for general distribution, a special run would be made on quality paper and delivered to the palace to be read by the royal family. Typographical errors practically disappeared in the paper, because the workers now saw their tasks as something more than a mechanical routine; they saw beyond the immediate operation to a reader who would enjoy the paper and whose enjoyment was of concern to them; they were no longer merely doing a job, they were creating a newspaper. "If men understand what they are about, if they see the whole process of which their special work is a necessary part, and if they have concern, care, for the whole, then the mechanizing effect is counteracted. But when a man is only the tender of a machine, he can have no insight and no affection; creative activity is out of the question" (*Human Nature*, p. 144).

To operate mechanically, that is, solely on habit, is to operate without thinking. Thought only occurs when habit is disturbed. So the individual who is said to be doing something solely by habit without thinking of what he is about, is said to be doing it absent-mindedly; his mind is absent, it is woolgathering elsewhere. In spite of this fact, the moral ideal has always been a man who has perfect moral habits. Having perfect habits, i.e., habits adequate to every occasion, he would have no need for thinking and his life would be a mechanical round of literally pure thoughtlessness. Dewey points out that such a concept has as a matter of fact been offered as the ideal life in the case of Aristotle's God who has naught to do but to contemplate his own perfection, in the Indian concept of Nirvana, and in the way most Christians interpret heaven.

If, on the other hand, the essential nature of goodness consists in the activity that overcomes difficulties and opens up new prospects of activity, in short, if goodness consists in dynamic growth of personality to make for an ever richer and more varied life, the traditional static conception can hardly be held to represent moral perfection or to embody an ideal that men ought to strive for.

Dewey describes his version of the ethical goal as follows:

There is seen to be but one issue involved in all reflection upon conduct: The rectifying of present troubles, the harmonizing of present incompatibilities by projecting a course of action which gathers into itself the meaning of them all. . . . Good consists in the meaning [significance] that is experienced to belong to an activity when conflict and entanglement of various incompatible impulses and habits terminate in a unified, orderly release in action (*Human Nature,* p. 210).

Dewey's view is not a form of utilitarianism. The good does not consist in calculating *future* goods and ills: "good, happiness, is found in the present meaning of activity" (*Human Nature,* p. 212). This meaning depends upon "the proportion, order and freedom introduced into it by thought as it discovers objects which release and unify otherwise contending elements" (*Human Nature,* p. 212).

Thus the activity of growth is not a good simply as a means to some end. The activity is the end—but this is not true of any blind, brute activity whatever. Happiness is found in released and informed activity, released in that it removes a frustration of the past, and informed in that it is connected by intelligence with future activities, with other human beings, and with other parts of nature. So that instead of the present being a means to future good, the significance which the future gives to the present makes the future a means to present good (*Human Nature,* p. 266).

It is that activity which is pregnant with meaning and future significance that is moral activity. "Morals means growth of conduct in meaning" (*Human Nature,* p. 280). For Dewey the function of ethics is literally to find the meaning of life, or, more accurately, to give life meaning, or significance, and to provide for continual growth in that meaning. A life has meaning to the degree that there is "a widening and deepening of perceptions" (*Human Nature,* p. 292). "Good is always found in a present growth of significance in activity. . . . An activity has meaning in the degree in which it establishes and acknowledges variety and intimacy of connections" (*Human Nature,* p. 292).

To be meaningful is to mean, to intend, to refer to something else. So life has no one meaning, it has many meanings. The more connections and relations an activity has, the more meaningful is the life which the activity constitutes. There are infinite connections of any life with its environment; the ethical ideal—the meaningful life—consists in activity that provides a growing awareness of these relations.

Infinite relationships of man with his fellows and with nature already exist. The ideal means . . . a sense of these encompassing continuities with their infinite reach. This meaning even now attaches to present activities because they are set in a whole to which they belong and which belongs to them. Even in the midst of conflict, struggle and defeat a consciousness is possible of the enduring and comprehending whole (*Human Nature,* p. 330).

The type of growth which promotes a further awareness of these relationships provides for further growth, and thus satisfies the search for an ethical goal. It is a kind of growth which leads to new insights and new orientations, to a multiplication of sensed distinctions and sensed connections. It provides for a richer life, a life of greater significance, of increased meanings, and, in addition, provides for a reorganization and reconstruction of the quality of experience so as to free our energies for wider and deeper experiences.

Whether what Dewey thus describes is what we mean by happiness and by the good is a question which each must decide for himself. It does seem as though those moments in our lives in which we find the deepest satisfaction, when we say to ourselves "Life is good," are moments in which the significance of the present moment lies in its presenting a form of activity which solves a conflict of the past and opens up new vistas for the future. The doctor who discovers a new medical treatment, the artist who discovers a new form of expression, the politician who reconciles a schism in his party, the teacher who sees a class discover a new vision, or the mother who helps a child over one of life's rough spots—all experience the quality which Dewey is describing. The more connections with others that these moments make, the more expansive they are in the associations they include, then the richer they are, and the more meaningful is the life of which they are a part.

Dewey's approach culminates in that sense of community found in all of the pragmatists:

Within the flickering, inconsequential acts of separate selves dwells a sense of the whole which claims and dignifies them. In its presence we put off mortality and live in the universal. The life of the community in which we live and have our being is the fit symbol of this relationship. The acts in which we express our perception of the ties which bind us to others are its only rites and ceremonies (*Human Nature*, pp. 331–32).

THE CONSTRUCTION OF THE GOOD

The moral end is the object of ethical knowledge, and like the object of all knowledge is a reconstruction of experience in a way that resolves conflict. To discover this resolution demands inquiry and activity and the construction of a way of acting that will be successful as a resolution. One cannot tell at the beginning of any inquiry what the end result will be, for the end is a construct out of the process of inquiry. Accordingly Dewey does not know what the specific objects of ethical conduct ought to be any better than anyone else. We are all engaged in constructing them as we think and plan and execute plans for greater human happiness.

It is also the case that these constructs will not be the same for all persons. Every ethical situation is different; no one precept or goal will cover all persons or all situations.

If we still wish to make our peace with the past, and to sum up the plural and changing goods of life in a single word, doubtless the term happiness is the one most apt. But we should again exchange free morals for sterile metaphysics, if we imagine that "happiness" is any less unique than the individuals who experience it; any less complex than the constitution of their capacities, or any less variable than the objects upon which their capacities are directed (*Influence of Darwin*, p. 70).

We should also engage in sterile metaphysics if we sought to "find" the end, rather than to construct it. Obviously the ways of acting available in the world as we have it are not adequate to the resolution of the basic conflicts that face us. We need to construct new resolutions. "Thinking has to operate creatively to form new ends" (*Ethics*, p. 198).

To understand how Dewey thinks that we must go about it to construct new ends, we must first examine a distinction usually made in philosophy between what are called factual judgments and value judgments. A factual judgment is a judgment that something is the case; a value judgment is one that something ought to be the case. It is a factual judgment that men do fight wars, that some neckties are red, or that that chair has four legs. It is a value judgment that men ought not to fight wars, neckties ought to be orange, or that that chair ought to have three legs.

Factual judgments are taken to constitute the subject matter of science; value judgments the subject matter of ethics and aesthetics. It has long been a question in philosophy as to the proper relation between these two kinds of judgments. The ancient Greeks distinguished between the two and took the position that factual questions were to be answered in terms of value judgments. When Aristotle wanted to know what orbits the planets followed, he began by inquiring as to what orbit is the best for a planet, i.e., what orbit ought it to follow. Since on the Greek view a circle was the noblest of all geometric figures and since the planets were heavenly bodies and ought to follow the best paths, he concluded that planets therefore must move in circles. The universe was constructed by the best beings in accord with the highest moral and aesthetic standards, so that if one knew what truly ought to be the case, he would *ipso facto* know what was the case. And furthermore he would know without looking. It was upon this hidden premise, that truth is beauty, that philosophy as a branch of knowledge was founded.

Modern science began when scientists first made a clear distinction between value judgments and factual judgments, and insisted that a factual question could only be answered in factual terms. This led to the great schism between religion and science. Science dealt with factual matters and religion with value matters, and never the twain shall meet. In the Middle Ages this was called the doctrine of the twofold truth.

Dewey in his attempt to re-fuse the factual and value features of the universe does not make the mistake the ancients made. He does not hold that factual judgments are reducible to value judgments. But he does believe that the bifurcation of human experience, made by science, into value and factual issues is not an ultimate division. It is only an expediency, a methodology which, from the standpoint of science, promotes investigation. In reconciling these two facets of experience he does not hold with the ancients that factual judgments are reducible to value judgments, but rather that the converse is the case. The ultimate meaning and function of a value judgment must be expressible in terms of judgments about facts.

We have seen the distinction that Dewey makes between experience and knowledge. He makes a similar distinction in ethics between the desired and desirable, the valued and valuable, the satisfying and the satisfactory. To say that something is liked, desired, valued, or satisfying is, on his view, to make a factual statement. This is a report of an existing fact. To say that what is enjoyed is enjoyable, or what is desired is desirable, or what is satisfying is satisfactory is to make a value judgment. To say that x is enjoyed is to record a fact but not a value. Someone does enjoy x. To say x is enjoyable is to say x ought to be enjoyed; it is to make a value judgment, a judgment as to the importance of bringing x into existence or of keeping it in existence.

For most philosophers x is enjoyed would be a value statement. Dewey says not; it is a fact. What is enjoyed may not be enjoyable. It may be that arsenic tastes good, i.e., is enjoyed by human beings, but this would not mean that arsenic was enjoyable, that eating arsenic was an activity in which human beings ought to engage. A liking is not a value any more than an experience is knowledge. Liked, enjoyed, etc., state facts about experiences; they are merely factual judgments. To make value judgments about what is liked you must obtain further information. How are these objects which are liked and enjoyed created, how are they controlled, what are their consequences? When these facts are established, then one may make a value judgment.

Dewey uses as an illustration Charles Lamb's story of the discovery of roast pig. The first man to taste roast pig liked it. This was a fact. Whether he ought to set up eating roast pig as a regular end of conduct was, however, a value question. It could only be established by further inquiry. Suppose that upon investigation factual statements of the following order were discovered: Roast pork may be easily obtained by raising pigs and roasting them over a fire; roast pork is easily digestible; pork contains elements necessary to human nutrition; pork contributes to the growth of the human body; etc. Having obtained factual statements of this sort, he could *then* make the value judgment, roast pork is valuable.

On this view value judgments are not separable from factual judgments but are reducible to them. To say pork is enjoyable means pork is easily obtainable, digestible, contributes to human growth, etc. So, far from ethics being separated from science, it can only progress as science progresses.

The "desirable," or the object which *should* be desired (valued), does not descend out of the a priori blue nor descend as an imperative from a moral Mount Sinai. . . . The "desirable" as distinct from the "desired" . . . points to the difference between the operation and consequences of unexamined impulses and those of desires and interests that are the product of investigation of conditions and consequences (*Valuation*, p. 32).

Traditional hedonism defined value in terms of enjoyments that happened anyhow. Dewey elects to define value in terms of enjoyments that are the result of intelligent inquiry. The latter enjoyments lead to the only practical judgment—the only judgment that has to do with practical action, in short, the only judgment that gives an idea of value that can serve to direct practical conduct.

The connecting of value judgments and factual judgments

brings all of scientific knowledge to bear on our efforts to resolve ethical problems. It not only brings scientific knowledge
but the scientific method to our aid. We experiment. When
we fail, we can profit from our failures in our next experiments.

It is not pretended that a moral theory based upon realities of
human nature and a study of the specific connections of these realities with those of physical science would do away with moral
struggle and defeat. . . . Such a morals would not automatically
solve moral problems nor resolve perplexities. But it would enable
us to state problems in such forms that action could be courage-
ously and intelligently directed to their solution. It would not as-
sure us against failure, but it would render failure a source of in-
struction. It would not protect us against the future emergence of
equally serious moral difficulties, but it would enable us to approach the always recurring troubles with a fund of growing
knowledge which would add significant values to our conduct even
when we overtly failed—as we should continue to do. Until the
integrity of morals with human nature and of both with the environment is recognized, we shall be deprived of the aid of past
experience to cope with the most acute and deep problems of life.
Accurate and extensive knowledge will continue to operate only
in dealing with purely technical problems. The intelligent acknowledgment of the continuity of nature, man and society will alone
secure a growth of morals which will be serious without being
fanatical, aspiring without sentimentality, adapted to reality without conventionality, sensible without taking the form of calculation
of profits, idealistic without being romantic (*Human Nature*, pp.
11–13).

In the light of this relationship between factual judgments
and value judgments, we set about it to construct ethical ends.
We may begin by asking ourselves what an end would be. If
the goal of ethical inquiry is the freeing of activity, an end
would be something which would succeed in doing this. Thus
when a man finds himself in a situation where activity is

frustrated, he constructs imaginatively, in the light of available factual information, some end which he believes will, if attained, solve his problem. Keeping this end in view he then proceeds to act. The end-in-view thus becomes a means to freeing present activity. Its significance lies in the fact that it does facilitate activity. Without an end-in-view we do not know what to do, we are frustrated, activity is inhibited. With the construction in imagination of an end, energies are released and life moves on. The significance and the value of an end is that it thus releases energies and provides for continuing activity. Which is to say that an end is a means to action. This paradoxical notion of an end is basic to Dewey's thought. "The aim is as definitely a *means* of action as is any other portion of activity" (*Democracy and Education*, p. 124). "In a strict sense an end-in-view is a *means* in present action; present action is not a means to a remote end. Men do not shoot because targets exist, but they set up targets in order that throwing and shooting may be more effective and significant" (*Human Nature*, p. 226).

The reverse of this is also the case—means become ends. For having once decided upon the end, we must act not on the end-in-view but we must take the means which is next to us and consider it as our end of immediate activity in order that it may successfully be a means. "Means and ends are two ways of regarding the same actuality" (*Human Nature*, p. 233).

But even when ends-in-view are attained, they are not fixed and final points at which activity ceases. Every end is a means to new and further activity. This follows from the fact that an end provides for a reorganization of energies that makes further growth possible.

A mariner does not sail towards the stars, but by noting the stars he is aided in conducting his present activity of sailing. A port or harbor is his objective, but only in the sense of *reaching* it not of taking possession of it. The harbor stands in his thought as a significant point at which his activity will need redirection. Activity will not cease when the port is attained, but merely the *present direction* of activity. The port is as truly the beginning of another mode of activity as it is the termination of the present one (*Human Nature*, p. 226).

This fusion of means and ends forms what Dewey calls the means-end continuum. What life is made of is a continuous series of activities. We may, for certain purposes, cut a point in the series and call it an end as long as we realize that it is not a dead end but part of a continuing series and seen from a wider perspective is a means to something else. But what looks to be a means in a wider perspective will be an end on a short range view.

The fusing of means and ends is not meant to deny the value of either. Both are necessary. To concern oneself solely with means and to ignore ends is materialism; to concern oneself solely with ends and to ignore means is sentimentalism.

The construction of ends occurs when an activity is frustrated. It seeks to find an outlet by projecting in imagination a state of affairs which would, if present, remove the conflict. This state of affairs becomes an ideal to be striven for. The next problem is to discover how to construct it and to ascertain the consequences which will ensue if it is brought into existence. Inquiry, experimentation, investigation take place. When sufficient facts have been gathered to indicate how the ideal may be made a reality, to indicate that neither the process of creating it nor the consequences which follow from it will produce undesirable results, it is accepted as an ethical end, i.e., as a valuable object, and then acted upon. To discover the relationships by which we may go from where we are to where we wish to be, we must conduct scientific inquiry which will provide us with the cause-effect sequence through which we can realize the ideal. Thus ethics is intimately associated with science and cannot progress beyond it. "Every gain in natural science makes possible new aims" (*Human Nature,* p. 235). The construction of goods goes hand in hand with the results of inquiry.

All of this means that there are no fixed and final ethical ends. Scientific inquiry has no final and closed end which it is approaching. Inquiry is continuous growth in knowledge, and, as inquiry develops, new ethical ends and goals are discovered and may be constructed. But, after all, "A free man would rather take his chance in an open world than be guaranteed in a closed world" (*Human Nature,* p. 311).

10

Some Implications of Dewey's Naturalism

The relations between Dewey's ethical, educational, and social philosophies are so intimate that they may almost be said to be identical. Each is but a different facet of his central doctrine of the intrinsic worth of the fullest life for each individual. For purposes of exposition, it may be best to discuss first the relation between his ethical and social views and then the relation between his social and educational philosophies, concluding with a brief statement of his philosophy of religion.

SOCIAL PHILOSOPHY

That Dewey's ethics has social significance may be seen from his interpretation of right and wrong as deriving an important part of their meaning from social pressures.

Why, indeed, acknowledge the authority of Right? That many persons do not acknowledge it in fact, in action, and that all persons ignore it at times, is assumed by the argument. Just what is the significance of an alleged recognition of a supremacy which is continually denied in fact? How much would be lost if it were dropped out, and we were left face to face with actual facts? If a man lived alone in the world there might be some sense in the question "Why be moral?" were it not for one thing: No such question would then arise. As it is, we live in a world where other persons live too. Our acts affect them. They perceive these effects, and react upon us in consequence. Because they are living beings they make demands upon us for certain things from us. They approve and condemn—not in abstract theory but in what they do to us. The answer to the question "Why not put your hand in the fire?" is the answer of fact. If you do your hand will be burnt. The answer to the question why acknowledge the right is of the same sort. For Right is only an abstract name for the multitude of concrete demands in action which others impress upon us, and of which we are obliged, if we would live, to take some account. Its authority is the exigency of their demands, the efficacy of their insistencies. There may be good ground for the contention that in theory the idea of the right is subordinate to that of the good, being a statement of the course proper to attain good. But in fact it signifies the totality of social pressures exercised upon us to induce us to think and desire in certain ways. Hence the right can in fact become the road to the good only as the elements that compose this unremitting pressure are enlightened, only as social relationships become themselves reasonable (*Human Nature,* pp. 326–27).

The reader who is familiar with William James's essay "The Moral Philosopher and the Moral Life" will recognize the identity of Dewey's interpretation with the view put forth by James in the latter part of that essay.

But not only does Dewey's ethics have a social meaning; his social philosophy has an ethical meaning.

Government, business, art, religion, all social institutions have a meaning, a purpose. That purpose is to set free and to develop the capacities of human individuals without respect to race, sex, class or economic status. . . . Democracy has many meanings, but if it has moral meaning, it is found in resolving that the supreme test of all political institutions and industrial arrangements shall be the contribution they make to the all-around growth of every member of society (*Reconstruction,* p. 186).

The social meaning of Dewey's ethics and the ethical meaning of his social philosophy, when combined, give us the full meaning of democracy. "But if democracy has a moral and ideal meaning, it is that a social return be demanded from all and that opportunity for development of distinctive capacities be afforded all" (*Democracy and Education,* p. 142). A development of the implications of this statement results in the traditional doctrines of democracy.

The notion that a social return shall be demanded from all may be contrasted with the concept that a private return shall be demanded from all. The fullest growth of a personal life necessarily involves social contacts, for man is a gregarious animal. He does not live to himself alone, and he cannot do so if he wishes the fullest life. To satisfy his social impulses and to live a life of increasing significance, he must be part of a social community and participate in its ideals. But what is true for him is also true for others. He needs them, but they need him. There is thus a reciprocal relationship which calls for a social return from each of us.

The notion that opportunity for development of distinctive capacities be afforded all produces a negative and positive aspect. Negatively this notion involves what is called political democracy, or a classless political organization. The fullest growth of each individual "comes only when there is a responsible share on the part of each person, in proportion to capacity, in shaping the aims and policies of the social groups to which he belongs" (*Reconstruction,* p. 209). This participation in shaping group decisions is limited to specified groups in all forms of political organization except the democratic. Only in a democracy do we find a classless political organization in which all participate.

The classlessness of social democracy is implied in a similar fashion. If an individual is to be free to grow in those directions which his native capacities and desires indicate, there must be no class barriers which render movement from one occupation to another impossible. Further, since growth means an increased contact and communication with others, there must be no class barriers to the free expansion of experience. From the standpoint of the individual, democracy means a continuum such that he can move from any point on the social pattern to any other point without hindrance.

Positively, the notion of the opportunity for the fullest development of the capacities of all, involves the concept of freedom. Not freedom in the negative sense of no hindrance being offered, but freedom in the positive sense of a support and assistance offered to activity by intelligence. As Dewey sees it, science no longer offers us the closed world of Newtonian physics—where everything is fixed once and for all. The world of modern science is an open world—a world that is open at both ends.

Instead of a closed universe, science now presents us with one infinite in space and time, having no limits here or there, at this end, so to speak, or at that, and as infinitely complex in internal structure as it is infinite in extent. Hence, it is also an open world, an infinitely variegated one, a world which in the old sense can hardly be called a universe at all; so multiplex and far-reaching that it cannot be summed up and grasped in any one formula (*Reconstruction*, pp. 60–61).

Uncertainty becomes, then, a real fact about the world. "Upon an empirical view, uncertainty, doubt, hesitation, contingency and novelty, genuine change . . . are facts" (*Human Nature*, p. 310). Man finds himself in a world that is precarious and uncertain; problems arise because situations are indeterminate. A man who finds himself in a precarious situation may have all the barriers removed from his action, all the negative freedoms, and still not be free to act because he does not know what to do. Ignorance is the real barrier to solving problems freely. A physician who has a patient dying of some unknown disease is not free to cure him. Action is stopped, and the restraint is ignorance. He cannot choose among various alternative treatments and act upon the one that is best. What limits his thought and action is ignorance; what would free it and suggest alternatives upon which action might proceed would be knowledge. "A physician or engineer is free in his thought and action in the degree in which he knows what he deals with" (*Human Nature,* p. 303). It is intelligence that gives us "all the control of future possibilities which is open to us. And this control is the crux of freedom. Without it, we are pushed from behind. With it we walk in the light" (*Human Nature,* p. 311).

Just as Dewey's ethics was naturalistic, so also is his social philosophy. His basic belief is that human beings working cooperatively can, by their own intelligence, solve their problems. "The foundation of democracy is faith in the capacities of human nature; faith in human intelligence and in the power of pooled and cooperative experience. It is not the belief that these things are complete but that, if given a show, they will grow and be able to generate progressively the knowledge and wisdom needed to guide collective action" (*Problems of Men,* p. 59).

Individual intelligence functioning in a social context thus becomes for Dewey the key to the good life. Since the function of education is to provide citizens who can promote the fuller development of society, education must concern itself with developing citizens with intelligence that will function in a social context. We turn now to an examination of this process.

EDUCATIONAL PHILOSOPHY

John Dewey is perhaps most widely known for his educational philosophy. As the propounder of what came to be called progressive education or the activity curriculum, Dewey has been more highly praised and more sincerely damned than any educationist in history. It is one of the quirks of fate that this movement which has so often been condemned as radical had its inception in Dewey's efforts to develop an educational experience analogous to what he had found on the farms of Vermont as a boy.

Dewey seems to have begun developing his own philosophy of education when he began giving thought to the difference between the eager interest with which children learned from activities out of school and the lack of interest displayed in the school learning experience. He came to the conclusion that the industrial revolution had produced changes in our way of life that had basic implications for our educational system, but that we had not been aware of these implications. The factory system had replaced the household and neighborhood economy wherein household goods, clothing, building materials, food, etc., were fashioned in the home or in shops in the immediate neighborhood. In this economy children learned what things were, by participating in the activity which produced them, and by sharing in the beneficial consequences of the activities. "The children, as they gained in strength and capacity, were gradually initiated into the mysteries of the several processes. It was a matter of immediate and personal concern, even to the point of actual participation" (*School and Society*, p. 21).

Children did not learn that light was something that came by pressing a button; they followed the whole process of light-making from the killing of the animal and the trying of the fat to the making of wicks and the dipping of candles. Dewey feels that "No training of sense-organs in school, introduced for the sake of training, can begin to compete with the alertness and fulness of sense-life that comes through daily intimacy and interest in familiar occupations" (*School and Society*, pp. 24–25).

It was the effort to move this type of activity which had once gone on on the farm and in the home into the school that was one motivating force in the development of the new education. The other force was Dewey's theory as to what mind, or intelligence, was. The theory then common was that the individual person consisted of two things, mind and body. The purpose of education was to train the mind. Dewey says:

It would be impossible to state adequately the evil results which have flowed from this dualism of mind and body, much less to exaggerate them. Some of the more striking effects may, however, be enumerated. (a) In part, bodily activity becomes an intruder. Having nothing, so it is thought, to do with mental activity, it becomes a distraction, an evil to be contended with. For the pupil has a body, and brings it to school along with his mind. And the body is, of necessity, a well-spring of energy; it has to do something. But its activities, not being utilized in occupation with things which yield significant results, have to be frowned upon. They lead the pupil away from the lesson with which his "mind" ought to be occupied; they are sources of mischief. The chief source of the "problem of discipline" in schools is that the teacher has often to spend the larger part of the time in suppressing the bodily activities which take the mind away from its material. A premium is put on physical quietude; on silence, on rigid uniformity of posture and movement; upon a machine-like simulation of the attitudes of intelligent interest. The teacher's business is to hold the pupils up to these requirements and to punish the inevitable deviations which occur (*Democracy and Education*, p. 164).

In contrast to this view of mental activity as something separated from bodily activity, we have Dewey's view of mind, or intelligence, as active inquiry into the causes and consequences of things. "Mind is not a name for something complete in itself; it is a name for a course of action in so far as that is intelligently directed; in so far, that is to say, as aims, ends enter into it, with selection of means to further the attainment of aims" (*Democracy and Education*, p. 155).

Combine these two doctrines and you have the view that the most valuable and effective learning takes place when the child follows the development of a process from its initial problematic conditions to its final resolution, through actively participating in the situation by personal inquiry and investigation.

Add to this the fact that children are being educated to participate in community life. Traditional school procedures ignored this fact. They sought to educate children for social life in an unsocial atmosphere. A society is a group of people consciously working together to attain a set of common aims. This cooperative activity integrates the group and gives it a sense of sympathetic communion and shared participation. The school should be so organized as to develop this social spirit. "The school itself shall be made a genuine form of active community life, instead of a place set apart in which to learn lessons" (*School and Society*, p. 27).

When the native curiosity and intelligence of children are exercised on activities in this fashion, the change is from passive recipiency to active participation. Rather than the individual absorption of a quantity of facts, there is group concern with the quality of work. This type of program is not oriented toward indulging the child's every whim. But an effort is made to take matters which interest him rather than the teacher, to supply him with the factual material necessary to come to a solution of the problems posed for him by his interests, and to encourage him to work them out—through group action where desirable—in such a way that the solutions are his solutions and the experience of learning how to think problems through and work them out is his experience.

For the child simply to desire to cook an egg, and accordingly drop it in water for three minutes, and take it out when he is told is not educative. But for the child to realize his own impulse by recognizing the facts, materials and conditions involved, and then to regulate his impulse through that recognition is educative. This is the difference, upon which I wish to insist, between exciting or indulging an interest and realizing it through direction (*School and Society*, p. 57).

When these activities were carried on in the home or on the farm, their primary orientation was economic; the educational benefits were only secondary. In the school situation, of course, quite the reverse is the case. Every effort is made to make every activity a source of insight into nature and into scientific methods of control and use. These activities become extended into the past through tracing them back historically, and into the present through discovering their geographical spread. From any task the child can proceed to infinite connections with man and his development. One of the functions of education is to see that the child does this.

Permeating a classroom operating in this way is a discipline and organization which will not be recognized by the casual visitor because of its difference from the atmosphere of a traditional classroom.

Within this organization is found the principle of school discipline or order. Of course, order is simply a thing which is relative to an end. If you have the end in view of forty or fifty children learning certain set lessons, to be recited to a teacher, your discipline must be devoted to securing that result. But if the end in view is the development of a spirit of social cooperation and community life, discipline must grow out of and be relative to this. There is little order of one sort where things are in process of construction; there is a certain disorder in any busy workshop; there is not silence; persons are not engaged in maintaining certain fixed physical postures; their arms are not folded; they are not holding their books thus and so. They are doing a variety of things, and there is the confusion, the bustle, that results from activity. But out of occupation, out of doing things that are to produce results, and out of doing these in a social and cooperative way, there is born a discipline of its own kind and type. Our whole conception of school discipline changes when we get this point of view (*School and Society,* p. 30).

This type of approach to education satisfies Dewey's definition of education as "that reconstruction or reorganization of experience which adds to the meaning of experience, and which increases ability to direct the course of subsequent experience" (*Democracy and Education,* p. 89). It also fulfills the role required of education by his social philosophy: the development of citizens who can promote the fuller growth of society through the medium of individual intelligence functioning in a social context.

RELIGIOUS VIEWS

The anathema in which Dewey's views on education have been held in many circles is only surpassed by the vehemence of the attacks on his naturalistic philosophy by adherents of organized religions. This is in spite of the fact that Dewey is—in his own sense of the term—a deeply religious individual. However, his religious views will not fit the mold of any traditional religion. He is, in that sense, a reformer and a prophet.

For many years Dewey wrote very little on religion directly. His views could be inferred from passages in some of his writings, but little was said explicitly on the subject. In 1930 he explained his reticence as follows:

While the conflict of traditional religious beliefs with opinions that I could myself honestly entertain was the source of a trying personal crisis, it did not at any time constitute a leading philosophical problem. This might look as if the two things were kept apart; in reality it was due to a feeling that any genuinely sound religious experience could and should adapt itself to whatever beliefs one found oneself intellectually entitled to hold—a half unconscious sense at first, but one which ensuing years have deepened into a fundamental conviction. In consequence, while I have, I hope, a

due degree of personal sympathy with individuals who are under-
going the throes of a personal change of attitude, I have not been
able to attach much importance to religion as a philosophic problem; for the effect of that attachment seems to be in the end a
subornation of candid philosophic thinking to the alleged but
factitious needs of some special set of convictions. I have enough
faith in the depth of the religious tendencies of men to believe
that they will adapt themselves to any required intellectual change,
and that it is futile (and likely to be dishonest) to forecast prema-
turely just what forms the religious interest will take as a final consequence of the great intellectual transformation that is going on.
As I have been frequently criticized for undue reticence about the
problems of religion, I insert this explanation: it seems to me that
the great solicitude of many persons, professing belief in the universality of the need for religion, about the present and future of
religion proves that in fact they are moved more by partisan interest in a particular religion than by interest in religious experience.[1]

In 1934 Dewey was invited to Yale University to give the
Terry Foundation Lectures on Religion in the Light of Science
and Philosophy. These lectures later appeared in book form
under the title A Common Faith. Here Dewey says what he
can about religion.

In these lectures Dewey distinguishes religion as a noun
from religious as an adjective. The former refers to an organized and institutionalized body of creeds and ceremonies.
The latter has, for Dewey, no such reference. It does not,
however, refer to what is sometimes called a "religious experience" of the sort that mystics and others have, which attests
to the existence of a supernatural order. Religiousness is an
aspect of an experience which is itself of something else. An
analogy may help. One does not have an experience of beauty;
he experiences something which has among its properties
beauty. But the experience is not of beauty, but of some ob-

---

[1] *Contemporary American Philosophy* (New York: Macmillan, 1930),
II, 19–20.

ject. The beauty is an effect of the experience. So the religious quality of experience is not something in itself, but is rather an effect of certain experiences. This effect is a better adjustment to life and all that life means. Dewey describes it in these words:

But there are also changes in ourselves in relation to the world in which we live that are more inclusive and deep seated. They relate not to this and that want in relation to this and that condition of our surroundings, but pertain to our being in its entirety. Because of their scope, this modification of ourselves is enduring. It lasts through any amount of vicissitude of circumstances, internal and external. There is a composing and harmonizing of the various elements of our being such that, in spite of changes in the special conditions that surround us, these conditions are also arranged, settled, in relation to us (*Common Faith,* p. 16).

This experience is not oriented toward any supernatural deity. It need only mean an awareness of a harmonizing and integrating of one's self with the larger universe of which he is a part. Neither is the attainment of it a conscious matter of volition. It comes about unconsciously, and some day as we have an experience having nothing in particular to do with it, we suddenly become aware of it. Instead of saying that it is religion that has this quality, Dewey prefers to say that anything that has this quality is religious. This takes the religious out of the hands of institutionalized religion and frees it for entrance into the life of every individual in the course of his daily activities.

This harmonizing and integrating of the self with the universe is not completely attained by anyone. It is an ideal that men desire and for which they strive. Religious experience occurs with the realization that one has come closer to the ideal.

Such a description of religion offers no fixed creed or doctrines that are inviolable and hence serve as barriers to further religious experience, nor is religion taken out of the everyday life of natural man and thrust into a supernatural realm open only to the few.

So far as Dewey expresses a faith in something, it is a faith in the abilities of human intelligence operating to solve the mysteries of the universe and to provide man with ideals which may be accepted as goals which will result in the integration and harmonizing of the self with the universe. The result of this kind of faith is "the unification of the self through allegiance to inclusive ideal ends, which imagination presents to us and to which the human will responds as worthy of controlling our desires and choices" (*Common Faith*, p. 33).

For Dewey the term "God" denotes, not a living being, but the unity of all these ideal ends which we accept as working values and which thus become the forces which motivate our actions. As man progresses, these ideals will change and become richer and more significant. As they change, so man's conception of God—or the divine, as Dewey also calls it—in life will change. These ideals are not presented as something already realized in another realm, nor are they separated from man's own experience and growth; they come out of man's problems and his life, and they become ideal possibilities which he can make into realities through the application of human intelligence and endeavor. Thus the term God becomes not an abstraction that is only ideal but represents an ideal that is significant in giving direction to concrete activities in the present.

Dewey presents the contrast between the traditional religious position and his own view as follows:

The extreme position on one side is that apart from relation to the supernatural, man is morally on a level with the brutes. The other position is that all significant ends and all securities for stability and peace have grown up in the matrix of human relations, and that the values given a supernatural locus are in fact products of an idealizing imagination that has laid hold of natural goods. There ensues a second contrast. On the one hand, it is held that relation to the supernatural is the only finally dependable source of motive power; that directly and indirectly it has animated every serious effort for the guidance and rectification of man's life on earth. The other possibility is that goods actually experienced in the concrete relations of family, neighborhood, citizenship, pursuit of art and sciences are what men actually depend upon for guidance and support, and that their reference to a supernatural and other-worldly locus has obscured their real nature and has weakened their force (*Common Faith*, pp. 70–71).

If the emotional drive and the sacrifice that men have put into traditional religions were transferred to a naturalistic religion based on a faith in the ability of human intelligence, Dewey believes that new and expanding perspectives would open up for the life of man.

CRITICISMS OF CONTEMPORARY SOCIETY

Dewey's views on social, educational, and religious problems are not simply an effort to suggest new and different approaches to these problems, but are based on features of contemporary society which seem to him unsatisfactory. On the social and political level he believes that our behavior suffers from a lack of planning. He suggests that the doctrine of rugged individualism, or *laissez faire*, belongs to an outmoded view of political and economic activity. This view was first advocated by Adam Smith, who argued that each individual needed only to take care of himself and to work for his own best interests without regard for others. Controlling the activities of each individual was "the invisible hand of God," which so ordered the efforts of each that by doing what was in his own best interests he necessarily did what was for the best interests of all.

An examination of the course of economic history under this

doctrine—and most recently the depression of the 1930s—tends to cast considerable doubt on its efficacy. If we give up the notion that there is an invisible hand controlling human behavior, the only alternative is a type of community consciousness that will develop its own plan to promote economic and political behavior that will work for the best interests of all. The alternative to economic and political anarchy is some type of planning, worked out by those involved and cooperatively executed by them. This calls for knowledge of economics and politics as sciences, and for the application of them to human affairs.

We have already seen some of Dewey's criticisms of education on the elementary level. He is equally critical of higher education. He uses the term "liberal education," but he defines it in his own way. He asks us to recall that a liberal education means an education for a free man. It is an education that is liberating, that provides for growth and expansion. At different times in human history, different types of education will succeed in doing this. Among the Greeks and Romans, education for a free man consisted of geometry, music, gymnastics, rhetoric, and philosophy. None of these was a practical art. The practical work was done by slaves, for whom quite a different kind of education was thought necessary.

During the Middle Ages a liberal education consisted of those subjects which would free a man from the narrow confines of his times. There was nothing for the average intelligent European to learn about his own day and age because practically nothing was known of the world he lived in. The only way he could get knowledge was by a study of the civilizations of Greece and Rome. Accordingly Greek and Latin and the philosophy necessary to understanding Greek and Roman writings were an essential part of a liberal education for him.

A liberal education for our own day cannot be established in terms of what was a liberal education in Greece and Rome

nor in the Middle Ages. To determine the content of a liberal
education today, we must ask ourselves what subjects give
the greatest promise of liberating a modern man. Dewey's
answer is the study of the scientific method. This does not
mean the development of technicians. It does not mean that
every student is to be a chemist or a physicist or a biologist.
But it does mean that the core and heart of a liberal education today will consist in coming to understand how to judge
and interpret the world and the people in it in a manner that
is controlled by careful examination and observation, coupled
with a respect for facts and an elimination of personal prejudice and bias. If around the core of social and natural sciences
we establish those other studies which also contribute to the
growth of the individual—the fine arts and the arts of communication—we come to a type of education which holds
more promise for liberating modern man than could be hoped
for from the return to the Middle Ages advocated by many in
our own day.

In contemporary religion, Dewey objects to the view that
God is all and man is nothing. The function of organized
religion is to save man. But it cannot save him unless he is
first lost. Accordingly its basic doctrine is that man is by
nature fallen, and he can only be raised by supernatural means.
This orients man toward devoting his energies to deserving
divine assistance rather than toward the development of
natural arts of control and security that will enable him to
improve his lot by his own efforts. Evils and catastrophes
which befall man are, on this view, God's will. They are
punishments from on high. On the contrary, Dewey holds
that they are the result of human ignorance of the behavior
of natural forces. The cure for them is not appeal for for-
giveness but an inquiry into causes, so that their occurrence
may be avoided in the future.

From this brief examination of Dewey's social, educational,

and religious philosophies, it is clear that he is something of an iconoclast. But his criticisms are not merely destructive. He has, as we have seen, positive suggestions in each of these areas outlining plans of action which he believes will lead to a fuller life for all men. Whether his views are sound can only be determined by their trial, for he is, after all, a pragmatist, and a philosophy that would not work in practice would be more unacceptable to a pragmatist than to anyone else.

11

Conclusion

We began our examination of pragmatism by asserting that it was essentially a theory of meaning. This is more true of the pragmatism of Peirce and James than it is of that of Dewey. On Peirce's view, pragmatism is the doctrine that the meaning of a sign may be determined by ascertaining the practical considerations that would be true of any object to which the sign is applicable. For James, pragmatism is the view that the meaning of our idea of an object may be stated by indicating the sensations we may expect from the object and the reactions we are to prepare toward it. Dewey, however, gives a more general definition of pragmatism, which includes the views of Peirce and James, but goes beyond them to give pragmatism a wider scope. Dewey defines pragmatism as the doctrine that reality possesses practical character.

This formulation suggests several important points. In the first place, it constitutes the pragmatic rejection of traditional speculative metaphysics. Traditional metaphysics concerns itself with the nature of reality, but little if any consideration is given to the relation of such speculation to practical affairs. Presumably people in the practical affairs of everyday life are dealing with reality in some of its major aspects. Hence, it would not seem unreasonable to expect as one test of any theory of reality that it connect with practical affairs. Philosophers have not traditionally submitted their theories to this test, largely because of the influence of the Greek philosophers, who developed the art of theorizing but who had little contact with practical affairs—these being matters for slaves to deal with—and who thus divorced theory from practice. Dewey's concern with avoiding this separation may be seen from the fact that he defines pragmatism also as the doctrine of the unity of theory and practice.

A second important point in Dewey's formulation is the making explicit what was only implicit in Peirce and James —that pragmatism is a theory about real objects, not simply about ideas of objects. Pragmatism is the theory that reality has practical character. Thus pragmatism is primarily a theory about reality, although as a method for clarifying ideas it is a theory about meanings, and what it says is that ideas possess practical character—deriving this character from the practical nature of the reality to which they refer—so that to explicate the meaning of an idea one need only state its consequences in practice.

A third point that may be seen in Dewey's definition is his theory of the meaning of ideas, or instrumentalism, the doctrine that ideas are intellectual instruments for directing our activities when we are dealing with reality. Or, in the traditional pragmatic terminology, an idea is a plan for action. To find out what action the idea is a plan for, you put it into practice and discover the consequences it has for practice.

In our examination of the philosophies of Peirce, James, and Dewey, we not only have seen something of what each means by pragmatism, but we have examined an application of the pragmatic theory of meaning to one concept basic to each. In Peirce we examined the concept of reality, in James the concept of truth, and in Dewey the concept of the good. We saw how each of these philosophers explicates an abstract conception by expressing it as a concrete relation of an ambulatory type.

Peirce developed his notion of reality from his conclusions about the function of inquiry. The function of inquiry is to fix beliefs that will provide a trustworthy guide for action. If our method is to do this, it must be based on something that will have these characteristics: 1) It must control our thinking; our thinking must not control it; 2) it must be publicly observable; 3) it must lead to a common opinion. The scientific method seeks to fix belief in terms of these three characteristics by proposing reality as that which will fix belief. Reality is defined in its practical character as that which will be the same in all human experience. Out of this is developed the concept of the continuum of inquiry—the community of investigators. Combining this concept with the notion of reality, we see that we have a method which is self-corrective but which will not give us absolute knowledge in any finite period of time. While we may come to know reality completely in the course of investigation, we can never be sure that we know it completely until all investigation is completed.

James's analysis of truth was developed from the traditional correspondence theory, according to which an idea is true if it corresponds to reality. He argued that truth in its practical character means the property of an idea that will lead us successfully from one point on the continuum of our experience to some other point through a successive series of experiences. Absolute truth, like absolute reality, is, on this view, an ideal limit toward which, our hope is, investigation will lead us.

Dewey's analysis of the good is in the naturalistic tradition but is not a form of hedonism. He criticizes the traditional desire-satisfaction theory by saying that desires and satisfactions grow out of needs and are not fundamental because we continually evaluate them in the light of their costs and consequences. The good is not defined in terms of desires and satisfactions that occur anyhow, but in terms of a harmony of satisfactions and desires that is the result of intelligent inquiry. Goods are not casual as in traditional hedonism, but causal by virtue of understanding their causes and consequences and making them secure through arts of control. Rather than the satisfaction of a desire, good always consists in the resolution of a conflict. Good, in its practical character, is defined by Dewey as the awareness of the meaning and significance of a way of behavior that provides for an orderly, harmonious, unified, and informed release of energy in action. His view implies a continuum of means-ends which denies the distinction between them as ultimate, which eliminates ends-in-themselves and substitutes for them ends-in-view, and which declares any absolute moral end or absolute hierarchy of values impossible because of constantly increasing knowledge which makes possible the construction of new ends.

Although Dewey's ethics eliminates absolute moral values, he does not believe that the alternative to ethical absolutism is ethical anarchy. Ethical anarchy is avoided by associating ethics with science. Ethics is concerned with valuations, value judgments, what sort of thing ought we to desire. Science is concerned with factual judgments, what sort of things are the case. Science is not concerned with objects simply as causes or as effects but with the laws connecting them. Ethics is not concerned simply with impulses nor with ends but with the means connecting them. Science cannot get knowledge of the sort it seeks by resort to a Humean sensationalism which atomizes the universe and makes laws impossible, nor by a Kantian apriorism which places laws outside of experience. It can only find laws by a technique which observes the connections between things within experience. So ethics cannot obtain valuations by mere hedonism—an atomized casual universe of impulses and enjoyment—nor by an ethical apriorism that places the goal of ethics outside of human experience. Ethics can only attain valuations—judgments of what is valuable—by a study of experience; a study that reveals what is valued and the scientific causes and consequences of it. Just as scientific knowledge is not mere givenness but is control of the given, so ethical knowledge is not mere enjoyableness but is control of what is enjoyed.

The association of science with ethics does not imply that value judgments are completely reducible to factual judgments. The experience of goodness is a tertiary property. Science deals with primary properties. But also the scientist does not completely reduce experiences of secondary properties, such as the experience of greenness, to factual judgments. He recognizes that only the primary properties corresponding to the experience of greenness can be treated by scientific methods. So with value judgments.

The problem of the relation of science to values is so crucial for Dewey that he defines the function of philosophy in the light of it:

Philosophy thus has a double task: that of criticizing existing aims with respect to the existing state of science, pointing out values which have become obsolete with the command of new resources, showing what values are merely sentimental because there are no means for their realization; and also that of interpreting the results of specialized science in their bearing on future social endeavor (*Democracy and Education*, p. 384).

In terms of the above summary of the pragmatic theory of meaning, one of the major differences between pragmatism and the contemporary movement known as logical positivism comes into view. For the positivist, value terms are meaningless. They have no cognitive import. The only meaning they have is emotive meaning. Thus, for the positivist, science, or

intelligent inquiry, can have no connection with problems relating to the determination of ultimate values. For the pragmatists, on the contrary, the problem of the relation between
value problems and science is one of the major problems in
philosophy, if not the major problem. This point of difference
between positivism and pragmatism has been described by
Dewey as follows:

Under present conditions scientific methods take effect in determining the concrete economic conditions under which the mass of
men live. But they are not employed to determine freely and systematically the moral, the humane, ends served by engrossing practical conditions, the actual state of ends and values. Hence the
more important things are left to decision by custom, prejudice,
class interests, and traditions embodied in institutions, whose results are mostly fixed by the superior power in possession of those
who manage them. Under these conditions, a recent movement in
philosophy demands especial notice. It retains the notion that
philosophy's concern is with superior reality, taking its cue in
search for it, mainly from mathematics and quasi-mathematical
symbolisms, but completely repudiating that aspect of philosophy
that has gone by the name of search for wisdom. It converts the
practical neglect by modern philosophies of political and moral
subjects into systematic theoretical denial of the possibility of intelligent concern with them. It holds that the practical affairs of
men which are of highest and deepest significance are matters of
values and valuations, and that *therefore* they are by their very
nature incapable of intellectual adjudication; of either justification
or condemnation on rational grounds. The movement retains in
the most emphatic form possible the ancient Greek conception according to which "theory" is intrinsically superior to any and every
form of practical concern—the latter consisting of things that
change and fluctuate in contrast with the eternity of Being. But
the movement in question goes, so to speak, the classic doctrine one
better. The latter held that practical affairs were the material of
inferior sorts of knowledge. The present movement holds that
moral affairs, concerned as they are with "intrinsic" values, or

"ends-in-themselves," are wholly outside the reach of any sort of knowledge whatever (*Problems of Men*, p. 8).

Aside from its theory of meaning and its position that reality has practical character, the other basic doctrines in pragmatism may be summarized as follows: *Empiricism:* that there is no source of knowledge outside of experience itself. *Naturalism:* that the experience in question is human experience. *Scientific method:* that in order to learn from human experience our beliefs must be controlled by reality. *Social principle in inquiry:* the doctrine that these beliefs are not what any one individual concludes, but are the product of the efforts of the community of investigators. *Immediate perception:* that while we perceive things as they really are and thus have immediate perception, we do not have immediate knowledge; that knowledge is a construct out of the process of inquiry. *Do not block the road to inquiry:* that the one inexcusable fault in seeking to attain knowledge is to block the road to inquiry; this may be done on the one hand by a dogmatic absolutism which cannot be justified by the facts, or on the other hand by a scepticism that asserts that knowledge is impossible.

When these doctrines are applied to our lives, much that seemed precious appears to disappear. This is one of the major objections that many persons find to pragmatism. We cannot close our examination of pragmatism more appropriately than by quoting what William James replied to this charge in the 1898 essay which launched the pragmatic movement:

It is true that a certain shrinkage of values often seems to occur in our general formulas when we measure their meaning in this prosaic and practical way. They diminish. But the vastness that is merely based on vagueness is a false appearance of importance, and not a vastness worth retaining. The x's and y's and z's always do shrivel, as I have heard a learned friend say, whenever at the end of your algebraic computation they change into so many a's and b's and c's; but the whole function of algebra is, after all, to get them into that more definite shape; and the whole function of philosophy ought to be to find out what definite difference it will make to you and me, at definite instants of our life, if this world-formula or that world-formula be the one which is true.

Abbreviations

Peirce, James, and Dewey were all prolific writers. Some device is necessary to simplify references to their works. In the case of Peirce's *Collected Papers* the editors have numbered each paragraph. References to Peirce are by volume and paragraph number following the pattern established by the editors. Thus (5.585) is to be interpreted to mean volume V, paragraph 585 of *The Collected Papers of Charles Sanders Peirce*.

In the case of James and Dewey, each of their major works is given a short title in the list below. References are by short title and page, so that (*Problems*, p. 73) is to be read as *Some Problems of Philosophy*, page 73.

Short titles are also indicated for certain other major sources of reference used throughout the book.

Common Faith	*A Common Faith*, John Dewey, 1934.
Democracy and Education	*Democracy and Education*, John Dewey, 1916.
Essays	*Collected Essays and Reviews*, William James, 1920.
Ethics	*Ethics*, John Dewey and James H. Tufts, 1908.
Experience and Nature	*Experience and Nature*, John Dewey, 1925.
Experimental Logic	*Essays in Experimental Logic*, John Dewey, 1916.

How We Think	*How We Think,* John Dewey, 1910.
Human Nature	*Human Nature and Conduct,* John Dewey, 1922.
Knowing and the Known	*Knowing and the Known,* John Dewey and A. P. Bentley, 1949.
Influence of Darwin	*The Influence of Darwin on Philosophy,* John Dewey, 1938.
Letters	*The Letters of William James,* ed. Henry James, 1926.
Logic	*Logic: The Theory of Inquiry,* John Dewey, 1938.
Logical Theory	*Studies in Logical Theory,* John Dewey, 1903.
Meaning of Truth	*The Meaning of Truth,* William James, 1909.
Memories	*Memories and Studies,* William James, 1911.
Outlines	*Outlines of a Critical Theory of Ethics,* John Dewey, 1891.
Philosophy and Civilization	*Philosophy and Civilization,* John Dewey, 1931.
Pluralistic Universe	*A Pluralistic Universe,* William James, 1909.
Pragmatism	*Pragmatism,* William James, 1907.
Principles	*Principles of Psychology,* William James, 1890.
Problems	*Some Problems of Philosophy,* William James, 1911.
Problems of Men	*Problems of Men,* John Dewey, 1946.
Quest for Certainty	*The Quest for Certainty,* John Dewey, 1929.
Radical Empiricism	*Essays in Radical Empiricism,* William James, 1912.
Reconstruction	*Reconstruction in Philosophy,* John Dewey, 1920.
Rejoinder	"Experience, Knowledge and Value: A Rejoinder," John Dewey, in *The*

	Philosophy of John Dewey, ed. P. A. Schilpp. 1939.
School and Society	*The School and Society,* John Dewey, 1900.
Study of Ethics	*The Study of Ethics,* John Dewey, 1894.
Valuation	*Theory of Valuation,* John Dewey, 1939.
Varieties	*The Varieties of Religious Experience,* William James, 1902.
William James	*The Thought and Character of William James,* Ralph Barton Perry, 1935.
Will to Believe	*The Will to Believe,* William James, 1896.

Selected Bibliography

This bibliography lists the principal works of Peirce, James, and Dewey which are of interest in connection with a study of pragmatism. The volumes by James and Dewey are listed chronologically. A final section of the bibliography lists alphabetically by author other works relevant to a study of American pragmatism.

I. CHARLES SANDERS PEIRCE

The Collected Papers of Charles Sanders Peirce, 8 vols.
  Volumes I–VI edited by Charles Hartshorne and Paul Weiss, Cambridge, Harvard University Press, 1931–35. (To be re-issued in 1960 as three volumes, under the imprint of The Belknap Press of Harvard University Press.) Volumes VII and VIII edited by Arthur W. Burks, Cambridge, Harvard University Press, 1958.

II. WILLIAM JAMES

Principles of Psychology. New York, Henry Holt, 1890.
The Will to Believe. New York, Longmans, Green, 1896.
Varieties of Religious Experience. New York, Longmans, Green, 1902.
Pragmatism. New York, Longmans, Green, 1907.
A Pluralistic Universe. New York, Longmans, Green, 1909.
The Meaning of Truth. New York, Longmans, Green, 1909.

Some Problems of Philosophy. New York, Longmans, Green, 1911.
Memories and Studies. New York, Longmans, Green, 1911.
Essays in Radical Empiricism. New York, Longmans, Green, 1912.
Collected Essays and Reviews. New York, Longmans, Green, 1920.

III. JOHN DEWEY

Outlines of a Critical Theory of Ethics. Ann Arbor, Register, 1891.
The Study of Ethics. Ann Arbor, Register, 1894.
The School and Society. Chicago, University of Chicago Press, 1900.
Studies in Logical Theory. Chicago, University of Chicago Press, 1903.
Ethics. With James H. Tufts. New York, Henry Holt, 1908.
How We Think. New York, D. C. Heath, 1910.
The Influence of Darwin on Philosophy. New York, Henry Holt, 1910.
Democracy and Education. New York, Macmillan, 1916.
Essays in Experimental Logic. Chicago, University of Chicago Press, 1916.
Reconstruction in Philosophy. New York, Henry Holt, 1920.
Human Nature and Conduct. New York, Henry Holt, 1922.
Experience and Nature. Chicago, Open Court, 1925.
The Quest for Certainty. New York, Minton, Balch, 1929.
Philosophy and Civilization. New York, Minton, Balch, 1931.
Art as Experience. New York, Minton, Balch, 1934.
A Common Faith. New Haven, Yale University Press, 1934.
Logic: The Theory of Inquiry. New York, Henry Holt, 1938.
Theory of Valuation. Chicago, University of Chicago Press, 1939.
Problems of Men. New York, Philosophical Library, 1946.
Knowing and the Known. With A. F. Bentley. Boston, Beacon, 1949.

IV. OTHER WORKS RELATING TO AMERICAN PRAGMATISM

Buchler, Justus. *Charles Peirce's Empiricism.* New York, Harcourt, Brace, 1939.

Feibleman, James. *An Introduction to Peirce's Philosophy*. New York, Harper, 1946.

Gallie, W. B. *Peirce and Pragmatism*. Harmondsworth, Middlesex, Penguin, 1952.

Geiger, George R. *John Dewey in Perspective*. London, Oxford University Press, 1958.

Goudge, Thomas A. *The Thought of C. S. Peirce*. Toronto, University of Toronto Press, 1950.

Hook, Sidney. *John Dewey: An Intellectual Portrait*. New York, Day, 1939.

——, ed. *John Dewey: Philosopher of Science and Freedom*. New York, Dial, 1950.

James, Henry, ed. *The Letters of William James*. 2 vols. Boston, Little, Brown, 1926.

Kennedy, Gail, ed. *Pragmatism and American Culture*. Boston, Heath, 1950.

Lieb, Irwin C., ed. *Charles S. Peirce's Letters to Lady Welby*. New Haven, Whitlock, 1953.

Morris, Lloyd. *William James*. New York, Scribner, 1950.

Perry, Ralph Barton. *The Thought and Character of William James*. 2 vols. Boston, Little, Brown, 1935.

Schilpp, Paul Arthur, ed. *The Philosophy of John Dewey*. Evanston, The Library of Living Philosophers, 1939.

Thompson, Manley. *The Pragmatic Philosophy of C. S. Peirce*. Chicago, University of Chicago Press, 1953.

White, Morton G. *The Origin of Dewey's Instrumentalism*. New York, Columbia University Press, 1943.

Wiener, Philip P. *Evolution and the Founders of Pragmatism*. Cambridge, Harvard University Press, 1949.

Wiener, Philip P. and Frederick H. Young, eds. *Studies in the Philosophy of Charles Sanders Peirce*. Cambridge, Harvard University Press, 1952.

Index

Uncertainty, factor of man's life, 246 f.
Unicorn, term, 10 f.
Uniformity, nomalist, 85
Unity, of universe, 131 f.
Universals, problem of, 25 ff.
Universal term, *see* General term
Universe: law and order in, 3, 86; explanation of, 5; atomization of, 14, 144, 264; diversification and growth in, 86, 130; element of chance in, 87; religious hypothesis re, 128 f.; pluralistic, 131; reality as measure of, 167; qualitative and quantitative properties, 207 f.; closed vs. open, 246
Utilitarianism, 215, 232

Value(s): in verification of truth, 163 f.; properties of objects, 208; in actions and ends, 213 f.; science and, 265; pragmatism and, 266 f.

Value judgments, 235 f.
Verification: theory of truth, 168 ff.; as meaning of truth, 179 f.
Visual image, and meaning, 49
Volition, idea of, 40; and conduct, 43

Whitehead, Alfred North, 24; on causal relation, 81; doctrine of God, 90; "fallacy of bifurcation," 186
Will: individual, 93; subordination of, 214
William of Occam, 33
Will to believe, James, 66, 122 f.; *see also* Belief
Work, routine vs. creative, 231
World: real, 72 f.; external, correspondence to general concepts, 76 f.
Wright, Chauncey, 5 f., 74, 137
Wrong, and right, 243 f.